What
Debt
Demands

What Debt Demands

Family, Betrayal, and Precarity
in a Broken System

Kristin Collier

GCP

GRAND
CENTRAL

NEW YORK BOSTON

Grand Central Publishing
Hachette Book Group
1290 Avenue of the Americas, New York, NY 10104
grandcentralpublishing.com
@grandcentralpub

First edition: November 2025

Grand Central Publishing is a division of Hachette Book Group, Inc. The Grand Central Publishing name and logo is a registered trademark of Hachette Book Group, Inc.

The publisher is not responsible for websites (or their content) that are not owned by the publisher.

Grand Central Publishing books may be purchased in bulk for business, educational, or promotional use. For information, please contact your local bookseller or the Hachette Book Group Special Markets Department at special.markets@hbgusa.com.

Print book interior design by Marie Mundaca

Library of Congress Cataloging-in-Publication Data

Names: Collier, Kristin author
Title: What debt demands : family, betrayal, and precarity in a broken system / Kristin Collier.
Description: First edition. | New York : Grand Central Publishing, [2025] | Includes
   bibliographical references.
Identifiers: LCCN 2025026003 | ISBN 9781538764985 hardcover | ISBN 9781538765005 ebook
Subjects: LCSH: Student loans—United States—Management | Student aid—Government
   policy—United States | College students—United States—Finance, Personal | Student
   aid—Corrupt practices—United States | Debt—United States | Student financial aid
   administration—United States—Management
Classification: LCC LB2340.2 .C643 2025 | DDC 378.3/620973—dc23/eng/20250618
LC record available at https://lccn.loc.gov/2025026003

ISBNs: 9781538764985 (hardcover), 9781538765005 (ebook)

Printed in Canada

MRQ-T

1   2025

For every student debtor, past and present

Contents

Contents

Prologue

UNDER THE FLUORESCENT BANK lights, I was sweating. The loan officer had taken my Social Security number, birthdate, and signature with him to another room where, I presumed, he was feeding it into a computer that would tell him how trustworthy I was.

I am very very very trustworthy, I had attempted to tell him with my eyes when I sat across a desk from him moments before. I was still wearing the sweatshirt and sweatpants I'd slept in after waking up late from my serving job at a college bar in Ann Arbor. I'd brushed my teeth but not my hair. I tried to make my face say: in three weeks I will graduate from a highly selective university, after which I will enroll in a competitive teaching program. Soon, I would be in a room with twenty-five children helping them understand language and narrative, forces that translate and shape the world.

I studied the faded Social Security card I'd brought with me. I'd never had my own credit card before, and I was not familiar with the equation that would produce it. My Social Security number confirmed that I was alive, that I existed, and the numbers conjured from my credit history told a story about that existence. I wondered if my data would convey to the bank my need. Without a credit card, my transition into the adult world would be challenging. I was twenty-two years old, and I still thought that the bank would care.

I removed the thin fleece I'd been using in place of a real jacket and laid it across my lap as if it were a sleeping child, showing the bank how careful and gentle I was. I looked down at my old sneakers, sticky with tap beer. I needed new ones, but that's not where the card's invisible money would be spent: that money would go toward teaching clothes, soap, kitchen items, a printer, groceries, a train card.

Around me, I heard the churn of the bank. People giving and taking with a certainty and ease I longed for. The account I'd kept there since sophomore year had never grown fuller than five hundred dollars, and every time I used my debit card, my stomach hurt: I didn't trust that the account numbers on the ATM slips were accurate. Maybe, this time, my account would be empty.

The man returned holding a milk-colored folder. The smile he left with had deflated, and his lips were pressed into a flattened balloon. He was disappointed in me, and I didn't understand why. "I really appreciate your help," I heard myself saying. Always I was searching for evidence that people around me thought I didn't belong at college, and I calibrated my words and my smile to respond accordingly, to remind them of my gratitude, as if gratitude conferred belonging. Maybe the computer told him that he should not give me much credit, and he was embarrassed to tell me.

"You were not approved for a card," he said, resuming his earlier position, across the wood desk. He opened the folder and then began, sheet by sheet, to lay out the pages of a printed document, as if plating slices of bread.

I'd never seen a credit report before and now here was mine in front of me, and it contained more pages than made sense. I didn't look at it yet, instead waiting for the man to keep speaking. When he didn't, I asked, "Why?"

He pushed a page of the report toward me, and if he was speaking then, I couldn't hear him because the numbers bent and warped the world around me. Unfamiliar debts stretched big and wide across pages and years. A credit card for a gas station and one for an underwear store and an enormous student loan from a bank and then another, larger loan from another bank. The numbers gathered and blended: $13,625. $1,014. $30,561. $40,494. $865. $7,584. They went on and on. The bank had gone quiet, but the debt was shouting at me.

I couldn't have anticipated it then, but the debt would keep shouting at me for the next fifteen years as I searched through memory, history, and literature. As I talked to collectors, debtors, and experts, as I traced my body's changes in order to understand what debt had done to me and why. To understand what debt does to all of us.

I looked again and again, picking up sheets and then setting them down, seeing and not seeing them all at once. The debts totaled at least a hundred thousand dollars. "There has been a mistake," I told him, after the silence had ripened, and I sensed that he was waiting for me. "I know I have a handful of loans from the Department of Education, though how many and for how much I'm not sure. Nothing else on here is mine, though. I don't recognize any of this," I said to him. "It can't be mine." I forced myself to breathe.

"If there is a mistake," he said, "you'll need to take that up with the police." His conjunction, *if*, was a sharpened knife. He did not believe me. I needed to leave. I moved backward in time, re-piling the credit report, page by page, and then placing it in the folder. Waking the sleeping child of my fleece and clothing each arm with it, before rising beneath the sharp lights. Retracing my steps through the center of the bank, past the teller and the plastic brown coffee dispenser, out the glass doors into a cold, wet city. Walking just across the street, to my college home, a three-story co-op with chipping gray paint. Up the damaged front steps from which weeds would sprout between the boards in a few more weeks, into the carpeted front hall.

And then backward. To the dorm I'd first lived in, north of campus, surrounded by thick trees and deer, and then farther, traveling across I-94 to my childhood home, so close to Lake Michigan that sometimes seagulls landed in our park. Into my bedroom, its windows head-height so that as a child I stood on my twin bed to see the silver maple in our front yard or to see the moon. Backward to the other house, the tiny white one with a carport instead of a garage, a sandbox in the backyard, into my bassinet, into my father's arms, into my mother's arms and before that, her body.

This isn't real. It's a mistake, I thought, even as some part of me already knew it wasn't.

Seated on the floor of my room, I did not call the police, as the man suggested. Instead, I called my mother. Though we had not been close since before college began, it was still her that I went to when things went wrong. During my sophomore year, when I lost a tampon inside of me, I called her to ask what to do. She told me that it probably wasn't lost, just turned around, and that I could see an OBGYN for support. A few years later, when a UTI led to a kidney infection with pain and a fever, she counseled me again to get help. She reminded me to listen to my body's messages, which for some reason, I didn't trust. And now here was a message not from my body but from the bank, that conveyed another emergency of my well-being.

I dialed her number, a sequence so familiar it felt like coming home. She picked up immediately, and I told her what had happened. "I think I need to report this to the police," I said. I wanted her to say that we would figure it out, that there was, in fact, a way out of the harm that someone, a stranger, had done to me.

She paused for a long time after—a silence that would echo out past the call into all the years ahead—before she said, "Please don't call them. Honey, I'm so sorry. It was me. All of it was me."

Chapter 1

Lender	Date Opened	Outstanding Balance	Monthly Payment	Account Status
AES/NCT	08/01/2004	$24,193	$182	Open
US Department of Education	09/01/2004	$13,625	$118	Open
Citi	11/01/2004	$1,014	$10	Open
WFNNB/ Victoria's Secret	02/01/2005	$431	$20	Open
AES/NCT	06/01/2005	$30,561	$230	Open
Bank of America	08/01/2005	$7,584	–	Closed/Collection
AES/NCT	09/01/2005	$14,994	$113	Open
Shell/Citi	12/01/2005	$289	$44	Open
AES/NCT	01/01/2006	$29,166	$220	Open
AES/NCT	05/01/2006	$14,699	$110	Open
ACS/GCO Ed Loan Fund	08/01/2006	$30,246	$207	Open
AES/NCT	01/01/2007	$14,640	$129	Open
AES/Chase Bank	09/01/2007	$40,494	$357	Open
Cavalry Portfolio Services	07/01/2009	$11,448	–	Closed/Collections
		$233,384	$1,740	

THE CALL, AS I remember it, lasted only minutes beyond my mother's confession, stretching just past her apology. I'm not sure if I pushed her for immediate answers or accepted her promise that she'd explain it all soon. Alone in my bedroom afterward, I sat on the dirty carpet, flipping through the report, reading from the window's weak, ambient light. Sometimes, I paused to study a detail. What did AES/NCT stand for? I assumed that AES/NCT debt was an education loan, but I didn't understand who the lender was or why two lenders were listed. Was it connected to school? Could I have needed all this money, somehow, for tuition? Questions appeared and blended and dissolved and reappeared in new forms. Outside my door, I could hear my roommates talking, picking up their keys and putting on their coats. Their lives remained unchanged from an hour earlier.

There were so many debts for AES, similarly shaped but distinct. The smallest debt was over $14,000—more than two semesters of tuition and fees—and the largest was over $40,000. I picked up and set down the report, reading bits of information, and then pausing when it felt unmanageable, threatening. Why would they give my mother this money? And how? The only way I could manage the cold and breaking wave inside my body was to say, *Okay, this is bad, this is insane, this doesn't make any sense, but I don't have all the information yet, and this might not be entirely correct. Any minute, my mom is going to call me back and clarify everything.*

In my earliest memory of my mother, she presses my four-year-old face against her salmon-colored cashmere sweater. She smells like she always did: of hairspray, floral perfume, and lipstick, which smelled earthy, like the desert. A few moments earlier my two friends had sat

2

across from me on my daybed, tossing stuffed animals back and forth over a sort of no man's land between us. We reached into and out of the empty zone, gathering new things and then throwing them. I loved human-like toys—Barbies and dolls and books with people in them—and the older of the two threw a large plastic baby at me, hitting my nose, and releasing blood all over my face, and after I screamed and my mother ran in, all over my mother's sweater as she clutched me whispering, "You're okay you're okay you're okay."

At four I'd begun to understand my mother and I as separate beings with our own eyes and arms and voices, but I still collapsed us sometimes. I remember crying in my basement daycare, lying down for a nap, thinking that wherever my mother was, she'd know I was upset and that I missed her because she'd be crying, too. When my mother cut her long, straight blond hair into a bob around that time, I cried again. She'd been transformed and without my consent. Every part of her was sacred, statuary. I did not want her to change how she applied her makeup or for her to wear new clothes that I'd never seen: I wanted her to be knowable and constant, an extension of me.

As I got older, I allowed for our mutual and disparate evolutions. Her hair got larger and flatter and larger as she tried out new styles with more and less hairspray. My hair, blondish and thin as a kid, turned brown, grew fuller and frizzier, and I clipped it and braided it and straightened it—at first with her help, and then on my own. Even as my mother's wardrobe responded to trends, she always chose items washed in color: tangerine, fuchsia, kiwi, lemon. In middle school and high school, I stopped dressing like a child-version of her. I wore wool and earth tones, worn T-shirts from Goodwill, replicating styles I'd seen in magazines.

Our divergence wasn't only an aesthetic one. By the time I was a teenager, it was clear that we fit into the world in different ways.

3

My mother was loud, always talking, quick to share the story of a raccoon in our garage to a stranger. She never wanted to be still. Never wanted silence. Never wanted to spend too long in the interiors of her mind. Things swirled chaotically all around her, and she lovingly, excitedly, churned them. I was quieter, more apt to study people than to talk to them, and I resisted any moment in which people would turn their gaze and attention toward me. I hated having conversations with people I didn't know, unless I was interviewing them as a high school journalist. Even as a teenager, I'd walk to the swings in the park, located across the street from my house in a giant field behind the fire station and, with my CD player on, pendulum through the low sky, yellow field all around me, bats chirping and darting like thick black confetti. Sometimes my best friend, who lived a few blocks away, would join me, and we'd swing in silence until it was dark.

Occasionally, my and my mother's bodies would collide again. In elementary school, home with the flu, my mother pressed wet, cool rags to my forehead and braided my hair to keep it away from my face. In high school, after I dropped a frozen turkey on my foot, breaking it in three places, she helped me into the shower, and used the wand of a therapeutic ultrasound machine to massage the tissue above the breaks, warming and healing the fractures.

Our differences weren't essential—they did not need to dictate how we related to one another. And still: It had begun to feel to me as if our wiring meant there were things we could not understand about each other. Or maybe it meant that we didn't know how to talk to one another about what we did not understand. But it was her touch I wanted when I hurt.

———

In many ancient civilizations, debt collection was facilitated by a threat against a body, though whose body depended on social and legal customs. In ancient India and Ireland, according to bankruptcy scholar Louis Edward Levinthal, a creditor could sit at a debtor's doorway until the outstanding debt was paid, which it often was because "public opinion would have punished instantly and severely the debtor who allowed his creditor to become exhausted or to die of starvation before his door." Instead of threatening the debtor's body directly, the creditor threatened himself first. It seems to me that this decision was in part a calculation about what the community was willing to bear. It was the creditor's suffering that they could not tolerate. And it was the community's punishment that motivated the debtor to pay. What's left implied in this historical account is that the debtor had the money all along and was waiting for the right threat to extract it.

In Egypt, a debtor was compelled to pay by "spiritual sanction." He pledged repayment on the body of a recently deceased family member, most often his father. In the absence of payment, the creditor was given the right to open his family's tomb, remove his father's corpse, and reseal the tomb without it. When I read this detail, I thought of Antigone's quest to bury her brother, even in the face of her own possible death. An unburied body, or a body unburied, disrupts grief and the journey to the spirit world. I wonder what happened to these ancient borrowers that made repayment impossible—how many bodies were taken back. Levinthal does not write what the creditor did with the body afterward, though the resurrection suggests an eternal homelessness, a wandering far and wide away from family.

He notes that this pledge was enforced by the community rather than by the law, and that the debtors themselves could not be enslaved by the creditors because it was the state to which they owed their bodies for governance, labor, or war.

———————

A few days after learning about the debt, I took a walk by the Huron River and called my father. "Did you know?" I asked. By then I must have had a narrative for the debt's origins, albeit an incomplete one: likely, that my parents had run out of money and used the loans to survive.

My father's voice was sticky. It kept getting caught in his throat. He hadn't known, he said. At least not about all of it. He'd known there had been some loans, enough to cover school but not this other stuff. "Was it study abroad that got things all messed up?" he asked, a question I'd keep returning to in the years ahead. For five months, I lived in a small beach-side suburb of Sydney in a large co-op house a few blocks from the ocean—a strange, decadent impossibility, and a gift I didn't think I deserved, even as I got a job halfway through the semester to help support myself. He needed there to be a clear cause for what had happened, and it would be easier if I was that cause.

"My semester didn't cost over two hundred thousand dollars. And I got a scholarship for it," I said. That was beside the point; the bulk of the loans were acquired before the program began. The gray sky and the river met and blended. "It wasn't my fault." But I doubted myself. Maybe college was a giant pit, sucking us inward, scrambling the logic of our resources. Maybe I was to blame.

My father did know that our finances were really bad, he admitted. It was all a mess, and he wasn't sure how they'd get out of it, but they would. And then they'd turn their attention toward my debt, and they'd figure that out, too. I felt the futurity of his promise. How long would it be? How much would the debt grow in the meantime? And how would I make payments as I waited for support? As I walked back toward campus, I carried with me twin beliefs: I had been abandoned by my family, and they would never fix this, no matter how much they wanted to. And they loved me and would make it okay someday. These beliefs shifted around inside me, competing for space. I couldn't hold on to both for long.

My relationship with my father had always been easy, though less intimate than with my mother. When I was born and for many years after, my father worked at a factory that made tank systems, compressors, and pumps, and the repetitive movement of his hands on the machines, moving levers, touching products, rinsing in chemicals, meant that his hands were worn and chapped. In the winter, despite sleeping in gloves coated with Vaseline, his hands would crack open, exposing thin red rivers. In my earliest memory of him, he asked for another chicken nugget, and, scared to hurt him or perhaps scared of him, I dropped it into his palm so that I didn't touch him, before looking up into his gray-blue eyes and feeling ashamed. He was often tired, even when the nature of his work shifted, and he was moved into an office. When my sister and I left the basement lights on or dropped our wet towels on the carpet or forgot to close the door to the thick humidity of summer, he snapped at us in a voice both cold and angry.

He was funny, though, with a strong sense of comedic timing, delivering jokes about himself, or my sister, mother, and me that were insightful without being mean. He could grab a strange detail from one of our stories and recite it back to us later, repackaged with humor—a trick that showed he was listening and that dulled the alienating discomfort of adolescence. And he laughed easily, tapped into and cocreated bits that we could recycle into conversations later. We often sat together on our back patio or in our living room without talking, passing pages of the newspaper back and forth or reading our separate books in silence. In that way, we seemed more alike. Our silence felt desired and shared.

While my college matriculation preserved the warm distance I'd always had from my father, it widened the fault line between my mother and me. Neither she nor my father had gone to college—though my father would eventually complete a degree in the evenings after work—and none of their parents had finished high school. We all sensed that I was departing for a place from which I'd never truly return. My parents and I never discussed in detail how we'd manage college financing, either the processes that created it or the money that fed it. They completed the Free Application for Federal Student Aid (FAFSA) on my behalf. It never occurred to me that I might be the one to do it. I knew that I'd work part time during the school year, which I did for more and more hours as college went on, and full time during the summer to pay for whatever I could—my living expenses, and, by senior year, my rent. A combination of my parents and my future, in the form of debt, would pay for the rest, though it was never clear to me how much each of us was contributing in an individual semester. That I didn't know this or didn't think that I should ask about it was a testament to my parents' financial politics, which I'd inherited: We didn't discuss money, especially our own, and my mother managed everything because that's what she was good at. She'd worked at a bank since she was sixteen, moving out of the teller window and into an office where she approved, created, and dispersed debt to people in the form of automobile loans.

As college went on, my family's financial health frayed alongside my relationship with my mother. She lost her job and was out of work for a while; my parents fell behind on all their bills; there were lots of bounced checks; and my university bill was often paid late, sometimes after many e-mails and a red symbol that emerged on my student account, blinking sharply at me each time I checked the portal. I thought of these snags as painful, singular events, linked to one another, but discrete from everything else. We'd move through it and be on the other side.

In phone calls with my mother in the weeks after I discovered the debt, I tried to understand the scale of it. "Why so much money? Where did it all go?" Around that time, I wrote a short story about a young woman who gradually and then completely disintegrates. The first sign: She finds her toenails on the lawn, brightened by moonlight. Seeking answers from my mother was an attempt, more than anything, to shore myself up, keep myself intact. I didn't expect that the answers would be satisfying.

"We were going to lose the house," she told me in one phone call, as if that loss offered an explanation, as if I should be the one responsible to mitigate that loss.

I, too, loved our home, which my grandfather and father had extended and molded, and my mother had painted and papered. Every few years, the colors and patterns of its interiors shifted, and, outside, something new was planted or added. A dogwood tree. A basketball hoop. And when my father's father passed away and he received a small inheritance: a pool in our backyard. My footprints were pressed into the cement below the pool liner. Our home was the place we performed rituals of love and family, and it was a marker of the middle-class life my parents had climbed into. To give up our home—or, rather, to allow the bank to take it away—would feel like watching bulldozers at work on the architecture of our lives. The loss of our home, for her, was both real and symbolic.

And yet, accepting her explanation—that this debt was a

necessary strategy to keep our house—felt like being forced into a truce with something monstrous. It left me on edge, unable to sit in one place for too long. My parents couldn't tell me how much the loan payments would be or when they would begin or how we would afford to pay them. That spring, walking around the newly green and budding city, I studied every flower, every doorway, every petal for threats, which emanated from the landscape all around me, which seemed to emanate from inside me, too.

"I was always going to pay you back," my mother said in many of the calls, an assurance designed to soothe us both: Her harm had an escape hatch. But I understood that her and my father's combined middle-class incomes were not nearly enough for them to pay back the debt in their lifetimes. Sometimes, I threw my flip phone after our calls, daring it to break. There was no money for another one. *They have abandoned me.* I took turns holding each belief before I eventually set the first aside, realizing it was the second one I needed to survive. *They love me and will figure it out.*

———

Debt collection practices across the ancient world depended on collective surveillance and collective shame. And many depended on the participation of living family members, who never acquired the debt to begin with. How did these debts remake what was intimate and sacred between them? According to Hindu law, you could maim or enslave someone who didn't pay, or you could enslave his wife. In ancient Babylon, insolvent debtors were regularly sold into slavery, and if the debt was large enough, so, too, were their kin. Debt was rarely solitary in its cruelty. It didn't just wound one person but many: a mother, maybe, and a daughter, too.

In Roman law, recorded in the Twelve Tables, a borrower

pledged his own body to a creditor. If he was unable to pay back his debt, his creditor could have him executed or make him his slave, after which he could kill him or sell him to another country. Levinthal reminds readers of the old proverb, "He who cannot pay with his purse pays with his skin." Many penalties for unpaid debt confused what was owed with who owed it—a fusion of money and personhood. In other words, if you couldn't pay, then it was your body that you should give. And if your body was not enough, you should give away someone else's.

––––––––

For a few weeks, I carried the credit report with me everywhere, as if it weren't a compilation of financial harm but a favorite toy, a stuffed bear named Patches that I needed to fall asleep when I was away from home. I unfolded and refolded the report so frequently that its creases calcified into bones. With vertebrae, it was alive. I thought about it all the time: as I lay in bed staring out the window, as I read *Clarissa* beneath a tree in the quad, as I revised a final essay at the coffee shop, as I cried in the English Department bathroom in the stall with the W. S. Merwin poem: "Your absence has gone through me / Like thread through a needle. / Everything I do is stitched with its color."

Sometimes I used the report's contents to search something briefly online, information I couldn't hold on to: None of it meant anything to me yet. What I wanted from the report was to see something new, a detail that would offer me a key to unlock the puzzle. Why had the theft happened? What should I do to fix it? With a few of my closest friends I pleaded: *Look at this report and please tell me what to do.* When none of my friends could help me, and the report failed to give instructions for its own undoing, I threw it away. I didn't need it anymore, anyway. We had fused together, and it was part of me now.

Chapter 2

HALFWAY THROUGH MY TEACHER training program in July 2008, and for the first time that I could remember, my aunt called. Something was obviously wrong. Standing in my dorm in Queens, just out of the shower, a thin towel wrapped around me, I considered allowing the call to go to voice mail so I could receive her news, whatever it was, from a distance. But worried that someone was sick or hurt or dead, I picked up.

"Your mom has been arrested," she explained to me, not pausing for a response, but using the inertia to carry her through the rest of what she needed to tell me. My mother had been charged with workplace embezzlement and health-care fraud, both of which she'd done in her position managing medical billing at a dentist office. I imagined the office, which was in a repurposed ranch-style home, a couple of miles from Lake Michigan.

I spun slowly as we talked, taking in the dorm room. With the exception of the clothes in my closet, there was almost nothing of mine in the room. The posters I'd made for teaching, the binders full of pedagogical theory and planning support, and the stack of papers waiting to be commented on had little to do with me and nothing to do with home—with the place I'd come from before moving here. I felt the urge to touch something that knew me or was part of me, some object cloaked in memory or meaning. I had nothing.

"I'm sorry, Kristin," she said. She sounded sad. And tired. My father had asked her to call because he couldn't. It was unclear if it was my sorrow and confusion or his that he couldn't face. I didn't ask my aunt to clarify.

I learned that my mother had a severe gambling addiction and had borrowed money from many of her family members, maxed out all her credit cards and, then, when all the credit lines had collapsed, she'd taken money from her employer. I sat on the twin bed, looking out the window. In Michigan, the peaches would be sweet and full. The farms that fanned out from the lake smelled like manure and rotting fruit by midsummer. I missed it.

"She wanted to pay it all back and she thought she'd be able to," my aunt said to me, leaving another sentence implied: Of course that would be impossible. As we spoke, my mother was in jail waiting for her parents to pay her bail—my parents had no money—so that she could return home where she'd remain until the trial. I felt something familiar coil and uncoil within me.

After we'd hung up and I dressed, I sat on the open lawn away from the dorms. My aunt didn't mention my name in the list of people my mother had either borrowed or stolen from, and it didn't occur to me that I should demand inclusion. What my mother faced was life-destroying—addiction, criminal charges, the pang of an empty bank account that would never be refilled. She no longer had a job, and my father's modest salary would go toward her defense and everything else. Even if she avoided incarceration, they would lose everything.

I felt myself dissipating—breaking up into smaller and smaller pieces with wet and softening edges. I bled into the campus, the classroom, my summer school students, my mother, our debt. To demand that my mother and family contend with what had happened to me would require me to solidify again. I would first have to insist on my own existence, and I couldn't.

———

Steph acquired the first of her loans when she was sixteen and enrolled in Simon's Rock (now called Bard College at Simon's Rock), a college that serves high-achieving young students who are ready to attend college before their peers.

I spoke with Steph, who was thirty-nine and white, on a virtual call in the fall of 2023, each of us sitting with a square of our home behind us: mine, an unfinished basement where I worked, and hers, what appeared to be a living room. "My chimney is being repaired today," she warned me, "so there may be some loud knocks."

Steph would have stayed at the arts magnet high school she'd been attending—she adored it—but because of a busing issue, that high school was no longer available to her, and she didn't think a traditional school would be a good fit. Though she was awarded some need-based and some merit-based aid, she still needed to borrow money to attend the college, whose tuition, she recalled, was $28,000 her first year and $2,000 more each year afterward. Signing the loan papers, she remembered fearing the debt's impact on her future, to which her mother said, "You can't get blood from a stone." Steph understood that to mean: If you don't have money, then the lenders won't be able to take it. I considered that this aphorism obscures the fact that you still might try everything possible—to the detriment of your career, dreams, relationships, and health—to have enough money to give them.

"I don't regret it," Steph said, despite this school leaving her with an incredible amount of debt. She met her husband there and had a great educational experience. After graduation, she took a year off and then enrolled in a Master of Fine Arts in Creative Writing at the University of Pittsburgh. She'd wanted to be a creative writing professor since high school, facilitating the kind of rich and imaginative classroom that she had loved her entire life. Getting her master's degree was the next step.

But after graduation, Steph could not find a full-time position. "It was 2005," she said to me, "so the idea of getting a job in academia was not as much of a pipe dream as it is today." Though she couldn't find the job she wanted, she did become a part-time adjunct professor while working full-time at a law office. One semester, she used up all her sick days so that she could teach her once-a-week writing course to nursing students. The writing course only paid Steph $1,200 for the semester, not even enough to cover her loan payments, which were about $600 each month.

"It felt like"—she paused for a moment, grabbing for language that would clarify her experience for me—"a horrible joke that I took out all this debt to be able to do this job. It's a real job," she said, emphasizing the word "real" as if to remind herself that she had not conjured this job from nothing. It had existed. "And then the job wouldn't pay me enough to cover the debt that I took out to get the job and the ridiculousness of that was really crushing." Before she gave up on becoming a professor, she taught a few more classes, one of which met during her lunch break at the law firm. She commuted by bus across town to teach before returning to her office to finish the rest of the day. In the end, these jobs did not pay her enough, and she needed the vacation and sick days that she was using to teach, so she quit. "Adjunct faculty are paid, on average, $3,894 per class taught, with the annual income of the lowest-paid adjuncts near the minimum wage, and given that most of them have advanced degrees, they also bear the burden of the $1.7-trillion student debt crisis," according to *Business Insider.* I'm certain Steph was a good teacher.

Steph and her husband, who also had student debt, sometimes called themselves "poor with an asterisk." She said, "On paper we were not rich, but we should not have been so poor." The asterisk was a drain, slurping up their resources and making it impossible for them to care for themselves, despite working full-time. So overwhelmed by the stress of the constant calculations of how to—just barely—get by, Steph developed severe panic attacks and a condition in which she struggled to swallow. "I would chew up food and move it to the back of my throat and then would feel this flare of panic, like, *I don't know how to swallow. I'm going to choke.*" It was as if Steph was drowning in her own body, nearly dying doing what should have been a restorative, nourishing act: feeding herself.

After an endoscopy and swallow therapy, a doctor asked her if perhaps what was plaguing her had less to do with her throat muscles than with a grief, anxiety, and depression that she couldn't manage. "It didn't occur to me that my anxiety could be the root of a physical symptom," she said. "It was eye-opening." Steph did learn to swallow again, in part by helping her body understand what represented a threat. The food did not. The debt burden that she could not manage, that would not go away, that was hurting her, became something else entirely. It had texture and flavor. It could choke her. This transmutation allowed for the specter of choice, which ultimately, she didn't have; she needed to eat. Still, I understood this urge to resist collection in another form.

———————

In a 2013 paper in *Social Science & Medicine*, researchers studied debt's impact on general health outcomes—the first study of its kind, they noted. Earlier scholarship traced the impacts of socioeconomic status on health and the impact of debt on mental health, but before this study, no one had drawn a clear, thick arrow between debt and a body. Because of Americans' rapid accumulation of debt since the 1980s—including medical, credit card, student loan, payday, and mortgage debt—more people are experiencing indebtedness than ever before, and it's hurting them. It's hurting us. The study, which focused on young adults between the ages of twenty-four and thirty-two with personal debt, found that debt is "a significant predictor of health outcomes."

Indebtedness, and just as importantly, the *feeling* of indebtedness, corresponds with high blood pressure, stress, depression, and worse health outcomes. Chronic stress can be especially dangerous because it continually triggers the body's fight-or-flight response without allowing the body to recover when the stress has passed. The body's attempt to protect itself impacts all of the body's systems, leading to hypertension, heart attacks, and strokes. It gives us stomach aches, bloating, heartburn, acid reflux, and weakens our intestines, making us vulnerable to bacterial infection.

The *Social Science & Medicine* authors note that some kinds of debt, such as a manageable mortgage, can be a positive predictor of general health. In these cases, the debt often correlates with higher income levels and other assets. What the researchers don't say is that this kind of debt, this positive debt, is also racialized. Good debt is enabling, according to scholars Louise Seamster and Raphaël Charron-Chénier, and bad debt is a hindrance—and they highly correlate with what Seamster coined as "White debt" and "Black debt."

Debt cannot be understood in isolation. It follows that even small amounts of debt can be devastating if the complete picture is bleak, if it includes other layers of precarity that follow from race, disability, wealth, sexual orientation, immigration status, etc. In an op-ed on food and housing insecurity in the college population, Professor Sara Goldrick-Rab recalls a student she interviewed who slept in "libraries, bathrooms, and her car." Stretched for money, she sold her plasma and often didn't eat. When this exhausting cycle left her unable to focus, her grades dropped, and she lost financial aid, after which she left college, homeless, without a degree and with debt that would follow her for years, maybe the rest of her life.

———

In late fall of 2008, a couple of months after program training, I was slumped against my boyfriend, waiting for the pharmacist to fill a prescription for an antibiotic to treat a kidney infection, the first of many I'd have that year. I was getting UTIs all the time, no matter when I peed or how much water I drank or what steps I took to mitigate infection. Sometimes, the pressing urge of the infection alerted me quickly enough to get medication, but this time the infection traveled before I caught it, climbing its way through the urethra, up the ureter, and into my kidney. I felt its presence in a wave of fever and a heavy, steady punching in my kidney. It got so bad that I couldn't think, could hardly walk.

"Will the meds be ready before you close?" I heard my boyfriend, a first-year med student, ask the pharmacist. "She's in so much pain.

She can't go home like this," he said. Since I'd discovered the debt six months earlier, no one else had advocated for me. Hearing him demand my medication and explain my pain to a stranger brought me to tears—he'd brought something invisible to the surface and announced it as real.

While managing the infections, I'd been answering calls from debt collectors all over New York City, from the Upper East Side where I lived, to the South Bronx where I taught, to the program office near Penn Station, where I made copies of lesson plans late at night. My student loan payments had been deferred while I completed my graduate degree in education, but there was no such pause for the fraudulent cards. Collectors representing four different lenders called me all the time. The credit card debt that my credit report had listed as being sold to a collection agency, was, from what I could tell, dormant, waiting. I thought about searching for it, but decided not to, hoping it would go away.

The collectors learned the rhythm of my days and increasingly called me in the late afternoons and evenings when I was most likely to pick up. At first, I answered these calls in hopes that my explanations might help me. I didn't have another plan.

"The debt isn't mine," I told someone on one such call that fall as I walked down Seventy-Eighth Street toward my apartment, which was at the top of a walk-up building two blocks from the East River. The collector had reminded me of my outstanding balance—a sum I can't recall now, but it totaled more than all my wealth, which, with the exception of the day I received my tax return, was always less than $800. I often ended the month with an empty bank account.

The calls usually began with what seemed like a genuine performance of empathy: *I really really get it. I've been there. I am on your side, and I want to help you make a plan. Together, we can figure this out.*

Together. I wanted more than anything to share my burden with someone else, even a person who didn't care about me or justice more broadly.

"Okay," the collector replied after I insisted that the debt didn't belong to me. I tried to read belief into his tone and into the exhale that followed. "Whose is it, then?"

"My mother's." I passed my apartment as we spoke, walking toward the river. I never took the collection calls inside with me, worried that my roommates would overhear them, even though I'd already told them some of the story. Because my credit was ruined and I had no money for a security deposit, one of their parents had had to cosign and cover my share. My boyfriend lived in a dorm in a hospital, and when I stayed with him, I took the calls in the hospital courtyard, or sometimes in the hospital itself, as far away as I could be from anyone who'd overhear. It never occurred to me that many of these people were probably taking their own calls, or would be soon, when their loved ones had been discharged and they were left with enormous medical debts.

Couples walked their dogs along the path by the river, and runners moved quickly by in spandex. *Do they have debt? How much?* I wondered of every person I saw. On the phone, pressed tight against my ear, the collector said it was not his job to handle "this information" and I would need to talk to someone else about it, maybe the police. He suggested a payment plan in the meantime, asking for a small amount of money: "Even twenty dollars will help." I considered giving him the numbers to my debit card. It would not meaningfully reduce the debt but it might keep him from calling me back for the rest of the week. His voice, and all the collectors' voices, formed a chorus of debt. I heard their songs all the time. I didn't pay him because I couldn't afford to.

Before hanging up, he reminded me that the lenders would ultimately collect, whether I gave them money willingly or not—a court could force me to. Leaning against the railing, I allowed this threat to swirl around me and over me, before I turned back toward the city to walk home.

Unable and unwilling to give the collectors my money, my body paid, just as bodies had across the ancient world. In addition to the UTIs, I developed ulcers and intense stomach aches. Often these aches would begin as heartbeats, growing hotter and larger throughout the day until eventually, my whole core aflame, I puked. Their origin was inexplicable. It was the beer I had the night before. Or, it was coffee in the morning. Or it was too much of a certain kind of lunch or not enough. I could identify accelerants but not sparks.

———

In Jacinda Townsend's *Mother Country*, Shannon, one of the novel's protagonists, owes Sallie Mae $112,530.37 for a student debt burden that began as $45,000. Despite an undergraduate and graduate degree and two financially stable but distant parents, Shannon is hardly able to care for herself. Her apartment remains largely barren and dirty; she eats just enough; and she drives an old and failing car to commute to her underpaid job as a temp for Humana. When reflecting on the "flotsam" of the loan burden—the domestic, necessary, and sometimes unnecessary items that she'd purchased in college—she remembers herself as a young woman, standing in front of a mirror in a little black dress as she prepared for a date. She recalls the purple lilacs her date gave her and feels the warm ache of a cavity in the back of her mouth. "People didn't understand how you could work all your life and die with rotten molars, but here it was."

Shannon has just received a new notice from Sallie Mae that they have added a 25 percent collection fee to her loan balance, on which she wasn't making payments previously because she couldn't. She smoothes the letter out with her hand, like you might use an iron to massage a shirt's wrinkle, and then she tears it up into smaller and smaller pieces. Next, she takes "the tiny bits of Sallie Mae's letter, put[s] them into her mouth, and swallow[s] them in one fierce, mulchy gulp." As the shredded loan mass moves into her digestive system, she imagines a future of penury and debt imprisonment. When she bleeds from one nostril, she uses the heel of her hand to stop it, breathing through the other side.

Keeled over on the floor, her stomach gurgling loudly, she calls Sallie Mae, though she doesn't consider what she will say when connected with a representative, whose primary allegiance is to the debt and the debt's owner, not the student borrower. Instead of a human, a robot greets Shannon with a "spoken word essay" of menu options, and unable to tolerate the robot's voice, which sounds as if it's smiling, Shannon hangs up, in pain and alone. Unlike Steph, the debtor who forgot how to swallow, Shannon's body remembers, and she eats the debt whole, waiting to see what her body will do with it.

———

My stomach aches increased in frequency and intensity until I couldn't stop throwing up for two days. I tried to lie on my side so that there was no pressure on my stomach, but the fire moved upward into my chest and down into my calves. Inside me, I could hear the acid moving like a crashing wave. I tried resting against a stack of pillows before that became unbearable, too. After I threw up, each time, I lay flat on the tile floor in the bathroom before I started shaking—back to bed to begin again.

I had broken up with my boyfriend for reasons I could not articulate to him or to myself—I loved him—but I sensed it had to do with the debt. I felt unreachable. We moved through different worlds now.

My roommates were out for the night, and I was unsure if my bank balance would allow for a cab, so when I realized that I was in danger of becoming dehydrated, I walked to Lenox Hill Hospital, where I puked so hard in the waiting room that I shit my pants. In my hospital room, a nurse handed me a kidney-shaped pan and another and another, cleaning them out each time she returned. I needed to drink a cup of metallic-tasting medicine that would allow the doctors to see my insides, she said. She touched my arm with her cool hand, maternally, and I cried. I was released the next afternoon with a prescription for a different antibiotic: this time, a stomach infection.

I got a cystoscopy and an endoscopy, and my teacher's union health insurance allowed me to see specialists across Manhattan. I changed my diet, took acid blockers. Though each flare-up of illness was treated and the pain abated, it always returned in a new form. No doctor could offer a thesis that connected these illnesses.

Visiting a college friend in Boston around that time, I changed clothes in her room, which, unlike my bedroom, had a full-length mirror. I didn't recognize the shape I saw before me. I'd grown small. I was sharp and thin, and in the light, nearly watery. Unable to look at myself, I turned away quickly to dress.

———————

Very often the health outcomes, like interest, are compounded because people with debt don't seek out medical care to save money. In a 2023 survey, 36 percent of working adults with medical or dental debt said their debt burdens caused them to delay care. Or avoid it altogether. In the same survey, more than half of respondents said the care they opted out of or delayed caused their condition to become worse. Debtors' bodies erode, and then because they cannot afford to tend to them, they erode some more.

Economists writing for the Federal Reserve Bank of Atlanta examined debt and creditworthiness's relationship to mortality using a sample of US consumers and household members from 1999 to 2016. "Without exception," the authors write, "as severely delinquent debt increases, by any of our [measures reported], mortality rises." The transition to severe delinquency, or having a debt that is at least ninety days past due, corresponds with a 5 percent increase in mortality risk. As credit risk improves, mortality risk declines, as if a person's credit "worthiness" translates to something more devastating and profound: their right to be alive. "Taken as a whole," the authors write, "our results imply that financial policies are health policies."

———

On Edie's first date with Eric in *Luster,* by Raven Leilani, he takes her to an amusement park. His choice of date winks at their difference in age: He is in his late forties, and she's in her early twenties. Their age gap is one of many gaps between their lives. He is white and wealthy, in an open marriage, and living in the suburbs. She is single, Black, and indebted, barely able to pay rent with her low-wage work as a children's book editor, a job she loses soon after they meet. At the start of their date, she reflects: "Eric's enthusiasm is infectious. After the first two rides, I am enjoying myself, and not just because dying means I won't have to pay my student loans."

Loan collection thrums in the background of the book, as Edie and Eric's relationship deepens during dinner dates, sex in her bleak apartment, and then sex at the house he shares with his wife and adopted pre-teen daughter. Edie moves into his home against his wishes after she loses her job and her apartment. Following her termination, Edie thinks: "I find myself becoming sentimental about what I will leave behind, the whiff of Lysol and ink, the stack of someone's homemade zines on the sink, and this very stairwell, in which I have regularly pleaded for student loan deferrals and set up pelvic exams." In the first call, she is asking collectors to pause collection on her student loans so she can pay rent and feed herself. She very often can't. At one point Edie considers that what Eric believes are dates are actually opportunities for her to consume calories. The next call is a request for reproductive health, a right she's entitled to but will lose anyway when her job loss ejects her from her company insurance plan.

Edie replicates this call rhythm—loan collection, health, loan collection, health—from Eric's home in a rich New Jersey suburb, where she is very obviously an outsider. "I walk around the cul-de-sac," Edie says, "take long calls with Sallie Mae. I defer my student loans, schedule an appointment with a gastroenterologist in Hackensack." These loans are both spectral and fleshy: They float behind the central action of the story and then, occasionally, make material, bodily demands. According to the scholar Annie McClanahan, in her seminal book *Dead Pledges: Debt, Crisis, and Twenty-First Century Culture*, "The trust on which credit claims to depend is secured not through the alienation of the debtor's morality but by the power of the state to act on her body..." It emerges from "capital's ability to remove the debtor's capacity to feed and educate and house herself."

While alone and poor and sick, Edie navigates these loan payments not because of shame or allegiance, but because the debt makes real and bodily threats.

———

That fall, as I led my first reading and writing workshop with the eighth graders I was teaching, my mother called me frequently for support. Her trial was approaching, and she was convinced that her intentions should guide the criminal-legal system's process and outcome. "I've tried to be a good person in my life," she said to me in one call. I paused before my apartment door, just as I did with the debt collectors, so that I could finish the conversation on the stoop. Beside me was a coffee can that had been nailed to the wall so the apartment's smokers could ash their cigarettes. When it rained, the cigarettes floated up like thin canoes before tipping over onto the sidewalk. "I have no record. I don't deserve jail." My mother said this to me as if the repetition would make it real. She needed me to agree, and mostly I did. I couldn't conceive of how incarceration would fix anything for either one of us.

It struck me that while my mother understood that stealing from her employer was not the right choice, her sorrow was almost entirely directed toward her own pain. She was terrified. She didn't seem to believe that the theft had hurt the dentist, and I wondered how that translated to what she'd done to me. I was angry at her but from a distance. I couldn't hold on to it. Our debt had sickened me, and it felt as if I had no dependable body, no container, to hold these feelings.

"Things could be worse," I told her. "You have a family standing by you. You'll get through this."

I'd signed up for a free monthly credit report, and occasionally looked at it, but often didn't. The debt was growing, I knew that. Though the loan payments were paused, interest was accruing. Occasionally debt would capitalize, and the new loan total would be used to calculate the new monthly interest, and so on, forever and ever. On a loan of $30,000 with an interest rate of 14 percent, the accrued interest each year was over $4,000. And there were eight loans. To track the accumulating interest was to watch myself be buried alive.

The court file tells me that my mother pled guilty to embezzlement so that a secondary charge of health-care fraud was dropped. My mother was sentenced to two and a half months, a duration that meant she'd serve her time in a jail a couple of hours from our house rather than a state prison. A family member told tell me that following her sentence she howled, and late at night for weeks afterward, I heard an echo of that howl from across the country, sorrowful and wild.

While incarcerated, she wrote me a single letter, which I cannot remember, save for the stamp she used, which was a green sketch of a coniferous tree. I wondered how she'd found something beautiful there. I didn't write her back, and she never wrote me again.

———

Not long after my mother was incarcerated, I dropped off my laundry at a cleaner near my apartment. I normally washed my own clothes but hadn't had time that week and had run out of things to wear. When I picked up my clothes after work the next night, I sorted through the pile, which smelled, strangely, of nothing: underwear, socks, bras, T-shirt, pants, and then a gift my mother had given me the Christmas before, something I hadn't meant to include with the laundry: a thick wool sweater the color of cranberries. I wore it all the time and loved it.

As I unfolded it, I noticed that something was wrong. It had shrunk, turning felt-like. I held the sweater up before me. It was so small that it would fit a toddler. Seated on the floor of my living room, I pulled it in different directions to enlarge it, with no luck. I searched the internet for proof that its evolution, with the right intervention, could be temporary, that I could take it backward to what it was before, the thing that I cherished.

I knew then that I would leave. When my two-year program was finished, my loan payments would be due, and a quick scan of the credit report told me my monthly payments would be nearly $2,000. I already felt I had nothing left to give the collectors. I could not generate more money, at least not meaningfully, but I could live somewhere cheaper. *Maybe Chicago*, I thought, *I know people there.*

When I went to bed that night, in my bedroom without blinds, a luxury I told myself I could not afford, I felt the city watching me. I held the sweater as I waited for sleep.

Chapter 3

DURING MY FIRST WINTER in New York, not long after I ruined my sweater, I dropped my cell phone down a flight of stairs at the Seventy-Seventh Street subway stop. The fall cracked the screen of my flip phone into a jagged scar, drenching the phone in pixelated light and making it impossible to text or see who was calling. In the month before I got a new phone, I answered every phone call, unsure if who awaited me on the other end was a friend, a family member, a colleague, or a collector.

When my phone rang in the bread aisle of a grocery store, for example, I answered it. My mother was still incarcerated, and, in her absence, my father had been calling more to check in on me, so I thought it must be him. It wasn't. On the ground beside me was a basket of food, and in my ear was a collector telling me that to be a good person, I needed to give him money. I can't remember if I spoke with him in the store or left the basket to speak outside. I'm not sure if I bought groceries at all.

I liked grocery shopping, the act of picking out produce, damp from the mister, still smelling of earth. The experience of scanning the tomato sauces for the loveliest jar before choosing what I could afford. In a grocery store, everything was full of possibility and potential. The basil and the garlic and olive oil waited to become pesto. The parsley and bulgur: tabouli. The experience was domestic, reliable, even hopeful. Because of their calls, I brought the debt collectors everywhere; they *were* everywhere. What felt imaginative and connective and loving about the city—museums, parks, the crowded basement antique store a few blocks from my house—was transformed into threat. Nowhere was beautiful, nowhere was safe, nowhere was mine.

People who have significant student loan debt are living in a different world than people who don't, Jim, a borrower, said to me. In Jim's thinking, these people from different worlds might tread the same paths—to the grocery store, the park, the bank, the library, the gas station, for example—but their alikeness is on the surface, only a shimmer. "People without student debt bind to different parts of society," Jim said. And then he revised that slightly. "These people *live* in a different society." We'd been talking for an hour at this point, and our conversation had bounced around across timelines and debt burdens, tracing his and his family's loans alongside their biography.

Jim was sixty-three and white and had recently completed a nursing program, a second career, which he'd been pushed into because of his family's massive debt, most of which was from student loans. During his clinical rotations, the doctors and nurses he met were incredulous that he would need to do this grueling work so late in life. Jim had become exhausted from explaining to people that without this job, he'd never be able to retire. He'd thought of every option, every payment plan, every way to make money, and decided that he needed this career, which was not only fulfilling but dependable and well-paid, to survive. "I'm not discouraged about becoming a nurse," he said. "I have a pretty good attitude about that." What's exhausting is the explanation itself, which I sensed included some political education: He had to alert his colleagues to the fact that lots of older folks nearing retirement age have debt burdens so large that retirement is impossible.

"It's just awkward trying to tell the story of your life during a fifteen-minute break. But I do like storytelling," he said before taking me backward to an Occupy Wall Street event at which he first began to consider how it would feel to talk about his debt.

Sometimes, when I spoke to borrowers, I waited to ask for specifics of their debt, a question that felt complicated: I didn't want them to share anything that made them ashamed or uncomfortable, though I wanted to understand the shape and the size of what they owed. Jim offered up this information without my asking. His son borrowed around $36,000 in federal loans to attend school; his wife borrowed around $200,000 in a combination of Parent PLUS loans for their son (loans given to parents on behalf of their children) and for her own graduate program in social work; and Jim borrowed around $63,000 in private loans for his own education because he could not take out federal loans after refusing to register for the draft. "The moral peace of mind I got by refusing to be involved in the military was worth the higher interest rate," he said. Altogether, they were nearly $300,000 in student loan debt. Though his wife's career as a social worker meant that she should qualify for debt relief someday, Jim wasn't sure that she'd last that long. The work was too difficult.

I'd heard this before—this calculation of how long to keep unsustainable employment because it's the most promising pathway to paying down debt, either with accumulated wages or through a relief program. Other debtors in old age have shared their experience of working more hours, as their colleagues in similar fields work fewer and begin to ease into a quieter life. Jim was practical in his calculation: He explained which loans they would pay off first, along with the possibility of refinancing. If he was incredibly frugal, and he was planning to be, he thought they'd be able to pay off all the loans in a few years. That wasn't true of many people I spoke with. One borrower, a therapist unable to save for retirement, shared that she hoped to die of a heart attack so that her children wouldn't be financially responsible for her. She understood that her Social Security benefits would not be enough to sustain her.

"What do you think people without debt misunderstand about what it's like to have it?" I asked Jim.

"People who have a lot of money do not know what it's like to struggle," he replied. "For example, people who are never tired can't understand what it's like to be tired all the time, to have stayed up all night." He didn't make clear if this was a metaphor or a fact of his own life, that his nursing degree had meant he hadn't slept enough, but I suspected it was both. Large burdens often come with working long hours and multiple jobs. It's hard to imagine this level of exhaustion if you've never experienced it. Exhaustion like that coats everything around you, every movement, every skyline.

After our call, on a walk, I found myself studying the landscape around me, searching for another world floating just above it. I was moved by this idea of a secondary world, a place I began to think of as a shadow world. If you aren't looking closely or don't know where to look, you might miss it—though it's there, lightly clouded and squirming like heat over asphalt. In *Doppelganger,* Naomi Klein traces her own shadow world, which she names "the Shadow Lands"—a realm not bound to the United States. She writes, "They are the mangled and dense understory of our supposedly frictionless global economy." They can be found in the mines and industrial farms, the factories and slaughterhouses, the trains and ships, the warehouses and trucks—each location carrying "a distinct yet numbingly familiar story of depredation." She doesn't say that the people doing this work have debt, but many of them certainly do, just as the nations they belong to do. These two darkened spaces overlap.

The shadow world is populated by people at work all the time, facilitating trust, intimacy, healing, and joy, experiences made more challenging for the caregivers through the work itself. When I spoke to borrowers, it was not the numerical dimensions of their debt burden that I was left with, as shocking as those numbers sometimes were, but the specificity and banality of what they missed from the other world, the one over which they hovered as they managed kidney dialysis, checked someone into a psychiatric care facility, or brewed someone's coffee. Jim wished he could go out to eat. The shadow world has the same restaurants, but no one who lives in it gets to eat at them, though they deliver and wash the dishes, grow and pick the food that adorns the plates, or transport it in trucks. Jim was careful to clarify, as borrowers always were, that his desire was small in comparison to all the unfulfilled desires across the big, suffering planet. It was probably even small in comparison to his own suffering—his need to push his body to draw blood and clean bed pans for long shifts with few breaks. Yet, his longing mattered.

A different borrower shared with me that standing outside looking in for so many years had changed him, hardened him, closed him off. Because he could not live fully in the world, he retreated from it.

———

When I think of New York City now, I see a shadow city mapped atop the real one—a topography shaped by debt. The diner a block from my apartment, with the mosaic floor and art deco tiles, was not just the place where I occasionally ate fries at 3:00 a.m. with my roommates, tipsy and flushed from a night of dancing. It was also the place where I ate dinner alone even though I knew I should not, that I should make a sandwich instead. The terror that I might run out of money colored everything that I did, every thought that I had. I felt distant and different from the people around me. And, still, after particularly hard weeks when I was lonely and exhausted, I ate dinner there, selecting the cheapest thing on the menu, sitting in a corner booth near a window, watching the city as I ate.

I cannot think of Central Park without imagining the large boulder near the castle, where I perched as a debt collector demanded repayment. "I don't have anything to pay you," I said, atop the rock's cool, firm surface, hoping I'd sense where I ended and the earth began. I remember a handful of stores across the city in which my debit card was rejected as I waited for my teaching payments to clear. "Do you have another way to pay?" the cashiers asked. By that time, my uncle had offered to cosign a credit card for me, the limit of which was five hundred dollars because of my debt-to-income ratio. "I do," I said, watching them swipe it as if waiting for results from a high stakes scan. *Please work.* I always got by, just barely.

Steph, the borrower who longed to teach creative writing, shared that during her time working at the law office, debt collectors called her at lunch. Seated in her cubicle, while the office buzzed around her, she cried as she spoke with them. What was supposed to be a break from her job was transformed into a secondary job: managing debt and hiding it from her colleagues. No one wants their boss to hear them explain to a collector that they cannot afford to pay their bill.

When I think of this detail now, I imagine her cubicle as gray and empty. I wonder if this regular experience with collection shaped the way she inhabited space, in addition to the space itself—what she added to her walls or opted not to. If she kept eating lunch there or took it outside. If she began to see the slim partial walls as a symbol of the debt that drove her to this job, which she needed to pay the debt. Absent the loan payments, she told me that she would have chosen something kinder and freer, not the law firm that required her to tell people in need of Social Security Aid that despite their disabilities, they'd need to wait two years just to have a benefits hearing. Day after day, she heard stories of poverty and hunger and felt powerless.

———

Debt's topography is shaped by presences and absences. The presence of collection, a yearning shadow, leaching the light and coloring the landscape. And absence: everything that should be there but can't be—very often, homes. Because many borrowers can't own homes, they rent, and the rental process is also shaped by indebtedness. In the novel *Writers & Lovers*, by Lily King, the twenty-something protagonist's large debt burden means she cannot afford a comfortable one-bedroom apartment in Boston, despite her grueling work schedule. The only place she can afford is through a connection: her brother's college friend rents her a tiny room attached to his garage. "The room used to be a potting shed," she narrates, "and still has a loam and rotting leaves smell." The former gardening shed contains a twin mattress, a desk and chair, a hot plate, and a toaster oven that must be stored in the bathroom. In addition to living beside the intense smell of earth and clay, Casey must also consent to walk her landlord's dog each day, in exchange for a rent within her budget. Her landlord doesn't need to charge her rent. He has a relationship with her and her family and he doesn't need the money—but he does. The rent itself confirms something: that she should be grateful to him. There is little privacy; he often finds her at her desk writing, where he interrupts her work to give her envelopes from debt collectors "stamped with bright red threats."

In an essay in the debtor-zine *In the Red*, Leona Lee writes about the experience of finding housing as a borrower and someone with a disability. In 2018 when she was living with her partner, Craig, they learned that he had lung cancer after his initial concerns were dismissed by doctors as a winter cold. By the time of diagnosis, the cancer had spread everywhere, weakening his bones and leading to a series of falls that required Leona, along with a hospice team, to care for him around the clock. I cried when I read her description of her final month with him when she slept three hours each night, listening to him breathe on a baby monitor. When his breathing stopped in the fall of 2018, she was holding him. As is true for many working class and poor people, Craig had no life insurance, and after he died, he left Leona with only enough money to cover his half of the apartment for several months, but after that, it would be unaffordable.

Though she'd tried to negotiate one of her private loans five years earlier, the servicer refused her efforts, and in the chaos, urgency, and heartbreak of her partner's medical crisis and death, Leona missed payments and warning letters. Two months after Craig died, she opened the door to a sheriff who served her papers, which eventually lead to two judgments for unpaid debt, marring her credit report, alongside the thousands of dollars in debt she'd accumulated to pay for medical expenses. While managing her grief and her own medical needs—recovery from lumbar vertebrae fusion—Leona had to find an apartment, a nearly impossible task. Her Social Security and Disability Income was one barrier, because it wasn't three times the rental amount, but the deciding factor in her many rejections was the default judgments on her credit report. Eventually, Leona was forced to move into "a dark, cold, overpriced basement apartment" that was not up to code.

———

What makes renting precarious makes ownership even more challenging. Student debtors often have debt-to-income ratios that disqualify them for mortgages; sometimes late debt payments or defaults have led to lowered credit scores; their debt likely means they are unable to save money for a deposit; and the presence of debt often means they lack the family wealth that facilitates many first home purchases. This hardship is especially clear for Black borrowers. Recent research by the Urban Institute on student loan debt and homeownership for borrowers of color finds that the ownership rate for young Black borrowers with a bachelor's degree (ages twenty-five to forty) is lower than young white adults who did not finish high school. As of 2019, it showed that only 23 percent of young Black households were homeowners, about half the rate of their young white counterparts.

These ownership statistics don't just reflect a lost opportunity to build wealth; they represent the loss of *homes*. Writing about renter exploitation in *The Irish Times,* novelist Sally Rooney unpacks this loss: "Even aside from the financial toll of renting, consider the psychological hardship of trying to make a life for yourself and your family in what is ultimately someone else's spare house. Your home—your place in the world, your refuge, the stage for all your private dramas of your intimate life—can be taken away from you at any time, through no fault of your own, for the financial benefit of someone wealthier than you are." Annie McClanahan complicates this thinking. Your home, too, can be taken away if you cannot afford to keep paying the bank. She argues that with the existence of a mortgage—a word from the French for "dead pledge"—"...neither the pleasures of ownership nor the protections of domestic privacy are given..." Rather, she points out, "they depend instead on the ability to continue to pay over and over and over again." If a new hardship—a lost job coupled with high student loan payments—means that you cannot pay your mortgage, then the home ceases to be yours.

In a 2017 Federal Reserve Report, researchers found that each $1,000 increase in student loan debt lowered the rate of homeownership by 1.8 percentage points for borrowers in their mid-twenties who attended a public four-year college. For the years of their study, this meant an average delay of only four months, but there is nuance to that finding. This delay flows outward—a delay in one generation of homeownership means a delay in the next. And because home ownership is a major wealth builder in the United States, they write that "even a small change in home ownership can have wide-ranging effects." The cohorts they studied were in their mid-twenties before the housing and financial crisis, so the researchers acknowledge that the impact is likely greater now. Among the policy recommendations they offer to combat this impact on ownership is an oft-cited relief—student debt forgiveness.

The homes that are not purchased by borrowers are purchased by someone else, sometimes real estate investors who will flip the home and sell it for more money or turn it into a rental property. According to the *New York Times*, during the last quarter of 2021, 18.4 percent of the homes sold in the United States were to investors. Rents on these properties will be raised from year to year, sometimes wildly, eventually forcing tenants to move, sometimes to neighborhoods less suited to their needs, loosening their ties to their community and to what was, once, their home.

Debt shapes our relationship to where we dwell—whether we can mark these spaces as ours, put holes in the walls that we don't have to fill, make lasting changes that reflect us, because the walls and the homes are ours. It dictates whether we plant a garden, press bricks into the earth to make a patio, if it's our own children's handprints pressed gently into the cement sidewalk. And most of all, it impacts if we stay, if we *can* stay. When we are forced out by rising rents or a dispute with a landlord—or because we've been issued a predatory subprime mortgage, as was the case for millions of people during the financial crisis—we are robbed of the chance to build life-long friendships with neighbors, for our kids to walk or bike to their neighborhood schools or to be babysat by the teenager next door, to plant a tree that we can watch grow year by year, to move through the familiar, sometimes intimate, world of a neighborhood that is ours.

Keep zooming out this way: from bedroom, to house, to street, to neighborhood, to city, to state. Outward and outward. Soon we are looking down at all of the United States, across mountains, lakes, forests, prairies, and plains. Debt is shaping us across landscapes and generations.

Chapter 4

TWO YEARS AFTER I arrived in New York City, I completed my teaching program and moved back to the Midwest. A friend from Chicago flew out to help me load boxes and a few pieces of furniture into a small U-Haul. When I think about this move, I wonder why I brought anything with me, instead of selling or donating it, and flying home instead. The mattress I packed, a used hand-me-down from a friend's roommate, had a russet-colored stain on it from my period, which I remembered as two distant friends shimmied it out of the apartment door. My Chicago friend sprinted after them with a quilt, covering the stain just as the mattress greeted the sidewalk. None of what I owned was nice. Most of it was barely functional.

In New York, the terrain of my life felt unfamiliar, the geography of a life in crisis. Perhaps if I repopulated my new world with items from my life before debt—my oma's dishes, blue flowered sheets, a cheap IKEA lamp—I might help these two worlds to collide and overlap. If nothing else, I could keep the old world in view and perhaps enter back into it again one day to find everything loved and known waiting for me.

I left the city, in part, because I could not afford to live there. The student loan payments would be collected now that my graduate program was over, in addition to the credit card debts. Because my mother had listed her contact information on all the fraudulent loans, I didn't know what was due and to whom or even how to find out. I was pulled at by opposing forces: I needed absolute clarity about my finances, and I didn't want to think about any of it. I don't remember now what I did to track down this collection of passwords and servicers and payment start dates, but at some point, I did.

In e-mails from the time, I find traces of myself asking for loan information, which sometimes my mother knows and sometimes doesn't. I find an e-mail from my mother telling me she is sorry about a "mix-up" and that she's sent over "confirmation of a payment" to ACS ED Services, a Department of Education loan servicer whose contract was later terminated after repeated violations in loan collection and management. The document that's attached doesn't open anymore, or maybe never did. It appears that a payment was late, and ACS contacted me and then I contacted her.

I wonder if my credit, already low, had plunged further, into a weakened pulse. In her e-mail to me, my mother gave me the account password and username, which was her name. Her e-mail suggested that at the time we were navigating this debt incompletely but in tandem. A payment was missed, I was alerted, I alerted her, she paid, she alerted me, and then the cycle began again. There was no mention of how much the payment was for or how she, unemployed after her incarceration, managed to pay it. Likely, she and my father still shared an account, and it came from his paycheck.

———————

Patricia joined me from a small room in her home in Hamden, Connecticut, that she used as an art studio. Behind her, I could see a few acrylic and oil paintings—one of glaciers that she clarified were melting. Another, a swirl of reds and oranges, documented the 2019 fires in Australia. Much of the art she made—paintings, drawings, beadwork—engaged with the natural world, especially its extraction and degradation.

This house was hers now, and Patricia could hardly afford it. She inherited it from her mother after working full time as her caretaker until she passed away. Her mother had a line of credit on the house, and because of Patricia's credit score, she was unable to take it over. Instead, she needed to apply for a mortgage which she also did not qualify for until her sister offered to be a cosigner. When Patricia became her mother's caretaker and moved in, she spent the money she'd saved from a long and varied career. Her father had passed away from pancreatic cancer, and soon after his death, her mother was diagnosed with Alzheimer's. "I cared for her for ten and a half years," she told me. Her care allowed her mother to stay at home, to live and bathe and eat somewhere familiar to her body, even if, at the end, it was gone from her memory.

Patricia's debt, at its peak, approached $200,000, though she wasn't sure of the exact number because she'd stopped checking her balance. The seed of this debt was $35,000 in federal loans she had acquired to get her master's degree in physics.

Though we talked about what this debt burden had done to her finances, to her credit—the way it shrank her ability to qualify for things: a good rate on an automobile loan, a mortgage without a cosigner, etc.—we mostly talked about her home, which she loved.

I imagined it reminded her of her parents and of the life she gave them. "What beautiful paintings and a beautiful studio," I said.

Her academic journey was an interesting and long one. She received her undergraduate degree from Empire State College, now called Empire State University, part of the SUNY system and based in Manhattan; it's a nontraditional school in that students make choices about how they learn and how they demonstrate that learning, including the possibility to turn in portfolios. After graduating, Patricia received her master's degree, with a concentration in astrophysics, from Rensselaer Polytechnic Institute, taught for a year as a sabbatical replacement in Michigan, not far from my childhood home, worked on the Hubble Space Telescope, was a sub-contractor for NASA, and then taught as an adjunct again in institutions across the country. Though her degree might have allowed her a highly compensated job in research, she chose to teach. The work was hard. At one of the last jobs she had, she didn't have an office. "I had no place to meet students, no place to put my coat, or my hat, and it was the middle of winter in New England. I had to take everything around to whatever class I was in." What haunted her was not the poor salary or lack of labor protections but the idea that this university chose not to offer itself up as a real community. In the community she desired, everyone has access to and ownership over space.

The studio Patricia worked in had a leaky roof which had led to a collapse a while ago. Because she did not have the money to repair it, she applied for a grant from the city, which she was lucky to receive. But there were not enough grants to cover everything. "My hot water is working again. Finally," she said to me at the start of the call. She'd been without it for a week and had just paid to have it fixed, which she could not afford to do. She also applied for oil assistance from the city, and each year the application was different—

a new hurdle to jump in order to attain heat. The previous year they had run out of funding, and it was her Temple that helped her.

Tending to her home meant deciding what could be mended or replaced from her scant bank account, and what she, in her early seventies, could do herself or what would be left as is. There were always plants in her gutters. Her yard had become overgrown. "It almost looks like a meadow," she said, acknowledging the beauty in wildness. The backyard was filled with the invasive plant Mugwort, which she was allergic to, and her front yard had been taken over by Wild Asters. She was worried that a neighbor might have her ticketed for blight.

Patricia had recently applied for debt relief using one of the applications on studentaid.gov. Her loan was thirty years old, and she'd been enrolled in a form of IDR—Income-Driven Repayment—for most of that time period. When she first graduated, while working in Michigan, she paid off $5,000 of the debt, and then her wages were too low and rent was too high to make meaningful payments. "I asked about IDR at the time and was told there was no such thing," Patricia said about the servicers who misinformed her about repayment options. Eventually, after requesting forbearances in which interest accrued, she found her way to the IDR plan. When we reconnect a year later, she'll tell me that her application was approved—the debt was gone now. "But I'm still poor," she'll say. "I still rely on SNAP. My credit hasn't changed. I'm still poor," she'll emphasize again. "I still have to put medical care on my credit card." She was enrolled in a Medicare plan, but it didn't cover dental, vision, and hearing.

I reflected on the way in which the inside and outside of her house had grown porous. When her ceiling collapsed, her studio, like a garden, received rain from the sky. And in another room, she'd told me, there was a broken window. That gap would stay until she'd pieced together something new to patch it. "I have no money to fix it."

In Molly McGhee's novel *Jonathan Abernathy You Are Kind,* the titular character begins his job auditing dreams after recruiters meet him within his own dream and tell him that this work will offer him student loan forgiveness, among many kinds of forgiveness. His debt is enormous: "His loans, IOUs, and bills so diverse ecologists would be within their jurisdiction to classify the collection as an 'ecosystem.'" His student debt alone is a quarter of a million dollars. In addition to the low wage that will be offered for his nightly labor, the job comes with an additional incentive: each pay-period that he works will award him another hundred dollars of loan forgiveness. Dream-work will make his waking life possible

On Abernathy's first night of work, he falls asleep and awakens into someone's dream. He walks through a thick bog surrounded by thin trees and ferns. The mud moves up his legs, warming him, holding him, yanking him in. In the distance, a train whistles, but when he turns toward the sound, he doesn't see a train but a child, bloated, face down, dead. Suddenly, he's aware of another presence near him, a woman who is attempting, desperately, to turn the dead child over. The woman, who is the dreamer, is crying. Though he can't hear her, he knows she is talking to the child, maybe begging him to come back to life. Abernathy has been witness to this chaotic braiding of memory and longing but has not audited any of it.

Later, Abernathy will return to this dream and to the sleeper's other dreams, all of which include her dead son, her daughter, and a separated husband. His task, taken on behalf of the dreamer's employer, will be to remove what brings her anxiety and sadness. The dream landscape has been anesthetized and sanitized until the dream world is emptied of everything that matters to the dreamer. What matters to us often hurts us. The scraped-away world of the dream bleeds into the real world. What cannot be dreamed cannot be remembered, a realization Abernathy has too late.

Early in the novel, as Abernathy undergoes his training, the third-person narrator reflects on life's two labors, work and sleep: "Every day of your life, you will dream. You will work. Today, yesterday, tomorrow. To work and to dream is to forget." What I think they mean is that most of our day we are captured, first by work and then by sleep, and it's only in the few slippery hours outside of that that we really get to live. Many of the sleepers Abernathy audits are also in debt. Like him, their debt drives them to work and when the tender, humiliating, wonderful, terrifying parts of their real life make them, in the eyes of their employer, inefficient, the employer hires Abernathy to scrub their dreams, a process that will make them better employees, willing and excited to work more hours. Their memories, the narration of their very lives, are shaped and eroded without their consent.

———

Beginning when I was in high school, my parents gambled together, on Friday and Saturday nights, following long weeks of work—in their day jobs and sometimes, as bartenders for the events-arm of the community college or at the German soccer club my opa helped to found. I imagine that the opportunity to win money was appealing; they'd been working-class their entire lives, juggling low to middle-class wages with the financial demands of a four-person family. But I wonder if, more than the money, what they really wanted was to be transported and transformed. The casino at which they gambled was located on a giant boat that set sail at regular intervals, traveling along a river into Lake Michigan.

For a few hours on weekends, they underwent a role reversal: Rather than serving drinks to wealthy members of the Economics Club, people brought them drinks, remembered their names, and encouraged their participation in the casino through coupons and raffles. In one photo of the casino's gaming floor, the carpet is thick and reddish orange, interrupted by a gold pattern of something circular, nearly bursting. Machines are in rows in the foreground and clustered in the back. From the ceiling hangs an enormous chandelier. Red material threads a hundred small lightbulbs. It looks like a bouquet of glittering dandelions.

Suspended in casino-time, my parents lost their money, but probably felt, for a few gleaming hours, rich, afloat, connected to a reality different from the one that awaited them on land. The more money they lost, the wealthier the casino made them feel, awarding them domestic items that they brought home with them and gave to my sister and me: toasters, coffee makers, radios, CD players, etc. As the casino blended with our home, it became unclear where one ended and the other began.

Eventually, my mother began gambling alone on work breaks or afterward, disappearing into gaps of time, unaccounted for. "We can't find Mom," my sister called to tell me during my sophomore year of college—the "we" included my father, who didn't know where she was either. My mother emerged, eventually, without a convincing explanation, but then disappeared again, sucked into what casino designer Bill Friedman thinks of as the sanctuary of play, a space of constriction in opposition to gambling itself, which Friedman thinks of as boundless and smooth. Though a larger percentage of problem gamblers are men, women become problem gamblers more quickly after their initial gambling experience. My mother became an addict during the four years I was in college. She stopped bringing home presents from the casino, though I imagine they must have been giving them to her, and instead brought home debt collectors who called the house and sent mail.

When I was home from college, years before I knew about the theft, I noted my mother's return from work each afternoon. She drove too quickly down our residential street, running from the car to the house and asking me, "Has the mail come yet?" If it had, "Has your father seen it?" Often, his workday began and ended before hers. I remember her hands moving rapidly to sort a stack of envelopes, searching and searching for something I didn't recognize as a collection notice—though I would someday, receiving hundreds of my own. The collectors, whom I did recognize and with whom I spoke regularly, always asked for her.

We were always behind on something—the internet, the phone, a credit card, etc. My mother had an explanation for each outstanding payment, which I tepidly believed. I knew that we did not have money anymore, but I didn't understand that we, and that I, had so much debt. I grew to dread unfamiliar numbers on the caller ID, the sound of the phone, and even the corner of the kitchen in which the phone was housed. Eventually I dreaded the entire kitchen, its bone-colored tile, its cream cabinets with gold handles—the room in which I had once helped my mother fill deviled eggs and roll out dough for cookies. I passed through it quickly on the way to my bedroom.

Before my debt followed me, my parents' debt followed them. The debt scraped and wearied our kitchen, the interiors of our homes, and then the interiors of our lives.

———————

When Abernathy thinks of his own dreams, he is "filled with tenderness." In his mind there are farms, creeks, attics of books, "the ordeal of growing older. His parents. People he loved." There are, the narrator explains, "large homeplaces of people living inside of him, somewhere, no longer accessible." These dreams are not perfectly happy but they are complete, connected, and complicated worlds, restored and kept alive through the act of dreaming.

Toward the end of the novel, after Abernathy begins to suspect that his work might be more sinister than he realizes, he goes to the Dream Archive—where all the bits of stolen dreams are stored—to look for a colleague who has gone missing and stumbles, accidentally, into his own dream. He enters the attic bedroom of his childhood which smells like garlic and warmth, radiating from the kitchen below. His mother's perfume predicts her arrival as she ascends into the attic bedroom. Adult-Abernathy looks around his bedroom, noting the living, granular detail of his childhood.

From his position, his mother is backlit, and he sees her hair and a small patch of forehead. "He needs to see her," the narrator explains. "If he sees her, all will be fixed. He knows this somewhere deep within himself. Seeing her will fix him." But then two dream auditors arrive, and despite adult-Abernathy's urgent, hungry attempts to intervene, his mother is taken from him as he watches—sucked into a machine that will eventually make her into a nightmare. Her hands disappear into the hose and then her arms. He never sees her face. This means he will forget her entirely—that she will die twice, first in life and then in memory.

Abernathy has replicated this capture in the dreams he audits, including the dreams of the one living person whom he loves,

Rhoda. Cut off from memory and the social relationships that orient her life, Rhoda becomes zombie-like, shuffling between work and fitful sleep. She decides, like Abernathy's landlord and all the homeowners in the neighborhood, to sell her house to the city. The money the city offers her will be used to pay down her vast debts. And then the city will bulldoze her home and all the homes, which were containers for and the material of rich, meaningful lives—so that they can build a highway.

These extractions, of money, home, and memory, have loosened debtors' ties with the world—Abernathy's, Rhoda's, and all the other dreamers being audited. They are floating, untethered, bobbing in something vast and unfamiliar.

———————

When I was in college, my mother had managed, in the words of Abernathy's narrator, "an entire ecosystem of debt," in my name. As I gradually tracked down the information on each of the loans, I found her fingerprints everywhere. In another e-mail from around the time of my move, I told a friend that I tried to update information for a different account but was kicked out when I couldn't correctly answer the questions that would confirm my identity: How much was my monthly mortgage? And, from what company did I acquire my automobile loan? In becoming me, my mother had retained some of herself, and that residue made loan management impossible, forcing us back into contact every time I wanted to update an address or figure out what was past due. Though attached to me, the accounts were blended spaces—neither entirely me nor her.

If I did not know better, I would think that Abernathy scrubbed away my memories of those first years in Chicago, sucking up bits of my dreams as I slept off a ten-hour day of teaching at a college prep high school. Debt does not just shape landscapes, it shapes the act of remembrance, our reconstruction of the past. I know that collectors still called me—none of the debts had been paid off—but unlike the phone calls in New York, I can't remember them. My e-mails tell me collection was happening, and payment, sometimes, was not.

I do remember my first apartment in Chicago. Because of my large debts and poor credit, my initial application for the apartment was denied, reprocessed, and accepted after my uncle, the one who cosigned a credit card for me, offered to cosign on the lease. The one-bedroom was located just outside a newly gentrified neighborhood west of downtown, wedged between a highway and an elementary school. I picked it because I could afford it and because it had wood floors, was walking distance from a friend, and was on a bus line that would take me to work.

Of the six or so apartments in the building, all but two were empty, which I did not know when I moved in. One of those apartments housed two women, who hosted loud potlucks filled with music and laughter. I listened to these gatherings with longing from my apartment just above theirs. They moved out halfway through the year. The second apartment housed my landlord. He asked me to deliver my rent to his flat, and once when I dropped off the check, he opened his door wide to his own studio apartment, which featured a wooden Jesus—the size of a middle school kid—crucified and hanging on the wall, a box spring (no mattress), and stacks of books and Bibles. Soon after, he was forced into psychiatric care, and I lived alone in the building, sending my rent directly to a bank.

When the water heater went out or when my door to the outside didn't shut correctly, there was no one to talk to. I called the bank that I sent my rent to, and they told me to call someone else who told me to call the bank—an endless, bureaucratic loop.

In my three-story building, where the life of every unit had been blanched away when the tenants left, I filled the red kitchen pots that my oma had given me with water, waiting until each pot boiled and then emptied them into the tub. It was two more days before the bank would fix the hot water, and I wanted to clean myself. The process was slow. I only had four burners. By the time the water in the tub was deep enough to bathe in, it was cold. I got in anyway.

Chapter 5

SOON AFTER MOVING BACK to the Midwest, I met with a lawyer—introduced to me by a friend's parents—in a law office conference room in Michigan in a city three hours from Chicago. My commute took me past the highway exit for my childhood home. At a farm just off the highway, I used to pick blueberries. When I'd dressed that morning, I'd chosen clothes that were vaguely professional. I wanted to convey that this meeting mattered to me, that I was taking this opportunity, one that I would pay for, seriously.

This was not my first meeting with a lawyer. I'd spoken to someone when I was still living in New York. A high school friend had told her father, a corporate lawyer, about what had happened to me, and he had spoken to another lawyer friend, Dean, who said that he would be willing to talk with me about next steps. The little bits of advice I got over the years often worked like this: A friend with intergenerational wealth spoke to a parent who spoke to another wealthy friend of theirs. Wealth, like debt, webs outward, rewarding instead of punishing. The accident, or luck, of my birth circumstances—born into a middle-class town where most of my classmates went to college, many of them had college-educated parents, most of them were middle class, most of them, including me, were white—meant that I had resources where many others did not.

I'd delayed the call with Dean for a few weeks: As long as my action was still in the future conditional—*I would call soon*—there was still the possibility that I would receive relief. My friend's father had explained most of the facts of my predicament to Dean, but not all of them. In the year since I'd graduated, I'd learned that the fact my grandparents had cosigned the loans might complicate my efforts to extricate myself from them.

Their connection to the debt echoed and inverted our familial ties: It was no longer varicose veins and Christmas pickles that we shared, but a growing burden etched into our Social Security numbers and birthdates. The debt made us threats to one another. Either I paid, or they did. "You're right to be worried," Dean said to me after I voiced my fear. If I defaulted on the debt or, potentially, pursued legal action against my mother, the loan companies would try to collect from my grandparents. They were semi-retired. My oma was working at the jewelry counter at a department store, and my opa was doing contract work—he was a cabinetmaker by trade—for a handful of clients, after selling his tool and dye business years earlier. They did not have much disposable income, but that wasn't the point. The debt was not theirs either.

My oma was orphaned as a child in Eastern Germany just before World War II began. During the war, she lived with nuns, working in the kitchen of a children's home before distant relatives in Michigan offered to sponsor her immigration, which she undertook as a teenager after the war ended. She traveled alone, spent the entire voyage seasick, tasting crusted salt on her face after leaning over the railing to puke. "The key is to keep your eye on the horizon," she told me later. She never learned to swim and remained fearful of water her entire life. My opa traveled a similar pathway, from east to west across Germany during the war—while around him, cities burned. He remembers the sound of starving horses crying out for food and when a bridge collapsed behind him, wagons, horses, luggage, and children churning in the river. He remembers Russian soldiers offering him shots of vodka when he was only ten years old, hungry and dirty, covered in lice and fleas.

In Michigan, my grandparents became members of a community of German immigrants, always negotiating their relationship to their old home and to the war. "No, you're not," my oma said to me each time I told her that I was "starving." My grandparents were ever-present but distant, part of the regular patterns of my family life—attending my sister's and my soccer games and music performances and birthdays—but uninterested or unsure of how to talk to us about our feelings. My oma, especially, seemed just out of reach to me, closer with her pet dogs than with most people, except for my mother, whom she spoke to on the phone almost every day.

It didn't surprise me that she and my opa had cosigned the loans. Not just because they didn't understand the lending system, but because they were deeply attached to my mother. Their brand of love was material. If my mother needed money or said that I needed money, it was their responsibility to give it to her, even if they didn't have it. Much later, when my oma was in the earliest stages of Alzheimer's and I lived far away, we began to talk on the phone regularly, and she told me that she'd given my mother a lot of money over the years. She understood that some of it—or even much of it—had gone to casinos, but she didn't seem to care. "She needs you," she always said to me eventually, a turn in the call I dreaded. She loved me but she loved my mother more. "It's time for you to forgive her."

"I don't want my grandparents to be implicated," I said to Dean. It wouldn't feel like relief to me if the dark clouds gathered around me reassembled around someone else, especially them. From my living room in Manhattan, I imagined my opa in the wood shop in his garage, feeding a plank into the mouth of a table saw; my oma in the backyard, whispering to her roses in German.

"I'm sorry to say this, but I don't know if there is actually anything you can do, then," Dean said. Left implied: If you don't do anything about it, at this point, it's your fault. There will be no more help, which felt like another way of saying, you don't deserve it.

———

In the seventeenth century, the British colonies in North America modeled their punishment of debtors on English Common Law, establishing debtors' prisons to house those who were unable to pay their debts and did not have family or friends who would or could pay for them. Debtors' tenures had no terms. "You weren't sentenced for a month, a year, a decade; you stayed in jail until your creditors were satisfied," according to historian Jill Lepore, writing in *The New Yorker*. Because it was challenging to earn money while in prison, debtors depended on charitable donations, kind friends, or shifting laws to receive relief.

In the absence of those possibilities, their new life would replace their old one indefinitely. In Marshalsea Prison, one of the English prisons on which the American colonies' prisons were based and the infamous setting of Charles Dickens's *Little Dorrit*, the world outside the prison walls was known as the "Living World" and the world inside was known as the "Dead World." This nomenclature acknowledged that what was lost through incarceration was often that which made one feel *alive*: freedom to move, to work, to host friends and family for celebrations, to travel, to receive medical care, to worship, etc. It also acknowledged the inverted temporal experiences of life in and outside of prison. Outside the prison, where one was a living person, their existence had an expiration date; someday, they would die. Inside the prison, where death had already occurred, no such date existed. To be dead is to be without time.

In early American debtors' prisons, as was true in English prisons, poor prisoners were subjected to worse conditions than their wealthy counterparts. In New York City, wealthy prisoners, according to Lepore, were housed in the "sun-bathed" upper stories of the prison, while poor prisoners "sat in darkness, day and night. They had no rooms; they slept on the floor in the ground-floor hall or were shut up in the cellar." It occurred to me when I read this that without sunshine and sky, one cannot track the hours, days, or years as they pass. Everything is present tense.

In the Marshalsea, where poor prisoners lived in quarters called the "common side," prisoners regularly, especially during the reign of a particularly brutal warden, died of starvation. In *Mansions of Misery*, writer Jerry White's chronicle of Marshalsea—colloquially known as "The Castle"—the author notes that if prisoners became sick enough from starvation and could somehow raise what was the equivalent of a day and a half of working-class wages, then they would be sent to the common nurse in the sick ward, where they qualified for prison rations before, usually, dying anyway. A committee investigating the jail documented that seven women wearied by hunger lay on the floor in the sick ward because there were no beds, and in the men's ward, eleven men, described as "living skeletons," were dying for the same reason.

Though less documented, debtors in the colonies and early United States suffered in similar conditions. While felons received food, bedding, and fuel, debtors had to pay their own way, which meant that without money they sometimes starved to death. They were dependent on charitable donations or forced to beg from people on the street. Many prisons had "beggars' gates" where prisoners could reach out their palms from below-ground to passersby. Debtors' prisons were outlawed in 1831 in New York and, due to a federal law in 1833, outlawed everywhere else after that. It was not just that elected officials and the populace understood the conditions to be horrible, but historian Donna Murch notes in *Boston Review,* "Unleashing the appetite for capital investment and experimentation in America required forgiving bankruptcy so that potential entrepreneurs could start over."

———

After I'd returned to the Midwest, my mother and I fought a handful of times, loudly, standing across from each other in the kitchen of the rental she and my father had moved into after they lost their house in the bankruptcy process that followed my mother's incarceration. This kitchen had timeworn wood floors and echoed in a way the old kitchen hadn't. The cabinets, which my parents had repainted a warm white, tipped inward toward the floor, as if they were interested in what we were cooking. The kitchen sink clogged regularly, forcing my parents to use a plunger after washing dishes. There was less storage—so they kept pots and pans in the oven, and dishes packed high and dense in the cabinets. Each time I opened a door to grab plates or a cup, I worried about its contents collapsing onto me.

"I can't change the past," my mother said at some point during each argument, a sentiment that felt useless to me. Of *course* she could not change the past, and her repeated assertion of this human limit suggested that I was requesting her to rewrite history to afford my forgiveness.

I saw the past not as a fixed point that we walked away from, but something that lived beside us. I didn't want her to rewrite the past but acknowledge its continual presence in our lives. Similarly, forgiveness was not a future we walked into, never to return, but an evolving state of being. It was not an object that I could hand over willingly, a singular gift, but a space we could exist in together, moving toward and away from each other in response to pain and joy and memory.

"You think that I am withholding forgiveness from you. That I can just choose forgiveness and then everything is different," I said. "But I don't think it works like that." I had tried. Just as the past was still with us, so, too, was the debt. She and my father, out of shame or fear or denial, had left me with it. They had not done any research or contacted any lawyers or specialists to determine what was possible for me. What they proposed instead was that we would pay this debt together, indefinitely. Their plan meant that I would live with this enormous debt burden until I died.

My mother's responses to these fights were always the same: "If it would make you feel better, then you can send me to jail," she would say, her voice bubbling and acerbic. When she was unable to account for their shared lack of action, she reframed the argument through the lens of incarceration. Perhaps having been ensnared in a system whose goal is to punish, not to heal, she could only imagine that her suffering was what I wanted to be free.

And she was not entirely wrong. Though I didn't want her in jail, I did believe her intentional discomfort might be part of our redemption. I was angry that in the years following her sentence, she had moved into and out of jobs, going periods without regular work. "How can you ever pay me back if you don't work as much as possible?" I asked. Her felony record meant that equitably paid employment was hard to find. I thought a decision to take underpaid work, even work that she hated, would be a meaningful gesture with real consequences. But there was a kind of sentencing in that desire, an implied punishment, that maybe I wanted after all.

———————

My life in Chicago felt like one long day: a constant present tense. I awoke each morning at 6:00 a.m.—first bused and then later carpooled with a colleague at 6:45—and arrived at the charter school at which I taught by 7:15 to begin my workday at 7:30. The school day ended around 3:30, after which I sometimes monitored homework detention and at other times led clubs or night school for extra money until 4:30 or 5:30 or 6:00 at night, after which I commuted home. At home, I took a brief break to run and to eat, before I finished whatever work I hadn't finished at school—lesson planning or giving feedback on essays, wrapping up by 8:30 or 9:00 so that I could go to sleep and do it all again the next day.

By the time I left the building in winter, it was dark, so I tracked the sunlight hours through the four windows of my corner classroom, watching the room grow orange, the light catching the snow or reflecting off the icy streets. I taught three sections of tenth grade English, and each lesson was a replication of the one before it with slight adjustments. So, I helped students close-read a passage about Esch running in the woods in *Salvage the Bones* three times. Between these triplet discussions, I answered calls from debt collectors facilitating the same conversation each day. Did I know how much I owed? When did I plan to pay? That I answered these calls at all surprises me now. There was something hopeful in its desperation and naïveté: If I kept talking to another human, even to tell them that I couldn't pay, maybe I could prevent the collection from escalating. There was also a kind of penance in it: If I answered enough calls, listened to the servicers' accusations and occasionally their cruelty, then it would all add up to something.

Teaching was nourishing and collection was not, but together they formed a sort of extended choreography. Thinking about the relationship between austerity, debt, and time, higher education researcher and writer Eleni Schirmer notes: "Austerity leads not just to unequally distributed money but also to unevenly distributed time." I often forgot which day it was, what class period I was in—noticing the end of my workday when the light from the window had thinned.

In scholar Jodi Kim's unpacking of debt in the play *Harvest*, she writes that "we can speak of debt as a 'shifting grammar of life,'" borrowing a phrase from anthropologist Kaushik Sunder Rajan. This shifting grammar—its requirements, its payments, its potential end-date—"perpetually recedes before our horizon into a future tense, a vanishing point through which a 'not yet' freedom is perhaps glimpsed but always foreclosed." Relief existed but was always out of reach. My work would end, or at least lessen, when my payments stopped, but their conclusion was always on the horizon, extending into a future I never accessed.

———

When I met with the second lawyer in Michigan, I had no faith that his answers would be different than the last, but the monthly payments were unmanageable, and I had to try. It was the first time I'd explained the story to a stranger in a couple of years, and I felt myself trying to add context to my mother's decisions to soften their edges. "She had an addiction," I told him as we sat at a wide oval table. "And she feels bad about what she did."

As I summarized the story, I was not just conscious of what he might think of my mother, but, also, what he might think about me. "I should have taken a more active role in understanding my student debt while I was in college," I said, anticipating a question I knew he wouldn't ask: *How did you let this happen?*

"This is a really big mess," he said. He asked if he could bring in his colleagues for consultation, mapping out the key actors on a white board. He placed me in the center, and then drew a line, like a thin arm, reaching skyward at the end of which he wrote "father." Then he drew another line, another arm, reaching sideways to my mother. Two more legs, to reach down to each of my grandparents, and a bunch of other lines to connect them to one another. For emphasis, he drew a circle around me that thickened with each stroke of his marker.

"Kristin doesn't want to press charges," he shared with his colleagues, "but even if she did, she can't. Because of the statute of limitations on identity theft, that's not a possibility anymore." Many of the loans had been acquired more than six years earlier. He hadn't shared this information with me yet, and hearing it said so casually, so finally, made the ink walls encircling me feel real. "Without an identity theft charge, I doubt the loan companies would release you of this debt," he said. "Why would they?"

I imagined all the years I hadn't known mattered parading past me. Years in school and years filled with an incredible amount of labor. There was no alternative history in which I would have pressed charges and yet it still felt like a loss for these years to have slipped by, unrecognized for their ability to bring financial relief.

"I think, if you can, you should just keep paying on these debts," the lawyer said to me at the end of the meeting, offering what would amount to a life sentence. I was paying nearly seven hundred dollars a month, and my father, recently, had started paying an additional thousand. Even with those payments, the debt was growing larger.

Now, I saw my future—not like a line but a puddle, spreading around and away from me, deepening into a lake. There would be no career switches or graduate school or medical leaves. No summer breaks because I would need to teach summer school and tutor for extra income. Every pause in one kind of labor made space for another kind. And this would go on forever, until I died.

Chapter 6

DURING MY SECOND AUGUST in Chicago, when everything pulsed with heat and moisture and my classroom window unit couldn't keep up, I received an e-mail from HR with the title "Wage Garnishment." The e-mail was clear and brief, language meant to convey what would happen to me without judgment, or, perhaps, acknowledge what I had *caused* without judgment, though I doubted the sender felt as neutral as her language suggested.

Starting the following pay period, several hundred dollars would be deducted from each bi-monthly paycheck and sent to a collection agency in Michigan that had recently won a default judgment against me for an outstanding $13,700 credit card debt.

I felt embarrassed that something from my personal life had leaked into my professional life. As if the very walls of my classroom—walls I had spent hours reimagining into canvases for celebration, learning, art, and poetry—had been punctured. I had tried to create a space in which students invited in things that made them feel safe and everything else stayed outside. But I had not even been able to do that for myself.

After the shame diluted, I felt the shock of the news: that this collection effort, which my mother told me she was managing, had gotten to this point. I didn't know about the lawsuit and had not attended the trial. How could all of this happen without my knowledge?

I called my mother and shared with her what I had learned. "I don't understand how this is possible. Did you know about any of this?" As we talked, I kept my eyes on the door to my classroom, ready to hang up the phone if anyone entered.

"Yes. We received papers a while ago. We told you. Remember?"

"You didn't tell me," I said, my voice small and sharp. Everything seemed to slow and shine around me. I was transported somewhere else that looked like my classroom but wasn't. "I think I would remember if you'd told me there was a lawsuit against me." I wondered for a second if I was wrong, if this news had been so disturbing that I'd folded it into a box and slipped it into some unused corner of my memory. But I wasn't. I wasn't. I wasn't wrong. My parents had received a court summons for me and because they were ashamed— I felt myself, already, trying to rationalize their decisions so that I could bear them—had opted not to tell me and, instead, allowed me to find out from my employer who was going to take my money to pay off another of my mother's debts. "If you'd told me, I would have refuted the debt. I could have taken it to trial. I could have defended myself. My employer wouldn't have been involved," I said.

My mother would not concede even as I desperately tried out new tactics. *This is cruel. This is insane. How can you do this to your daughter?* After the call, the room came into focus. I was still at work—

65

though soon that work would be worth less to me. Between the $600 in garnishment and the $700 in loan bills, it was going to be very difficult for me to afford everything else, even with the extra work I did on top of my full-time teaching job. The debt, our debt, which had not been dormant but had quieted into a steady march, seemed to be announcing itself. It would not be ignored. Or forgotten.

Consumers can have their wages garnished for defaulted debts on credit cards, student loans, and unpaid medical bills. According to authors of a 2024 paper published in *American Economic Review: Insights,* about one-third of individuals have at least one delinquent debt in collections, and as of 2019, "more than one in one hundred US workers experienced a creditor wage garnishment in any given month." Those workers pay, on average, 11 percent of their gross earnings to creditors each month, a share that's larger than the average US household's monthly food budget. The study's authors write that, "the magnitude of these collections raises the possibility that unexpected wage garnishment could severely strain workers' budgets and cause them to fall behind on other bills, thus potentially perpetuating a cycle of debt."

In 2014, about 0.8 percent of workers faced wage garnishment, and by 2019, 1.1 percent of workers did. The leap of 0.3 percent over the course of five years was largely driven by student loans. Unlike with private debts, with student loans, the federal government only needs to send a notice to a borrower to start the garnishment process, rather than using a court order. In addition to wages from employment, the federal government can offset Social Security checks and seize tax refunds and Child Tax Credit Payments, making it, in the words of a report by Student Borrower Protection Center, "one of the most aggressive debt collectors in the nation." Borrowers who have a loan in default are sometimes unable to qualify for housing or find employment that will allow them to begin to make payments. These defaults are especially hard on borrowers who are on fixed incomes, such as older or disabled borrowers.

When Congress passed the Coronavirus Aid Relief, and Economic Security (CARES) Act in March 2020 in response to the pandemic, they required the Education Department to stop using collection techniques, including wage garnishment—among other kinds of relief, including a payment and interest pause—but 2022 investigations and court filings show that they ultimately were unable to do so. So borrowers, sometimes sick, often in and out of work or working less, continued to have their wages taken from them, even when the US government tried to stop it.

In June of 2021, the Education Department's Office of Inspector General reported that more that 392,600 defaulted student loan borrowers experienced more than one million instances of illegal wage garnishments between March and September 2020. What was taken from them totaled more than $582 million—money that would have fed and housed borrowers. The FOIA documents show that these illegal garnishments continued into August 2021, 18 months after they were supposed to cease. In SBPC's report they note that the Education Department did *try* to end the collection but could not successfully find a way to dismantle the collection machine, which chugged on hungry and unresponsive. Servicers could not locate employers or located employers who did not respond and in some cases gave up trying to contact employers altogether.

In hundreds of pages of complaints made public through a FOIA request, borrowers shared enraging and harrowing details about their inability to care for themselves and their families in the face of collection. In March of 2020, one borrower wrote, "I was told my loan was paid in full and was just informed more money is being taken without notifying me." They noted that their wages were being garnished at 15 percent. Similarly, another borrower was told their account was also paid in full but had their income taxes seized due to an administrative error. One borrower would have liked to go back to school but was unable to because she could not access financial aid while her loans were in default and being garnished and she'd been unable to meaningfully negotiate with the department to pay off the outstanding balance of five hundred dollars. A borrower with a disability was having his wages taken for a school that shut down for defrauding the government.

The stakes were higher for some borrowers. One person called asking to end the wage garnishment because she had begun a loan rehabilitation program. The debt got away from her because she was unable to make payments when she was undergoing treatment for her brain tumor. She didn't realize her wages were going to be seized until they were—missing whatever notification had been sent to her. At the time of her contact with representatives from the Education Department, she was facing eviction from her apartment. People explained that they were unable to pay for life-saving medical treatment. That they were homeless. Many of them were single mothers. "I was not aware that my [tax returns] would be stolen from me. I am out of work, my husband just received a kidney transplant, & we need that money for bills & to continue to provide for our son," a teacher wrote.

In February of 2021, a woman complained that her wages had been garnished since December 2020, despite the pause in collections and garnishment ordered by the CARES Act. These wages, she said, were taken without her notification and despite being a student. She was told she would be reimbursed and was waiting. Borrowers were desperately saying, "We thought this was supposed to end," and from what I can gather, the representatives were mostly saying, "You're right. It was." They didn't understand why it's wasn't. One representative recommended that a borrower go to the federal aid website to "read about the CARES Act" as if reading about it would somehow, magically, end the collection that the federal government was unable to halt.

In the documents, the Education Department clearly knew that many loan servicers had stopped answering the phones in order to avoid addressing borrowers' urgent questions about their stolen wages. ED Employees explained that servicers had stopped picking up "due to volume," essentially saying, it's your fault that they are not picking up because too many of you are calling.

A few weeks after I received notification of my own wage garnishment, I drove an hour from my apartment to Gary, Indiana, so that I could call the collection agency before parent-teacher conferences and record what they said to me without them knowing. In Illinois, it's illegal to record someone without their consent. My uncle's friend, a lawyer, had given my uncle advice to give to me. Recently, I found an e-mail from that time when I asked the lawyer if he would represent me officially. "I'm finding it difficult to follow all the advice, and I think it would be easier if you took me on as a client. I'm confused and I need help. I want to pay you for it," I wrote, to which he responded, weeks after the call, that he'd help.

In an e-mail from the same time, I found a recording of the call that I'd made that morning from an empty parking lot just off the highway. I remember driving past an old train station on the way to make the call. I remember locking my doors in the parking lot as I watched people waking from corners of the abandoned big-box store—ashamed but also aware that I didn't know the area and was scared.

I was wearing a brown corduroy skirt and tights with tiny golden-rods on them, an outfit I remember because I loved it. In the backseat was my work backpack with a collection of essays and corresponding feedback that I'd show to parents in two hours. I remember think-ing "this is absurd" as the phone rang to reach the collection agency. It didn't feel real.

In the recording, a man picks up right away. Before he speaks with me, he asks me to recite my Social Security number. He then asks me to verify my address, but my address is not the address they have on file for the outstanding debt. They have my mother's, and it's this discrepancy which is the focus of the call. I need to prove that I never received the court summons, and he needs to prove that I did.

"I've never lived at _____," I say, reciting my parents' address, which I'd had to record in a notebook in preparation for the call. The home they live in is a home I have never lived in. He does not respond to my assertion but says that he is familiar with the case; at one point, he spoke with my mother, who explained that she had used my Social Security number to apply for the card.

I don't comment on his conversation with my mother. I vaguely remember now some instructions from the lawyer about pushing him to become angry. If he violated the "harassment or abuse" clause of the Fair Debt Collections Practices Act, the lawyer said, I might have cause to get the judgment dismissed.

"My concern is that I never received the papers. I was never served," I say. He remains quiet, a pause long enough to fill a glass of water. In the recording, I hear us both breathing in the silence and am struck by the intimacy of it. In Sampson Starkweather's poem, "What if We Call This Tenderness," the speaker navigates collection voice mails that populate their answering machine several times a day. They try to transform this connection into a kind of closeness. What can't be tolerated must be changed. "Please leave me / something tender" they say at the end of the call, a nod to tender's dual meanings. They won't get money, but they might get something else.

In the moments I expect him to become angry, he forgoes language altogether. Eventually, I hear myself say, "Do you have documents showing that I lived at the address? And if you do, would you be willing to send them to me?"

"The court has the necessary paperwork," he says before adding something about documentation that's garbled in the call. And then he says that my mother confirmed—whether to him or to the person who served the papers, he doesn't say—that I did live at the address but do not anymore. He pauses and then says, again, "She verified that you did live there."

But I didn't! I say aloud to my computer just as the past me says nothing, perhaps stunned that my mother told him something that wasn't true. Before that moment, our versions of the past had often overlapped, at least at the margins. I wonder now if she was so fearful of authority that it felt easier to lie, to acquiesce to whatever allowed her out of the exchange sooner. I also wonder if I'm too quick to give her an exit.

"Okay," I say toward the end of the recording, a turn toward a new strategy. I sound clear and measured. When I'd remembered this call, I'd thought that I'd been crying. I'm unsure now if I was crying quietly or if that had actually been on the way home. "Would you agree to set aside the judgment if I could prove to you that the lawsuit was never served to me?"

He does not need to prove that, he says, because if I *did* live there, which was confirmed by my mother, then they did not need to track me down out of state. We go around in circles. I ask, "What about the fact that I never took out the card and that's not my debt?" I push this question again and again, asking in slightly revised versions.

He can't advise me, he says each time. And also, "With this particular client, I really don't think they would ever agree to set aside a judgment." Collection companies often purchase outstanding debt for cents on the dollar. So this company might have bought my $13,000 debt for $500—this debt, which the collector admitted, they would be very unlikely to release no matter what I could prove. This debt which my mother explained she had used my Social Security number to attain.

"Those are all my questions," I say at the end of the call, proof that I'd grown weary or that I'd decided I should begin the commute back to the city to start my day of work.

As I've reflected on myself navigating the debt, I've always forgotten some details, and that forgetting creates a distance between the past version of myself and me now. But as the recording plays, I'm in the room with a me who feels very present tense, who comes to me unfiltered by memory and time, who speaks in the same voice that I have now.

I feel the urge to climb inside the car beside her, to hold her, to talk to the collector for her, to ride with her back so that she's not alone.

Chapter 7

THE LIGHTS WERE DIMMED in the hospital post-op room. Across from the bed was a small Christmas tree, knee-high, and loosely wrapped with lights that were too large, their end trailing outward like a limp, glittery tail. My mother and sister had gone home to rest, and I was alone with my father for the first time since his brain surgery. It was just before Christmas. My father wanted to watch holiday specials on television, but the lights and sounds gave him a headache, so I was reading aloud to him from *The New Yorker*, something reported and long about US imperialism. It was wrong for the moment, but I didn't feel that I could pause to flip through the magazine to find something better. I needed to keep reading, as if my voice could carry us somewhere softer.

My mother had called me the weekend before Thanksgiving 2013 to say that my father wasn't feeling well, and she was worried. He'd been lethargic for months. Instead of mowing the lawn, washing his car, or organizing the garage, he was going to bed right after work, sleeping through dinner and into the morning. He'd lost weight, and his head hurt all the time, despite a steady intake of pain relievers. They were going to the emergency room the next day, she said. I suspected then that he had cancer, though I didn't say that to her. I hoped I was wrong.

The following afternoon, my sister, who had recently graduated college and was working as a nurse in our hometown, called me. He had cancer, and it was everywhere: in his spine, kidneys, spleen, liver, and all over his lungs, which is where it originated. Lung cancer metastasizes quickly, and patients often don't experience symptoms until the disease is advanced, so he'd been living with it for a while, unaware as it made replicas of itself that were dispatched to new parts of his body.

One of his brain tumors needed to be operated on immediately, she said, because it threatened to make his body's basic functioning impossible. As we talked, I stood beneath paper globes that my roommates had hung from the ceiling for a party we were hosting that night. The globes spun slowly, turned by the breeze from the ceiling fan we kept on. After the call, I climbed onto our dirty tile floor to watch them. Around and around they went, and I didn't move at all. He was going to die and soon.

A I sat next to him in his hospital bed before surgery the next day, he told me about the events that preceded his diagnosis: He went to the ER, answered questions, was given an MRI, and before speaking with a care team or having his diagnosis explained to him, a doctor asked him if he'd like to meet with someone from the hospice team. "They told me I was dying without actually saying it when I was alone without telling me anything about treatment. It was nuts." As my father, who was fifty-seven, had grown older, the corners of his words had been chiseled off and rounded; he talked about painful experiences with a bounce as if everything was a little funny and manageable.

"I'm so sorry. How devastating and cruel," I said to him. The timeline of his illness had collapsed into a single day: First there was a single question—what made him sick? And then there was a second—how would he like to die?

Now, I wonder if he'd dressed his fear lightly in humor to deliver it safely to me, hoping that I might echo it back to him unchanged. If I found what happened to him as ridiculous as he did, attributed it not to a breach in protocol and kindness, but instead to an obvious oversight or lie—there were treatment options!—then he might believe he had a shot to beat it all and live. The doctor wasn't cruel, he wanted me to say, but mistaken.

Before the surgery, doctors warned us that the operation would be long and came with the possibility of complications. When someone asked about what came afterward, they cautioned us to take it one step at a time. First, they'd remove the largest tumor, which would alleviate the headaches in addition to saving his life. Then, we'd decide on a comprehensive treatment plan.

I was conscious of what the moment seemed to ask of us. We should not, I sensed, say anything that might be misconstrued as a good-bye. It was unlikely that my father would die during surgery but not impossible. We should also avoid discussing the treatment and the life that awaited him on the other side. We should talk about the surgery as a discrete event.

To be an *us*, a set of connected family members working in concert to provide love and care to my father and to one another, was unfamiliar. Though my debt had bound us, it was not *ours* in any real sense. My father was still making the largest portion of monthly payments on the private, fraudulent loans and I was making payments on the rest of them, just barely. The credit card garnishment was paused, caught up in legal bureaucracy as my uncle's friend and I communicated with the collection agency. There was some hope that we might negotiate a payment plan and have the judgment thrown out. But the loans lived on my credit report. Their collectors communicated with me, over e-mail or the phone or through mail. If my father ever needed to skip payments because of financial hardship or because he forgot, I would still need to pay. It would be me who would not qualify for a mortgage someday. It was me who'd been rejected for rental applications.

The weight my father had lost since the onset of his symptoms somehow aged him and made him youthful all at once. He was thinner, closer to the version of him I saw in family albums. But his face was hollowed, his skin loose.

As we waited to get an update on my father's ongoing surgery, it seemed an inversion of a different kind of waiting, like that during childbirth. We checked our phones and watches for the time. We tried to read but couldn't. We watched other people, wondering what they were waiting on, before looking away when they saw us. We refilled our coffee cups and water bottles and brought in food that we didn't eat. We imagined the shape and size of what they pulled from him.

In historian Virginia Hunter's exploration of public debtors in Classical Athens, she notes that there's no single word that translates to the English "public debtor," but a list of ways you might accomplish this status: You might not have returned public property, such as naval equipment; you might owe the state money from the taxes you collected for them; you might owe them for an outstanding fine.

While the "public" of public debtors traces the lineage of owing, their treatment is also public, in that everyone knows about their debt and collectively surveils and manages it. Once a person became a public debtor, their name was inscribed on the Acropolis, a visual center of the city, and they, essentially, lost their citizenship. Hunter writes, "They were barred from Athens' political space, The Agora, and forbidden to speak or move resolutions in the Assembly, hold office, sit as jurors, initiate lawsuits, or enter holy spaces," all of which was known as "atimia," loosely translated to dishonesty. The public was informed of their dishonesty—suggesting that it is a kind of lie to not repay what is owed—and then the debtor was no longer a part of the public in the same way. Their debt weakened their connection with the world.

Imprisonment was rarely imposed—only when a case was escalated, and a debtor still didn't pay or when a public debtor tried to step outside the bounds of their disenfranchisement and use rights that were no longer theirs. In Classical Athens, like eighteenth-century England, Hunter writes that debtors were motivated to collectively source their repayments because they were terrified to be incarcerated. So the debt became shared, as it often is, with the debtor's loved ones. While family members might not offer money to keep someone from becoming a public debtor, they would likely pay to keep the debtor from being imprisoned, when their severance from the world would become more complete.

Family members inherited the status of public debtor when their relative died. Because it was men who owned property and managed money, upon their father's death, sons became public debtors until they could repay the debt. But because of fines, it had usually doubled by that point, reaching totals that were impossible to pay off in a lifetime. Their property was then seized, their family made homeless. Though women could not own property, their father's status as a debtor often meant that no one would marry them, or that, sometimes, an already married woman would be divorced by her husband because if his wife was an only child, she would transmit the status of public debtor to him and their future children if they remained married.

One body, isolated by debt. Then another and another and another.

———

It was hard not to see my father's cancer through the lens of debt. My parents had smoked since they were teenagers, permanently moving their habit outside when I was born. In the summer, they smoked in our backyard seated at a picnic table that they painted a new color every few years. Raspberry colored one year, then corn, then sage. In the winter, they smoked in our garage, seated on a cement step just outside our kitchen door beside a rack of shoes. Occasionally, I crouched to smell my sneakers at recess, worried that they smelled like ashtrays, which they did.

For a few years when we were in elementary school, my sister and I wrote them notes, which we slipped into their cigarette packs, begging them to quit, a strategy that relied on the power of surprise—our young words leaping out unexpectedly with the next cigarette. *We want you to grow old with us. We love you and want you to stay alive*, we wrote. But none of their attemps at quitting lasted. Huddled on the step in the middle of winter, the garage door partially pulled up to reveal the snow, my father borrowed against his own body: each inhale, a tiny mouthful of time, that later his body would collect.

When my mother found out my father had small cell carcinoma, 89 percent of which is attributed to smoking, she refused to believe that his decision, that their shared decisions, had led to his illness. "This stuff is random," she said, "and unfair." Her refusal to acknowledge their addiction to smoking as the primary cause of his cancer was born from the same wellspring of shame, denial, and fear that made it difficult for our relationship to mend. Our communication had remained inconsistent in the two years since I learned about the wage garnishment.

In addition to the defaulted credit card, we were still navigating the rest of the debts, painfully and imperfectly, which often left me unwilling to speak to my parents for weeks or months, eventually relenting. Sometimes my parents didn't pay the fraudulent loans on time. I'd heard my mother was gambling again and that my parents had gambled together. My sister had confronted them about it, and they'd lied, before later admitting, "Yes. It's fun for us, and we like to go sometimes." When my sister called to tell me this, the news was so unbearable that I pretended she'd said something else entirely: *They've become addicted to gardening—tomatoes and peppers everywhere—I can't get them to come inside.* But afterward, I stopped responding to their text messages and phone calls for a few months.

Because of my father's illness, my mother and I started communicating regularly. Sometimes, his care required it: There were decisions to make about surgery, consultations, and meal trains. For the first time since I'd learned of the debt, we were able to have a conversation that was singular in its purpose rather than one in which each of us was having four conversations at once, every word tethered to history and metaphor and yearning.

Years earlier, when I'd first returned to the Midwest, I'd begged my mother to see a therapist, and after a few sessions that she found unhelpful, she refused to go back. I wanted her to examine not just what she had done but what had been done to her. Even then I sensed that there should have been guardrails to her borrowing, that someone should have stopped her. A therapist might pull back the layers of shame and fear and see what was beneath, help her to stop running away from what happened and stand still to look at all of it in its fully complexity. It was only through that kind of reflection that we might find each other again and decide, together, how to manage this debt and free me, freeing us both.

What she wanted was to pretend that she could sever herself from what happened, and that the severance would save us both. The past, for her, remained a land from which you flee without looking back

———

Between my parents' bankruptcy, my mother's restitution, and the fraudulent loans they were helping me to repay, they had very little money. None of us had any. And even with my father's relatively comprehensive employer-sponsored health insurance, there would be out-of-pocket costs to care for him. Soon he would be on long-term disability and would only receive a portion of his salary, which would be the only money he and my mother earned. She was not working outside the home so that she could care for him. Bathing was particularly challenging. In their rental home, they had no bathtub, and the shower was narrower than a telephone booth, its spout fixed so that water sprayed forcefully against the back wall. They moved a small chair in there, so that my mother could fill pitchers of water from the sink to pour over him, avoiding his bandaged head.

Because of a miscommunication in post-op instructions following his surgery, the bandages grew into his wounds, blending with his healing skin. Alarmed, my father called my sister to help him, and while he watched TV in the living room, she tried to use Vaseline to gently massage out the bandage threads, which proved impossible. "Breathe deep," she told him, before tearing them off, one by one, opening the wound. Blood pooled and then ran. Both acts—the pitcher baths and the bandage tending—were kinds of baptisms, pledges of vulnerability, need, and devotion.

Worried about how my parents would pay their rapidly accumulating medical bills on top of their outstanding debts, I started a crowdfunding campaign, like two hundred thousand people do across the United States each year—forcing us to become public debtors of sorts. Instead of writing a post that detailed the story of his cancer diagnosis, the treatment plan, and a clear delineation of associated costs, I wrote a short essay about my father's care for our homes over the years: how he planted new trees and landscaped our backyard, paved a patio, built a deck, reroofed our old house. I can't find the essay, but remember its thesis—my father had shaped our home and the world around us. I saw him everywhere I looked.

"It's beautiful," my mother said after I sent it to her, "but maybe it's important to explain what a good and kind person he's been, that he doesn't deserve this cancer." What did someone have to do to deserve cancer? I was not open to this suggestion. We didn't owe anyone a detailed story of his suffering, and I thought he deserved medical care regardless of his goodness. I did not want to perform our need for anyone even as I understood the need was real.

When I shared the crowdfunding site on my accounts, I was aware that some people in my hometown might read it as an epilogue to the reporting of my mother's arrest and incarceration. If she had not gambled, we would have had more money for my father's medical care, they might say, an idea I was not inured to. Most people don't need crowdfunding because of financial mismanagement but because of our privatized health-care system. Even so, no amount of financial mismanagement should mean people are denied access to care.

I was suspicious of my own occasional discomfort when a distant connection of mine gave us another hundred dollars. My father, though, seemed to be singular in his reception of the crowdfunding. He was only thankful, even joyful sometimes. My full-time teaching job and after school employment kept me from being at home during the week, but I drove the two hours to stay with my parents most weekends. As we watched action movies and reality TV, my father refreshed the website, calling out to us each time there was a new donation. "One hundred from_____! $One hundred and fifty from _____!"

These donations left me feeling naked, but they left him feeling affirmed. People loved him and wanted him to live. They wrote him messages that oscillated between nostalgia and hope. They were reminders that despite a handful of years that had been characterized, in part, by isolation and financial stress, my father remained an integrated, valued member of a world bigger than our household. During the weekdays, he texted me updates about the fund-raiser, sometimes sending messages from friends of mine he'd never met ("Do you know _____? They gave _____."). Perhaps this was another kind of salve for him. I, too, was a member of a bigger world, loved by people he'd never known.

Early on, I tried to respond to these donations with a personal message of gratitude. I've found these e-mails in recent years, and they make me feel a little unsteady. In the thick of grief and fear and loss, I was keeping lists and checking off people's names, using my lunch period to write personalized messages, doing what amounted to a kind of accounting. They gave money to my family which meant that we owed them something. I gave them what I could: acknowledgment and thanks.

At the time, it felt like the web of indebtedness had spun outward, wider and farther, thinner, more gossamer than the one with my parents, but there nonetheless. These days, it feels more complicated. In the absence of the health care that we deserved, we were cared for by other people.

For every web and landscape of indebtedness, one can also find a set of connections and relations built in joy, trust, and love. In total, our friends, family, my father's colleagues, and my colleagues gave us $15,000. We asked for $10,000. I stopped e-mailing thank you notes not because of a new sense of enlightenment about debt, but because I ran out of time. My father kept getting sicker, my teaching work kept piling up, the collectors kept calling.

––––––––

When I remember the winter he was sick, I remember a sense of abundance. The meal train, organized by a church my parents had newly joined, scheduled a delivery of food every couple of days: beef stews, roasted carrots, scalloped potatoes, chicken—everything cooked with extra cream and butter to offset my father's rapid weight loss. People were always dropping by, with cards and cakes, blankets, offers to shovel snow, or to pray, something I'd not known my father to do regularly until this time. There were always lights on in our house: lamps, the television, headlights moving in and out of the gravel driveway.

This abundance, however, was contained within my parents' home and did not follow me on my cold drives to Chicago, where the few groceries I had were often rotting in the refrigerator before

I could use them. Laundry piled up on my bedroom floor; I stopped cleaning. My apartment was not a home but the place I tried to sleep at night before I went to work and then back to Michigan. As I rotated between these spaces of labor and rest and illness, I tried hard not to think about my own future.

I understood that based on the type and spread of my father's cancer—stage IV lung cancer—my father very likely would not survive until summer. Already he'd stopped making the thousand-dollar loan payment each month, and going forward, I'd be left to pay the entire debt total, which—despite all our efforts to pay it down—had bloomed to $382,000 in the seven years since graduation. I could not afford it. And though the garnishment for the credit card debt might remain stalled, I knew there would be new rounds of garnishments for the loans.

What is going happen to me? I wondered all the time, a question that made me so ashamed that I couldn't voice it to anyone, though it thrummed around me, intensifying with each new notice from the collectors that I was past due on payment, each call of theirs I sent to voice mail. I did not want to think about my future and the debt alongside my father's death. I wanted the chance to grieve it for the tremendous, wild, impossible loss that it would be. The debt took that from me, too.

Chapter 8

"CAN YOU HELP ME?" I asked Todd, a bankruptcy lawyer, following a weekend home to visit my father that winter. Outside, it was snowing, flakes so heavy they piled in my eyelashes. My friend, a personal injury lawyer, had recommended that I speak with a Michigan attorney since it was in Michigan that I acquired my federal loans and my mother acquired the fraudulent ones. We both knew student loans were notoriously hard to discharge through bankruptcy proceedings. "You should try anyway," he said to me, a pleading which felt like a hug. He understood that my debt was an emergency, and he drove with me to meet with the lawyer, where he sat beside me so he could ask questions that I might not think to.

When my friend had contacted Todd, he'd outlined the plot points of my story, and in Todd's office I shaded in the rest. As with the other lawyers I'd met, Todd seemed fascinated by the thorniness of my case, the way the debt had woven like a vine among my family and wrapped around us, as individuals and collectively, slowly tightening. He asked me to repeat parts of the story that didn't make sense. How was it possible that the schools did not receive the loans that my mother acquired? Or that they could be dispersed in her bank account, rather than mine? I told him that I thought it had to do with their status as private loans but wasn't sure.

"I think you should write to the lenders directly and explain, again, what has happened," Todd said after I'd answered all his questions, advice that conveyed a faith in the lenders' desire to help borrowers. The office was orange in comparison with the light from the window. From Todd's tone, I couldn't tell if my case seemed too complicated to take on. I didn't ask him if he'd ever successfully discharged student debt through bankruptcy proceedings before, perhaps scared that he might say no.

Unsure of what to say, I looked to my lawyer-friend, who asked a few follow-up questions. I felt something recede in me, pulling my future with it. From a distance, I heard Todd answer the questions and begin to wrap up our meeting. I didn't think I'd be able to make the hour drive back to my hometown to drop my friend off without a promise from the bankruptcy lawyer that he would help me. I saw the drive in reverse—the cows, their thick heads resting on wooden fences, the pines and the spruces, the signs for u-pick berries and wineries, the apple farm just off the expressway, and the state highway that runs parallel with the St. Joseph River before crossing it when the river reaches Lake Michigan. I couldn't do it, not unless the world had shifted in an essential way.

"The lenders won't talk to me," I said, interrupting the shuffle toward a conclusion. "I've tried." Communication with the servicers was scattered and discrete. In the past, I would talk to someone and then the next person I spoke to had no record of the prior conversation. Even if I managed to get one lender to discharge the debt, which seemed unlikely, that was no guarantee that the next lender would agree. And in the meantime, I needed to pay an amount of money that was impossible. Even a negotiated monthly bill—or, rather, *many* negotiated monthly bills—would be harmful because the loan totals would still grow larger, bubbling, boiling over. "I want you to represent me," I said. "It's the only chance I have to get out from under this."

Perhaps wanting to spare me the cost, Todd suggested that my friend and I talk it over, maybe even try sending a letter or two first, and then if that didn't work, I could call him, and he'd help me. I called him later that week.

———

My student loans that weren't fraudulent were borrowed from the federal government through the Stafford Loan Program. For my first two years of college, my federal loans were unsubsidized, meaning that interest collected while I attended school. For the last two years, half of my loans were subsidized, so the government paid the interest until I graduated, a form of financial aid to families who are determined to need it through the complicated formula of the federal financial aid application (FAFSA). My mother lost her job at a credit union during my sophomore year of college and didn't find steady work again, at a dentist office, until after we'd filed our financial aid information for my senior year. My family got poorer, but school itself did not get cheaper for me; I just paid a little less interest on the debt.

The Stafford Loan program was created under the Higher Education Act of 1965 (HEA), the largest expansion of higher education in US history, though not its first (the United States created land-grant universities by expropriating eleven million acres of Native land through the 1862 Morrill Act; it also rewarded soldiers returning from World War II free education through the G.I. Bill, among other interventions). The HEA doubled the budget for higher education, gave the government authority over the entire system, administered necessary aid to historically Black colleges and universities, and increased grants for poor students. This kaleidoscope of aid was meant to make college accessible to students of color, poor students, and women and—though there is some debate among scholars about the extent to which that vision was realized—most agree that it worked. Scholar Melissa Cooper notes that by "redistributing the costs of education through the tax base, [President Lyndon B.] Johnson had made it possible for students without family wealth to access an institution that had once been a major conduit of class reproduction." During the 1970s, Pell Grants, which allocated federal funds to low-income students, were large enough to cover tuition, fees, and living costs, so students did not need to rely on their parents, according to Cooper. "For a brief moment," she writes, "the expansion of public investment in education replaced private, family investment as a means of access to eduction."

The Stafford Loan program was part of the guaranteed loan program laid out by the HEA, which was modeled on a smaller loan program that started with the National Defense Education Act of 1958 (NDEA). Essentially, the government paid private banks to issue loans to borrowers. These banks charged students relatively low, set interest rates and the government gave banks an interest rate subsidy. The government also promised banks that they would be repaid if the students defaulted. So there was a guarantee that, no matter what, banks would make money. According to Eleni Schirmer, it "proved to be a very profitable arrangement for private banks, which took all the profits but absorbed none of the risks."

The guaranteed loan program was also politically palatable. Rather than funding universities directly—as states do with K–12 education—both the Pell Grant program and the guaranteed loan program were tuition subsidies, supporting a higher education architecture that relies on a tuition model. In her book on the history of student debt, journalist Ryann Liebenthal summarizes lawmakers' ultimate approach: They aimed to "keep federal costs down, to ensure that private enterprise still had a role to play, and to prohibit students from getting a 'free ride.'" And as the costs of college increased and more and more students wished to attend, it was easier for the government to expand the loan program than to provide more money to students in the form of grants or direct money to universities. In *Indentured Students*, historian Elizabeth Tandy Shermer writes that this strategy was "part of complicated fiscal and political calculations rooted in thirty years of creatively underwriting, not generously funding, public-private social welfare guarantees." In a phone call, Executive Director of the Student Borrower Protection Center Mike Pierce summarized the impact of this strategy of "unlocking private capital" to pay for higher education: "The student debt crisis sits downstream from policy makers' failure to deliver broad, accessible, free public higher education."

By the 1990s, it was already apparent that people of color, women, working-class students, and middle-class students were struggling to afford college, complete their degrees, and repay the debts that they were left with. "Most undergraduates could no longer choose between paying out of pocket, borrowing, or working their way through college," writes Shermer. "Students and their families usually had to do all three."

After a 1991 Government Accounting Office report found that if the government issued their own loans, they'd save a billion dollars in the first year alone, President George H. W. Bush, President

Clinton, and President Obama gradually and then entirely replaced the guaranteed loan program with direct lending. This replacement was a fight: Republicans were interested in shrinking the government's role in higher education and protecting the banks that had fought hard to maintain their foothold in colleges. "An entire house of cards was built with an eye towards extracting as much money from working people paying for college and driving it into these private sector companies," said Pierce. "No sooner had I even mentioned this system than Congress was deluged with lobbyists," said Clinton about his intention to replace the guaranteed loan program with a direct lending one. This thinking was such a threat to the student loan industry that there was a coordinated effort by fifty student loan enterprises to defeat Clinton's legislation.

The Direct Lending pilot program was overwhelmingly successful: It was less complex than the government-guaranteed loans, which administrators noted "[had] been brutal for the kids and their parents." The paperwork was easier, and students received their credit more quickly. Feedback from colleges and students was glowing, and because of its success, many more colleges applied to use it the following year. Despite the program's success and affordability, Republicans blocked legislation that would enable incremental expansion of the program. They prohibited the Department of Education from either requiring or incentivizing schools to switch to the direct loan program.

As fights evolved over direct lending, lenders bribed aid officers across the country with concert tickets and fancy retreats if they recommended their loan products to students. Shermer argues that campuses were "beholden to bankers, who determined whether or not students would get the credit to enroll so institutions could stay open. Small, underfunded colleges especially needed the help lenders were more than willing to provide." Campuses depended on these student debt products, which means they balanced their budgets with students' future labor. Shermer cites a Wayne State higher-up who said that they were expected to make more than a million dollars a year from these financial products. A report from the New American Foundation summarizes: "In practice, those profiting from the guarantee system could use their substantial resources to lure or retain colleges and universities, while the direct loan program was not allowed to make its own case."

After many more legislative battles, President Obama's 2010 Health Care and Education Reconciliation Act ended the guaranteed loan program, altering the relationship between bankers, students, and universities. While this legislation didn't alleviate students' dependence on loans, which they needed in increasingly large amounts to cover tuition and educational expenses that had risen precipitously across the country, it did ensure that fewer students would be funneled into loans with high interest rates and few protections because every student who completed the financial aid form would qualify for direct loans at federally dictated interest rates.

The law maintained a relationship with private industries, however, since the government would pay them to collect and manage the debt through the process known as loan servicing. Borrowers know the names of these servicers well: Great Lakes Higher Education Corporation, Navient, MOHELA, Aidvantage, EdFinancial Services, ECSI, Nelnet, Default Resolution Group. It's these names that slide through mail slots, brighten caller IDs, and appear in in-boxes with new loan details, service transfers, and promises to answer questions that very often are not answered.

Today, student loan debt in the United States totals $1.753 trillion, over 90 percent of which is federal student debt belonging to 43.8 million borrowers. As of the 2019–2020 academic year, 61 percent of students graduating with a bachelor's degree took out student loans with an average debt burden of $34,329. As of 2021, over forty million borrowers had left school without a degree, which almost certainly means they do not have the credentials to pay back even relatively minor amounts of debt—for them, a few thousand dollars is not a minor debt burden at all.

Black college graduates are more likely to borrow, and when they do, borrow more than any other race, a debt gap that widens rather than shrinks in the years ahead. The poorest college students, those who receive Pell Grants, are more likely to take out student loans than their non-Pell classmates, and their debt burdens are higher even after receiving their grant aid. Nearly two-thirds of all outstanding debt is held by women.

———

Rather than entering into bankruptcy proceedings immediately, Todd suggested that we send paperwork to each of my lenders to indicate that the debt was fraudulent and hopefully negotiate with them directly instead of going through the bankruptcy process, which would be lengthy and expensive and, very often, did not result in discharged student debt.

I don't remember the conversation when we spoke about this strategy, or many of our exchanges in the year that followed. I do have a lengthy set of e-mails between Todd and me as we employed our early strategy of attempting to speak directly with the lenders about what had happened to me. A couple of weeks after I met with Todd, on January 10, I e-mailed him: "I am wondering if you have made contact with the loan companies yet. I am getting frequent calls now five to seven times each day, and I want to make sure that we have started this process so that I am not just ignoring this debt without taking action." I'd stopped paying the loans, because the payments were too large for me to make on my own, and collection efforts had escalated. I recall the sight of unfamiliar numbers appearing on my caller ID and the feeling of deleting the voice mails and throwing out the collection letters—only for collection to be resurrected the next day.

———————

In *Writers & Lovers,* debt collectors follow Cassie wherever she goes. The novel is set in the '90s, before most people had cell phones, so the collectors can't make contact in her rushed commutes between home and work as she bikes along a lake populated by geese, across a bridge, near a quad filled with college students. But at work, they can reach her, and they call her at the restaurant so frequently that she learns their names as she might learn the name of a regular patron. Cassie recalls that "a guy named Derek Spike from Edfund" has gotten her number and spoken to her boss about garnishing the wages that can barely sustain her right now. She needs and wants to write and grieve her mother's death, acts that are stabilizing and necessary, but the collectors offer her no reprieve, no reasonable payment plans, no guardrails on the collection window that might keep the calls from feeling like a haunting.

She is so exhausted by her life that at work one morning, she looks into the mirror to see someone unfamiliar: "I look into my eyes, but they aren't really mine, not the eyes I used to have. They're the eyes of someone very tired and very sad, and once I see them I feel even sadder and then I see that sadness, that compassion, for the sadness in my eyes, and I see the water rising in them. I'm both the sad person and the person wanting to comfort the sad person." Her debt has split her in two.

———

In response to the January 10 e-mail, Todd's legal assistant, Stephany, writes that after "many agonizing calls" with the largest of the loan servicers, American Education Services (AES), she was finally in touch with someone who knew about a form I could fill out that would allow my lawyer to speak with them. They were going to send it to me immediately. AES didn't send it that month or the month after that, despite Stephany and me each talking to them, requesting the form, and being told that the form had already been mailed but could be sent again. And again. And again. Reading the e-mails all these years later, AES's shifting, nonsensical responses and complete refusal to allow my attorney access is so absurd that it's nearly funny. My quest to receive and fill out the form becomes harrowing, takes on the mythos of a quest.

In early February, Stephany talked to someone who said that I'd needed to use the security questions to revise my authorizations, despite Stephany and me explaining, separately, to representatives that I didn't know the answers to the security questions, which I had not chosen because I did not open the account. A week later, I wrote to her: "I just spoke on the phone with a representative and they said under no condition can they authorize a third party via phone and I have to wait for the form. It should be in the mail in a few days." I tried to complete an online authorization form but was denied and then tried to call the office for several days, but AES was closed "for weather." By the end of February, I was getting ten collection calls a day, and Todd still hadn't been granted access to speak with anyone about my case. I hadn't received the promised form, though I was receiving collection notes that I piled on my desk, stacked high, into a cairn.

Of the eight hours I was at school each day, I had exactly an hour and a half when it would have been possible to call the lenders—the same block of time that I had to plan with my colleagues, to meet with students, contact families, provide feedback on student work, or to—very briefly—do nothing. I spent these precious minutes waiting on hold to talk to a representative and then debating, over and over, if they had mailed me a document that I could only receive through the US postal service and not online or through my e-mail.

On March 17—two and a half months since I first contacted AES—my lawyer was finally able to speak to them and initiate another minor process that we hoped would be linked to others and then maybe, eventually, to relief. Their conversation was not enabled through the mail-form, which never came, but through an opaque combination of phone conversations and security guesses that I accomplished, piece by piece, over my prep periods instead of working.

———

The loans that my mother acquired fraudulently were private student loans, which meant that she borrowed from a bank through a lending program not guaranteed by the federal government. At one point, every major financial institution offered private loans—Wells Fargo, Citibank, Sallie Mae, Discover, and Chase, which is where my mother acquired my loans, through their lending program known as Bank One.

Private loans are generally thought to fill the gap in the cost of attendance once students have exhausted grants and federal loans and contributed whatever they are able to through their own labor or family support. Historically, this gap did not exist because school was more affordable. In 1980, the average price to attend a four-year college full-time was $10,231 (including tuition, fees, room and board, and adjusted for inflation). For the 2019–2020 year, that price was $28,775, a nearly 180 percent increase. Wages, however, have stagnated. As of 2018, the average hourly wage had the same purchasing power as it did in 1978. Though Pell Grants and federal loans have increased over time, neither is enough to cover the cost of attendance for many students. So, first students borrow federal loans and then they often have to borrow again.

In *Student Financing of Higher Education*, scholar Jeffrey J. Williams tracks this rapid ascent of college cost, attributing it to a decrease in federal funding for higher education and a decrease in state-based funding to universities. In the 1960s, he notes, students could work fifteen hours a week during the school year and full time in the summer to pay for their tuition, negating the need for any student debt, including federal. By the year 2000, students would need to work fifty-two hours a week, yearlong, to afford school without financial aid.

Mike Pierce complicated the assessment that private loans emerged to meet student need in the face of escalating tuition. "When a student goes to college, that's a dollar sign to somebody," he told me. Private loan volumes grew rapidly in the period preceding the financial crisis, and then declined some as credit contracted before ultimately growing again in 2013. The story of private loans is one of a half-formed, still emerging mountain. As of 2024, there was nearly $130 billion of outstanding private student debt. While some borrowers have fared relatively well with private student borrowing, most of them acquired loans from companies targeting wealthy and high-earning individuals with favorable loans and refinancing. Everyone else, especially low-income borrowers and borrowers of color, face high and variable interest rates and predatory repayment plans. They often attend for-profit schools. They default at high rates and because of less oversight, they are subject to even more abuses in collection and management. The majority of private loans are cosigned, and according to the Consumer Financial Protection Bureau, older borrowers—fifty-five and up—represent 57 percent of all private student loan cosigners. Though these cosigners may have been promised opportunities to be released from these loans, for many borrowers, relief has never materialized, a strategy which the Consumer Financial Protection Bureau says is potentially illegal.

Nearly a third of the private student loan market—over $38 billion—falls outside of the only publicly available reporting structures, which are industry-led reports developed and released by private credit analysts. The industry reports are themselves incomplete. The SBPC calls this the "long tail" of the market. It drags behind the rest of the body. The tail is made of small banks, private nonbank lenders, specialty lenders, fintech firms, and other market actors who don't engage in the reporting structure. According to SBPC, "though these loans meet the definition of a private education loan under the Truth in Lending Act, regulators and researchers are left largely in the dark regarding their lenders' holdings and origination patterns, as well as borrowers' experiences in repayment." In short—none of us knows exactly how long the tail is.

During the years my mother was gambling heavily, many financial institutions were offering "Direct to Consumer" private loans, which means that universities did not need to certify the cost of attendance or what aid they or the government were providing as part of the loan application. Borrowers could take out as much as the lender approved—often a fixed number as high as $30,000—funneling the loans directly to borrowers' personal accounts, rather than paying the money directly to the school. In the case of my mother, the loans went to an account she opened in secret. This process allowed banks to generate a high volume of loans, which they packaged and sold to investors and made money on immediately. Banks competed to get on universities' "preferred lenders lists" and sometimes their loan products would appear as an option in the award letter, listed as a "companion loan" to the federal aid, a strategy which became illegal in 2008, after I had graduated.

What these private loans did require as part of the application process was a cosigner. From the incomplete paperwork that I've been able to track down, these cosigners included my mother, once, then my father, twice, then my opa, three times, and my oma, three times. There are two loans for which I have no documentation. The origination fees for private loans, like interest rates, are higher than federal loans. On the loan my oma cosigned on September 24, 2007, for example, because of the 14-percent interest rate and high origination fee, I would pay $100,000 over time, more than three times the original $30,000 balance.

I often wonder what it is my mother said to my oma when she asked for her signature and her commitment to pay back this loan if "I" could not. Though my oma's English was strong, it was not her native language. She'd never gone to college and would not have known that this single loan was more than three times my tuition for the year. Certainly, college must have seemed to her like a place of unending need. Soon after my oma cosigned one loan, college needed another $10,000 which her husband cosigned on only five months later, after he'd already signed on $40,000 the year before.

"Think carefully," Chase warned her in a note at the bottom of the loan document. If you don't think carefully, it suggests, if you do not pause to consider whether your loved one deserves access to this money, then it is you who is to blame.

In mid-March, Stephany e-mailed to say that AES would be sending paperwork that contained essential information about the loans. In early April, when it became clear I had not received it, Todd spoke to someone who was going to put him in touch with someone else to "find out why" I was not getting the paperwork that was promised, a copy of the loan origination documents—signatures, dates, loan types, interest rates—that would allow me to contest each loan.

I asked the loan servicer if they could just e-mail me a PDF copy of these documents, or fax them to the law office, so that we could print them ourselves, but that was not possible. The collection calls kept coming, and I passed on Todd's number to them, asking the collectors if they would please speak to him instead, but they didn't call him.

More collection letters came, which I made scans of on my work fax machine to send to Todd. In one small slice of memory, I was certain I accidentally left paperwork behind that my colleagues might find. I spent all of class worrying, imagining who might find these documents, and what they would think of me, leaving little attention for students' questions or ideas. I ran to the copy machine after class ended, but nothing was there.

As I waited for each subsequent round of paperwork that didn't come, or didn't come when it was supposed to, I also waited for my father to die. Each weekend, I drove from my apartment in Chicago to my parents' home in Michigan, following the swoop of Lake Michigan in a gentle U. I tried not to think of my father's deteriorating health, or my loan payments, or how I would make loan payments once my father died, but that's all that I thought about. My old car didn't have a way to play music from my phone, and each time the battery died—and it died a lot then—the entire stereo system would lock, so I kept a coffee mug in the cup holder, which I used as a speaker. Often, I would turn on an album and place my phone in the cup, prepared to sing to it as the city dissolved into sand dunes and thick trees, only to realize, two hours later, as I was pulling off my exit, that I hadn't heard any of it. Instead, I'd been buried inside myself, negotiating a future without my dad.

A friend of mine had recently gotten engaged to her long-time boyfriend. He'd invited us to the restaurant where they both worked—she as a server and he as a chef—and proposed to her in front of her family and friends, who'd waited for them in an upstairs room, warming with wine and anticipation. The next week, two friends and I recalled the night. She's so happy, we agreed. My friends talked about their ideal engagements—who would be there, where they would occur, and who they'd call right afterward. When they were done talking, I felt something gathering inside of me, wet and buzzing. I put my face in my hands and cried. I wasn't sure if I wanted to get married but that wasn't why I wept. "My dad won't be around to see any of it," I said.

My family had already stopped talking about the future, as we anticipated the first round of treatment. We did not say, "This summer we will go boating on Lake Michigan." Or, "This summer we will drive to the Upper Peninsula, where we'll camp together as a family for the first time in fifteen years." Everything was near-present, narrowed down to this week or today. To acknowledge a future was to open a door, on the other side of which might be a father-shaped shadow, but no father. I remember the day he received the results of his MRI after he'd completed his treatment. I was checking my phone every few minutes, waiting for a message from my sister who was going to the appointment with my parents, unsure each time I flipped my phone over if I would see the number of a debt collector, a text that told me that the chemo had worked and bought him a few more months, or the one that I actually received: "the chemotherapy didn't do anything. His tumors have grown larger, the cancer has continued to spread. There's not much else we can do."

After reading her text, I looked up at my class, my thirty students in small groups talking about a book. I felt an egg break open inside my chest. I messaged a work friend who came to relieve me, and I walked into an empty classroom down the hall so that I could cry alone. My father had probably lost a hundred pounds since December; he'd lost his hair; he was no longer strong enough to stand up from his chair or to carry anything. None of his clothes fit. Each time I came home, I was sure that it was the last time I might see him, and I watched him while he slept, tracing the skyline of his nose. I need to remember this, I thought, guilty for anticipating a life without him when he was right in front of me.

"I love you so much," I texted him from the empty classroom as I stood by an open window, watching people on the sidewalk. "I can hardly feel my body," I texted other people. "How is this real? He is going to die soon." And then I walked back to my classroom where I kept getting calls from debt collectors, where I e-mailed my lawyer, either that day or in the days that followed, to ask if we had gotten the paperwork we were begging for.

Chapter 9

IN THE YEARS AFTER I graduated, I hoped that my family's financial free fall, a force so large it sucked me down with it, had spared my sister, who began college the fall after I had graduated. *The government will see that my parents lost their home and that they have debts everywhere they look, debt that grips tightly to every surface of their lives,* I thought, *and then the government will respond to that financial reality by helping my sister, Kelsey, go to school.* At the time, I knew very little about higher education financing and still believed the government's aid was not just in proportion to a student's need but so comprehensive that it would be enough.

This vision of my sister's post-graduate life of relative ease sustained me. In it, her life was the inverse of mine. While I worked twelve-hour days, five days a week, commuting to work in the pre-dawn and commuting home after dark, my sister would work just one job, a nursing job, for the normal number of hours. She'd journey to work under buttery skies. Kelsey's loan payments would be reasonable. I couldn't even imagine what reasonable was at the time. Two hundred dollars a month? My dream emanated out of me. It was bi-directional in that it was forward thinking, hopeful about a future in which my sister did not suffer like I did, and backward thinking in that it infused what had happened to me with meaning: My suffering made my sister's life freer. What happened to me was not for nothing.

My projection was accurate and inaccurate at once. After my mother lost her job and struggled to find employment, my family's household income plummeted, dropping the family's expected contribution to a number that unlocked new kinds of aid, for which I hadn't qualified. Kelsey explained to me much later she was given around $3,000 in Pell Grants and $2,000 in Academic Competitiveness Grants (an expired program based on academic merit and financial need), two Perkins loans (an expired loan program in which schools offered federal loans), and $47,829 in federal loans, most of which were subsidized. She also remembered qualifying for work-study hours and securing a job through America Reads, a program in which college students tutor K-6 graders. She read to children for a couple of years before finding a more lucrative job that offered her more hours: nannying for two doctors she met through her nursing program.

———————

When searching for the Free Application for Federal Student Aid (FAFSA), my predictive algorithm directs me to a series of sponsored organizations that promise to support my or my children's journey to college. These organizations, all of which seem to be nonprofits, acknowledge that this journey to college will likely involve FAFSA and that the financial aid process will be for me, and the 20 million families that fill out the FAFSA each year, complicated.

So complicated that higher education scholar Sara Goldrick-Rab calls FAFSA "a small American bureaucratic tragedy all its own."

I find the federal website, four links down, and start to fill out a form. I begin by watching a series of animated videos in which people without any eyes but thick, sculpted eyebrows explain to me what FAFSA is. The speaker, a Black woman, tells me that the form will take me about one hour to complete. On a second video, I learn that the eyeless woman has a name, Taylor, and that she is in fact a "college counselor" tasked with answering my questions and not what she appears to be: an avatar of the federal government delivering me information in a one-way format.

The FAFSA I'm making my way through now is the product of a botched 2024 rollout by the Biden administration which supposedly eased the application burden for families and actually left schools and students scrambling to understand the scope of their aid packages as acceptance deadlines approached. This version, like all versions of FAFSA, is not a neutral collector of neutral data but, in the words of scholar Caitlin Zaloom, "moral technology" that "delivers and enforces cultural and economic mandates."

Though the information itself might take one hour to enter in the form, as counselor Taylor tells us, the gathering of the information takes most students and families much longer and often involves lengthy and challenging communication between students and parents and across households. Regardless of whether the student lives with both parents, both parents' Social Security numbers are required, along with their incomes, savings, investments and real estate (with the exception of the home the student lives in), educational levels, years of national service, and whether they receive aid from other governmental programs. The form supposes that students' families are comfortable sharing that information with the student, and that even painful separations between parents or estrangements between students and parents can and should be overcome in the name of the form. One borrower told me that the form was especially challenging for him and his family because his parents only spoke and read Spanish, and he was forced to translate the process, sometimes grasping for technical words he didn't know.

FAFSA's definition of a parent includes only biological and adoptive parents, excluding aunts, uncles, legal guardians, foster parents, siblings, and family friends who might be the student's parents in practice, the people the student turns to for love, wisdom, and financial support. FAFSA's exclusion neglects an opportunity to see the emotional contours of the student's life, but more importantly, it neglects the financial contours. The parent that they recognize on the form, for example, might be entirely out of the student's life, offering no material support whatsoever. Their income dictates what kind of aid the student will be offered, even if they won't be helping the student.

Some students' parents might be offering financial support to extended family and friends, as is true for many households of color and immigrant families, and they are unable to report this because it falls outside the guidelines for dependents. Because these extended family members are not biological or adoptive children, their care—however real and necessary and lifesaving it is—doesn't count. A student's parents also cannot report debt that they have related to medical care, transportation, utility, or credit cards. Debt that many of these families had to take on in order to live and work will make paying for college impossible. The form does not recognize the ways in which a poor family's wealth is diluted, shared with the people they love or taken by collectors. Conversely, the form does not see ways in which middle-class and wealthy families are able to keep their wealth. For example, parents do not need to report the equity they've accumulated in their place of residence or the value of their tax-advantaged retirement accounts.

These gaps amount to a sanctioning of a certain kind of family: one with two parents who are still married and living together, a retirement account, a mortgage which the family is making payments on, and an ongoing dialogue between parents and children in which finances are talked about openly. Zaloom writes that the form "fragments complicated and rich histories and relationships into informational bits. When that data is reassembled into an image of a family and its finances, it is often one that family members don't recognize."

"Every year the process of applying for loans was always stressful. It was something I had avoided. I had a lot of anxiety about debt, about a lot of things," Allison said to me about filling out the FAFSA form. Allison, in her mid-thirties, queer, and Asian American, approached the process as an outsider. Each of her parents was an immigrant: Her father migrated from England and her mother from southern China—both in their teens—and despite some brief interaction with the US higher education system, neither of them got a four-year degree, though Allison's mother eventually got her associate's, which she paid for out of pocket. At the end of high school, it was important to Allison's family that she be the first in her family to graduate college. The completion of her academic journey would not just be for her but for *them*. There was no college fund set aside for Allison, so the entirety of the net cost would be borne between the school—if they were lucky—and student loans.

Allison grew up in the Midwest, and a small, private school in a bordering state reached out during her senior year, asking her to apply and explaining that if she did well enough on a set of campus tests, she would qualify for a 100 percent tuition scholarship, leaving her to pay for room and board and other living expenses each year. Allison applied to the school, did well on the test, and was offered the scholarship. "That's when I learned that I had to take out quite a bit of debt," Allison said, around $13,000 a year to cover room, board, and fees. But she'd already been sold on the vision of the school and perhaps to some degree on the school's vision of her. If the tuition sticker confirmed that the school was valuable, then the scholarship confirmed that she was.

———————

Like me, my sister talks quickly, her voice electrified with what comes next. Kelsey has dark brown hair now, just a shade or two removed from black, a confluence of genetics and hair dye, but when she started college, her hair was blond. Her eyes are aloe-colored, like my mother's. When I think of her, I think of her first as she was at eighteen and in the years before when we lived together in my parents' house. I see her bruised knees and bowlegs and missing a front tooth. Because we were five years apart, even when we played together, we weren't playing the same games the same way. Once I set up a classroom in our basement, using a real desk my mother bought at a garage sale and a chalkboard she'd hung on the wall for us. This was school: I was her teacher and she was my student, and the classroom rituals and rules shifted often and quickly, without her consent. Neither of us understood if she was supposed to be learning through this process or if our exchanges were purely performance. I want to believe I was tender and patient with her because I loved her, but I worry that I was not.

The federal aid program worked as intended in that it was responsive to familial need. But I was wrong in imagining this responsiveness offered meaningful material support. Despite my mother's addiction and lost job, my parents' lost home, their maxed out accounts, and their inability to offer my sister money to transition her to school ("my friends' parents pooled money together to buy me a computer," Kelsey remembered), the government gave my sister, over the course of five years, essentially $5,000 to attend her in-state school—The University of Michigan, like me—with a yearly tuition of about $11,000, not including room and board and books and everything else.

FAFSA calculates something that was once called the Expected Family Contribution (EFC) and is now called the Student Aid Index (SAI). The Department of Education started using SAI rather than EFC because the old title was confusing: families assumed that the EFC would be *all* that they needed to pay for school, and that the EFC, along with the school's aid package, should cover the total cost of attendance. The SAI removes the word "family," noteworthy because the equation that determines it is still entirely dependent on the student's family wealth and makeup. "Index" acknowledges a measurement taken without suggesting that the family will contribute what has been measured. Often, they can't. And even when they can, there are still sometimes gaps between the school's aid, the SAI, and the total cost of attendance.

As parents and students move in and out of jobs or receive raises, the SAI adjusts accordingly. A family earning less than $27,000 in the 2022–2023 school year would have an SAI of zero, which does not mean that the family wouldn't pay anything for school. The SAI, in turn, generates a menu of aid possibilities: 1) A Pell Grant whose amount and value varies according to year and according to school (this money goes further at schools with more affordable tuition). In the 2022–2023 school year students could receive up to $6,895 if they were enrolled full-time. 2) A Federal Education Opportunity Grant of between $100 and $4,000. The schools themselves give out these grants, and once that aid has been exhausted, no funds are available. If a student applies for FAFSA too late or goes to a school serving primarily low-income students, they might not receive any money. 3) Federal Work Study. This aid is not a grant, but compensation for work, and like most jobs, it must be applied for. Schools serving primarily low-income students often do not have enough positions to support all the students who qualify for work study. 4) Whether students qualify for subsidized loans, which the government pays interest on while the student is in school. All US citizens are eligible for unsubsidized loans, and all direct loans, subsidized or unsubsidized, have yearly borrowing caps.

Sara Goldrick-Rab, in her intensive study of students enrolled in a Wisconsin aid program, notes that even when all grants are taken into account, "Pell recipients face a net price [a word she uses instead of "cost" to acknowledge institutions' choice in what they charge] of more than $8,000 per year—at the nation's least expensive option, the community college." In other words, students from the poorest families, attending the most affordable schools, still have a gap in what's been given and what they need. So they either borrow money or work full-time, making it hard to complete their degrees. They often need to do both.

"The racial wealth gap, high student debt levels, and unequal higher education access and outcomes for students of color—and particularly women of color—continuously reinforce one another," according to 2019 research coauthored by the Roosevelt Institute, the Century Foundation, and Demos. This racial wealth gap, born out of chattel slavery and its aftermath, is reinforced, according to the report, "in every key economic and social resource—from housing to banking to the K–12 education system." It means that Black children live in highly segregated neighborhoods, graduate from highly segregated and underfunded high schools, and then often attend for-profit predatory schools or schools with fewer financial resources, such as community colleges or historically Black colleges and universities, which translates, in addition to inequality in credit access, into Black students relying more heavily on debt and taking out riskier forms of debt. Absent a financial safety net and often caring for family or working while in school, Black students are forced out of school at higher rates, locking them out of the sorts of jobs that would make repayment possible. Even for those students who graduate, because of these interlocking inequalities, including discrimination in the job market, repayment is challenging.

Research by Ben Miller at American Progress shows that 32 percent of Black borrowers who entered school during the 2011–2012 academic year have defaulted on their loans, compared to 13 percent of their white peers. Black adults are almost twice as likely as white adults to have student loan debt, and Black borrowers with bachelor's degrees are more likely to default on their loans than white borrowers who did not finish school. Miller shows that twelve years after entering college, the median Black borrower had made no progress paying down their loans: the loan burdens had actually *increased* during that time period. In conversations, Black borrowers say it's like being in a sinking ship. You desperately try to scoop out water with a bucket, but the boat keeps filling. You are fighting hard to save your life and the lives of the people you love, and the water rises anyway.

The FAFSA process was so stressful for Allison's mother that the management fell to her father alone. Allison didn't think her father was irresponsible with money, but he was inexperienced with loans, so he signed up for the entire loan package, all the offered federal loans, along with a Parent PLUS loan. "We didn't even know if we had chosen the right amounts," Allison said. They believed that this was what was required to go to school; you just clicked "yes" on everything. "I guess we signed our lives away, and didn't even think about it." While the FAFSA process reflected and relied on all of them, so, too, did the debt itself: Each of them would bear loan burdens into their futures.

"We didn't really run into any hiccups until I was applying for my fourth year and got rejected," Allison said.

I tried to clarify which loans she was rejected for: Federal student loans are not dependent on a student's credit and don't require a cosigner. "Was it for the Parent PLUS loans?" I asked.

"No, it was for all of them."

While there are some eligibility guidelines for federal loans—you must be a citizen, enrolled in a degree-granting program, and not incarcerated, for example—Allison met all of those. But I didn't push her on that fact. Regardless of cause, she didn't have money to attend school senior year. Her mother insisted that they were rejected for tax reasons—she'd completed them late—and Allison suspected that it had to do with the fact her parents had lost their house through foreclosure that year. "We've never really come to a consensus about why that is," Allison said in reference to the rejection. In her parents' muddled, incomplete explanation, it was hard for me not to reach for the lie. Had her parents been dishonest about what happened? Or, had they, too, been unsure of why they'd been denied the debt that would allow their daughter to finish her senior year of college?

Her school allowed her to complete the fall semester, floating her a campus-based loan to cover the gap in her living expenses but would not allow her to complete her spring semester until she began making payments on her outstanding debt on the campus loan, which she was unable to do, so she left. This departure was especially painful around graduation, when everyone she knew—all her friends, her entire campus community—graduated but she could not.

———

My sister's federal debt today is $61,730. With the exception of the student loan moratorium that started during the pandemic, in which she did not make payments and interest did not collect, she's made payments on these federal loans, monthly, since her graduation in 2013. Despite these regular payments, which began as $400 and are now around $700, her debt burden has grown larger, not smaller.

"How does it feel for these debts to grow even as you pay so much money?" I asked her. It's a question I ask borrowers because I want to hear them describe their experiences. But it's also a question that feels strange—I mean, how do I *think* it feels to pay every bit of disposable income you have, and often money you don't have, toward a debt burden whose hunger is bottomless. I sometimes try out metaphors because the words I have available don't feel like enough. It's like throwing ice cubes into a forest fire. Like trying to empty a pool using a teaspoon. Even the metaphors I create feel flat.

"It feels fucking awful," she told me, acknowledging the situation's absurdity. She went to school to become a nurse. First, she worked in a post-op recovery wing in our hometown in Michigan, and then, in North Carolina, she moved into units that involved increased amounts of technological and physiological knowledge. Before the pandemic, she worked in a lung transplant ward, where she tended to patients waiting for new lungs and patients who found them. Many of her patients died. She spent a lot of her day with grieving families. During the pandemic, because she understood how to keep someone alive on an extracorporeal membrane oxygenation machine (known as ECMO), she was deployed to the COVID ward, where she worked long shifts terrified that she, too, might die. Following her shifts, we'd sometimes FaceTime, and I'd note the imprint of her protective equipment on her forehead. Despite offering herself to all these people, she now owed the government, ten years after graduation, *more* than she originally borrowed. She'd applied for Public Service Loan Forgiveness, a program that would hopefully provide her relief someday. But while she waited, she was suffering.

"What about the private debt?" I asked her. "What is that debt burden right now?"

"It's about nine thousand after being sixteen thousand at its peak when I learned about it," she said. Kelsey first learned about her private debt, a history which my mother disputes, in 2014, a couple of years after her graduation. Our grandmother, my father's mother, called to tell my sister that she'd been getting collection notes and calls for a Chase Bank private loan, a loan of Kelsey's that she had cosigned on. My grandmother was worried about her. Had she become financially distressed?

My sister hadn't known about the loan, and the financial distress was my parents'; they had been the ones making payments on the loan, mailing in checks each month. My grandmother called me around the same time asking, "What is going on with your sister?" I was worried for my sister and for my grandmother who had been living alone since her second husband had died fifteen years earlier, paying her bills through her work at a department store and as a home health aide, work that she loved but that was undervalued. She couldn't afford to make payments.

When my grandmother called, a memory surfaced from years earlier, one so submerged I'd lost track of it. Right after I graduated, and around the time my mother was incarcerated, my parents shared a strategy they had employed to manage the family's debts. They had taken out a private student loan of ten thousand dollars in Kelsey's name to pay down one of my debts, a process they implied Kelsey had agreed to. "It only seems fair," they said. It was a startling way to think about "fairness," and it was also myopic in its understanding of the scale of my debts. Ten thousand dollars wouldn't mean anything to me, but it would shift what was possible for Kelsey, and their relationship to her, for the rest of all their lives. Their misguided and heartbreaking strategy was evidence of their floundering in a vast and overlapping system of debts—student debt, mortgage debt, credit card debt, utility debt, car debt, and likely the sorts of predatory financial services designed to provide short term "relief" in the face of escalating precarity. They were drowning, and instead of imagining for themselves something entirely different, they conjured more ocean.

———

In *All in The Family,* sociologist Melinda Cooper explores the relationship between family and the state. Despite a vision of the family offered by the New Deal—one supported by a vast, though imperfect, set of social insurances—and new kinship models offered by feminist and queer activists, a convergence of political forces has repeatedly reinforced the nuclear family as a site of wealth transfer, care (especially in the absence of comprehensive medical insurance and social housing), and, increasingly, debt.

The Higher Education Act made a free or nearly-free education available to increasing numbers of women, poor people, and people of color, all without reliance on family support. If you had a single mother who did not have enough money to help you pay for college, you could still attend. Or, if your family did not want to spend their resources on you because they didn't believe in higher education or because your relationship was abusive or fractured, you could still go to college. Or if your parents were addicts who no longer had resources. Or if you were an orphan, if you fled violence, if your family was supporting a large network of kin, if your family faced health catastrophes, if you or your family experienced any number of common or surprising or complex kinds of suffering—you could still go to college.

This model of higher education funding recognized students as unique, autonomous people. While they might choose to be understood in the context of their family, while they might, in tandem with their family, make decisions about their future—their educational pursuits were not contingent on their family. This model was forward looking; it was hopeful. It relied on the idea of publicly funded social development that, according to scholar Christopher Newfield, "could not be reduced to growth or increased living standards, but was to be defined by a people in the active process of shaping their desires, dreams, interests, interpersonal relationships, and collective goals." It believed this social development was good for students and good for the world, and that all students were worthy of this chance, regardless of who birthed them or raised them.

It was precisely the political possibility of this open door to higher education that led to its partial closing. The demographic shifts in campus makeup helped to launch the student movement of the sixties, a relationship that Ronald Reagan, first as governor of California and then as the president, weaponized to make massive cuts to higher education. He tapped into anxieties of the white working class—who were benefiting from this increased access—by pitting them against radicals and people of color, whom he framed as a drag on social resources and the economy. Education should, again, be entirely a family matter. In the words of historian James Chappel in his consideration of Cooper's work: "Higher education, like housing, was transformed from a public good, financed by public spending, to family obligation, financed by private debt."

Chappel rightly notes that this debt-model of higher education financing creates a real and imagined relationship between family values and economic mobility: A good family has two heterosexual, married parents who, through their smart decision making, can meet their family's needs and, at the same time, save for college. This "good" family creates a shadow family that establishes a relationship between social inequality and family pathology. A bad family is one that cannot save, that is headed by a single, Black mother or queer parents or contains no parents at all because a young person is on their own. If they have insecure housing or not enough food to eat or cannot find stable work, if their life is hard, it is their fault because they have not created a good family and adhered to its values.

A few months after Allison would have graduated, had she been able to, the grace periods for her loans ended. The debt collector managing the campus debt eventually put her account into collections. "That was really scary. I didn't know what to do," she said. "And I remember having a panic attack because they sent me a letter saying you have to pay five throusand dollars in thirty days or we're taking you to court and if you don't go to court, you're going to jail." She recalled this memory in the same tenor she said everything else, as if none of it was scarier than the rest of it, all of it part of the same narrative of her debt that eventually resulted in her using a high-interest credit card through her bank to pay the collections on a monthly plan she negotiated. Though the outstanding campus debt was relatively low, it took Allison nearly six years to pay it off because of the monthly interest.

The full debt burden, not including the Parent PLUS loans, began as $40,000. Allison wasn't sure what it was when we met in 2024, twelve years after she'd acquired the first of her loans. She couldn't bring herself to look. Her loan payments were taken directly from her account, when they weren't paused for the pandemic. I sensed that it was not just the loan total that scared her, but the machinery that produced it: the website, its messages, the Education Department representatives, everything that had failed her. And I sensed that it was hard to engage with this debt without thinking about her family and what she still didn't understand about what had happened.

Allison thought she might go back someday, and what she said next surprised me. It wasn't for the career that the degree could give her or its ability to help her pay off her debt burden. She wanted to learn again alongside other people. She missed it.

————

I often think of my family's inability to contain our debt and its unwillingness to be contained. It stretched from my mother to me, from me to my grandparents, me to my father, my grandmother to my sister, my sister to me. I wish that after my parents shared their catastrophic strategy to take out a loan in my sister's name, I'd immediately called my sister, a lawyer, and another adult to do everything I could to extricate her. I imagine by the time I learned of the debt, they'd already spent the money—toward my loan or maybe something else—but I should have researched what was possible anyway, instead of what I actually did, which was nothing. I hung up the phone, allowing the news to float somewhere outside of me, and then finished my commute home from work. I couldn't take anything else in.

When my grandmother called me about this loan, she said she was sorry about what had happened to all of us, to my sister, to me, and to my parents. "When your mother showed up asking for money, she was just so scared and kept saying they were going to lose the house and they absolutely needed the loan. I didn't understand how much of the loan, if anything, was going to Kelsey or if it was all going to them. She asked me not to tell anyone, which I only agreed to because she was doing so bad." Later, my grandmother and I would have the same conversation again and again and again. She couldn't understand how everything had gone so wrong—and how we, as a family, would find one another again now that we'd become lost.

In recent years, my sister and mother have shared with me different understandings of this debt, whose payment they have begun to make together. My sister recalls this debt as a cruel surprise, in a lineage of cruel surprises. "Why would I ever agree to that?" she says to me. My mother says that my sister received half of this loan and seems to be unsure where the other half went. "Five thousand dollars went to her bank account," she says. "She signed the loan. I have her signature." My own memories confirm my sister's version, but it's possible that I'm wrong. That in the foggy swirl of incarceration and escalating debts and my outstanding undergraduate tuition they told my sister it was necessary to borrow this money, and she didn't really understand what she signed or where it was going. None of that justifies the debt's existence.

It's tempting to say that what was hungry and unyielding in our lives was not debt but addiction. But that's not right, as hungry and unyielding as addiction is. It matters that it was student debt—debt that weaponizes a person's desire to learn, that is unique in status and collection, that binds you to your family, that promises a world it very rarely delivers. It was student debt that ate us up and refused satiation no matter how much it was offered.

In a conversation about FAFSA with a former college financial aid director who wanted to remain anonymous, I asked if they could design an ideal FAFSA, what would it capture. They paused for a moment, and in my head, I filled that pause with some ideas of my own: How frequently do you struggle to wash your clothes? How many loved ones have you lost and who do you rely on? How many hours do you work? Where do you hurt and why? Do you have someone who can loan you money in an emergency? Will your parents need money from you to help pay the bills? Are you scared? Are your parents hungry? Are you hungry?

"FAFSA makes poor people prove over and over again in different ways that they are poor," they said. Wealthy folks, on the other hand, can more easily hide their wealth. The former aid director were interested in the direct data exchange that had been part of the FAFSA update which would allow better communication between the IRS and the Department of Education, and should, if it worked, offer the government and schools a more complete financial picture. However, they told me, "There are no changes to FAFSA that will yield anything significant for students." Expanding access around the margins is not enough. What we need, they said, is more free money to give kids to attend college.

Chapter 10

IN THE RACE BETWEEN my father's death and the mailing of the loan paperwork, my father won. I got the call early in the morning on April 14, in the pre-dawn, from my sister. "Dad just passed," she said, her voice small and bare. She left out the "away," as if he was walking from one room to the next or from the rocking chair he'd been nestled in for the last three months into the sunshine, strong and steady on his feet. I drove the two hours home in silence. It had rained in the night before temperatures dropped. Around me the world was dark, slick, and changed.

The loan paperwork finally arrived a month after his funeral. The scans from the servicer were, I noted, inexplicably scrambled in their order, as I scrolled through them, confused about which signatures and dates belonged with which interest rates and loan amounts. The batch begins in 2005 before ping-ponging across my college years. Some signatures appear to be several pages after the loan terms. It's remarkable that after five months of my lawyer and me begging AES to send this very paperwork, no one took the time to reshuffle it into its correct order so that we might believe they understood what they were looking at.

The first of the loans my mother fraudulently acquired, in July 2004, she cosigned herself. She borrowed $15,000 from Bank One at a 6.246 percent interest rate. The "finance charge," or the interest, is $21,662.40. The paperwork records the total amount I will pay on this loan when I finish making payments: $36,662.40. It is, obviously, a horrible deal. Had someone from the bank studied the paperwork they would have seen that my mother's signature and the one she forged for me are nearly identical. The first of the *l*'s in our last name is widened in the middle, like the center of a spoon, and the second *l* is thinner, like the spoon's handle. The *K* in my first name and the *R* in her first name swoop and cross at the same point.

On another loan from Bank One, my opa has cosigned. The loan is for $20,000 with an interest rate of 9.393 percent and a finance change of $37,765.60, which means the total amount of money I'll pay is $57,765.60. Over the years, the signature my mother uses for me varies. My real signature changed during that time, too, and I'm unsure if the shift in my forged signature maps onto what she notes in my real one or if it's just that her own handwriting has changed. Did she believe it mattered? That anyone would notice?

Though Bank One might not have checked the signatures, they surely pulled my credit, a standard step in the loan application process, the very step that necessitated the cosigner in the first place, which means they saw a growing record of private loans from their institution in my name, far more than I'd ever need for my tuition. I imagine, though it's never been confirmed, that the loan officers were instructed not to notice, not to care.

In the middle of the loan paperwork is a $10,00 loan, cosigned by my father. By the time I received the paperwork he had died, so

I never had the chance to ask him if it was his real signature or if my mother had forged that, too. In any case, I would have been scared that our final conversation would be shaped by the institutions that had made my life hard. I wouldn't have wanted to use our time together to wrestle with blame or interrogate our shared pain, so I don't think I would have asked him what I wanted to, which was: Did you know? Why did you let this happen to me?

———————

Once, I talked to a woman with student debt from an art school she attended in the Midwest. Growing up, her father was the sole financial provider, and his salary was enough to cover the family's needs, including the needs of her mother, who was ill. But the salary was not enough to cover the woman's art school tuition, which was nearly $32,000 a year by the time she graduated. Despite working multiple jobs, the borrower was unable to pay for school without taking on debt. About five years after graduation, she still owed $63,000 on her loans, despite her parents helping her with the largest of the loans with the highest interest. A few years before we'd talked, her mother had died, and the money from the life insurance was used to pay off one of the most expensive private loans. The woman cried when she told me this, and I cried, too.

"I'm ashamed that I had to use the money this way. I know my mother would have wanted me to do something else with it," she told me. I imagined her in the weeks and months after her mother died, moving through an altered, emptier world. Now, what in another context might feel like an enormous, life-changing gift— the end of a high-interest loan that could never be paid down—was instead linked to her mother's death.

What would you have done instead? I wondered afterward.

Another woman shared on social media that when she went to college, she and her mother agreed to share the student debt burden. She didn't say if her mother's debt was in the form of a Parent PLUS loan, but it seems likely that it was. Each of them borrowed $15,000, and though the writer was able to pay back her loan in ten years, she discovered, years later, that her mother had not, and that her outstanding debt burden had grown to $40,000. The daughter asked if she could pay for the loan, to ease this burden for her mother, and her mother said no.

Her mother, she wrote, "barely had enough money to make it through her retirement years." The difference between living in poverty and getting by was the $400-a-month loan payment she made each month. Her mother joked that she was "good at being broke." The mother saw the monthly payments as a gift to her child, whom she, her daughter wrote, loved more than "physics might suggest is possible."

The daughter did not know her mother was dying, but she did know that her mother was sick, and they spent the last week of her mother's life together, talking in part about the student loan. In the narrative of her mother's death, it's this fact that seems to enrage the writer the most. In the last unknown and fragile hours, they discussed what to do with this unpayable loan, rather than discussing everything else—a resonant memory of a birthday or favorite family recipe or a funny story.

Following her mother's death, when her daughter cleaned out her house, she found the paperwork for the loan and realized that it was twice what she'd been told: $80,000. Though the loan company—in this case, probably the federal government—had demanded that the mother pay them each month, upon her mother's death, the loan disappeared. Parent PLUS loans are particularly intractable, and death is one way the loan contract is nulled—either the parent's death or the child's. When I read this story, it called to mind debtors across the ancient world, the corpses of their loved ones unburied before them.

One body in exchange for another, a life bought with another life.

The last time I saw my father alive was during my school's spring break. I had driven home early in the week to be with my family, eating meal train dinners while smoking weed with my father, who needed it for the pain and nausea and was embarrassed to smoke it alone. His best friend gave him the weed, and it was tough and earthy, made us cough a lot before releasing us upward to float near the ceiling. We made up voices for the dog and tried to pretend we were sober when my grandmother dropped by with more food.

After spending a few days with my family, I drove to Detroit to see a friend before returning home again on the way back to Chicago. When I arrived, my father was napping on his bed in a white T-shirt that once fit him and now gathered around him like a swaddle. I watched him from the doorway for a second, unsure if I should wake him. *Which parts of you hurt the most?* I wondered as I leaned over to touch him lightly. His bones had thinned, his skin dried. When I'd hugged him recently, I'd worried that I might break his ribs. It felt like wrapping my arms around a bouquet of dried flowers. He woke, disoriented, his eyes watery and searching for too long before he found my face.

"Hi, honey," he said. This was the time to say good-bye. I felt it all around me, the sense that he was receding. But I couldn't do it. I spoke with him for a moment—Who'd visited that weekend? Had he been able to eat anything? My concern about food was compulsory and pointless. I already knew the answer to that. He'd stopped eating, almost entirely, two weeks earlier.

My father couldn't track the conversation, drifting off mid-sentence into quiet before reemerging somewhere new, where it was unclear if we were having a different conversation from months or years before, unclear if he knew it was me he was speaking to. I followed him in and out of this swirl of memory, worried that this disorientation might be scary for him, that my desire to sit with him didn't feel comforting but destabilizing. I eyed the spot next to him in the bed and considered, for a moment, that maybe I should climb into bed with him and spoon him on his slow walk away from me and the world. Then he was asleep again. It was a Sunday. I was supposed to work the next day and had lesson planning to finish, so I decided to leave. I couldn't afford to take unpaid time off.

"I love you," I said, watching the rise and fall of his chest as I'd heard mothers describe doing with their newborn babies. When I was four, in our first house, the tiny bungalow only a couple of miles from Lake Michigan, my father would wrap me in a robe after my bath and then lay me on my stomach in front of the heating vent, so that the warmed air inflated the robe like a balloon. In our second house, where we had no easy vent access, he used to replicate the process with a hair dryer. On nights we didn't have baths, he, my sister, and I lay in her trundle bed, playing a version of telephone on one another's backs. My sister drew an elephant on his back and then he drew what he thought she had drawn—a soccer net, say—on mine, and then I had to guess. "A sandcastle." We rolled over to reverse the order and began again.

"I'll be back next week," I said to my sleeping dad. I will be back I will be back I will be back, I said, crying as I left the room, hugged my mother, and drove two hours home. I will be back. Two days later, my sister called to say that he was gone.

———

By the summer of 2014, only a few months after my father died, something had developed in me, a sense of a world ordered differently than I'd understood it to be. "The security around the loan *paperwork* is higher than the security around the loans themselves," I said to my therapist. It appeared that my mother had been allowed to take out a loan that carried $37,000 worth of interest in less time than it took me to grocery shop. But it took over five months just to receive evidence of the loan's existence. "I don't understand how that's possible," I said, even as something thrummed beneath the surface, some sense that maybe I *did* know how it was possible, or at least why.

My suffering was good for someone else—financially and politically. Why else would the servicer trap me in this endless loop of phone calls, faxes, e-mails, and portal requests? Why else had the government not shielded me from this? Thousands of other borrowers had wandered this hall of mirrors. And trapped in another reflective dead end, many of them had seen what Cassie from *Writers & Lovers* had— a ghostly version of their own face—and quit.

There's a lot to be angry about, my therapist reminded me.

In June, I'd received fraud paperwork from AES. I'd also received a different set of fraud documents from a collection agency that one of my delinquent loans had been sold to, Performant Recovery, a name that suggests it was not demanding wages in escalating language and documentation but, rather, helping me to find something essential that I'd lost. Ten years later, in December 2024, Performant

Recovery would face legal action by the Consumer Financial Protection Bureau for allegedly illegally delaying borrowers the right to rehabilitate their loans so that Performant could generate more money in collection fees. According to the CFPB, when borrowers tried to initiate the rehabilitation process, managers would tell agents: "the objective is to delay as much as possible without getting Performant in trouble. "

As was true in the past, there was confusion about who sent what paperwork and when and who could talk to whom, and at one point a woman from Performant wouldn't speak to me because I had asked her to speak to my lawyer. Then AES stopped talking to Todd because the authorization I had given them in March had apparently lapsed in February, the month before I'd given it, even though he'd spoken to them all spring. But eventually, I filled out the fraud paperwork.

"Now we wait," Todd said. And if this failed, we still had bankruptcy as an option, however challenging it might be.

———————

In late September, nine months after we had begun contacting AES, Todd was still unable to talk to them. I wasn't sure what to do. "I can't print these forms from the website," I wrote to him, "and they keep telling me they sent the authorization forms, but they haven't." I asked him if I should keep logs of each call with AES in which they assured me that a thing had happened that hadn't, when they told me they did a thing they did not do. The debt collection calls kept coming, meanwhile, and the debt total grew from interest and late fees. I remember the feeling of hearing my phone vibrating in my desk while I was teaching—the sense of claustrophobia and predation. They were going to catch me.

For the first time in the e-mail, I voiced to him what I'd already said to my therapist: "It feels like AES and every person I speak with wants to make it impossible for me to have a lawyer. One man I spoke with yelled at me and said I wasn't allowed to have one based on my debt."

Reading this e-mail again, I wonder what the AES representative meant when he said I was not "allowed" to have a lawyer. Perhaps he meant that private loans are awarded the same protections from bankruptcy as federal loans and so my lawyer would be unable to help me. He spoke to me as if I was his badly behaved daughter. His tone echoed a broader, national paternalism that suggests that debtors are the country's badly behaved children and not who we really are: people who have gone to school or have tried to; people who have needed to put necessary medical care on our credit cards; people who have not paid off utility debts or stopped paying rent because we've lost our jobs or because other debts have made those payments impossible.

A month later, in early October, I e-mailed Todd again that I was "freaking out." There'd been no update to the authorization but the credit card debt from the default judgment that had seemingly disappeared had resurfaced. The garnishment that had been stalled had gone through and now my wages would be garnished by over $500. This garnishment would happen each month until $13,000 was paid off.

––––––––

Around that time, I cleaned out my bedroom desk, separating its contents into piles to be recycled, thrown away, or put back in its drawers. I'd bought the desk—used from a neighbor—because I'd hoped to write at it, but it was actually used to hold loan statements, collection notices, and medical correspondence—and the daily detritus of teaching: old lesson plans and notes I'd written myself during class: *follow up with* _____ *later.* Cross-legged on the floor, I shuffled through the documents. The collection notices from the loan company existed online, and I wasn't paying them anyway. Still, I wasn't sure what I should do with them: Was keeping them smart or punishing?

Tucked between communication from a private lender was a faded color photo of my father as a boy—probably four years old—posing with his two brothers on a beach. Lake Michigan is behind them, slate colored, its waves breaking against their ankles. They wear Speedo-style swimsuits and none of them are smiling, though their steely faces are obviously a performance. The day is bright, and I know they love to swim. Did his life turn out how he wanted? In his final days, was he thinking of debt?

Chapter 11

IN 1980, UNDER THE Higher Education Act's expansion, a new program was created to help middle and upper income parents with high assets, who were and still are predominantly white, pay for expensive institutions with fixed rate loans: The Parent Loan for Undergraduate Students (Parent PLUS). Though the interest rates were lower than parents would find on the private marketplace, they were higher than those in the federal government's student loan program, and the higher interest rate combined with the origination fees meant that these loans would be expensive over time. Today, most parents taking out PLUS loans have also received Pell Grants, which means that they have some of the lowest incomes and assets of families enrolling students in college.

PLUS loans are offered to any parents of dependent students and are most often used when all other forms of aid have been exhausted. Sometimes these loans are used in addition to private loans, but they are often used in place of them. Unlike federal loans, which have strict borrowing limits ($5,500 federal loans for a freshman attending school in 2024, for example), PLUS loans have none, which means that parents can borrow up to the full cost of attendance, including fees beyond tuition, such as room and board, books, etc. If the school is especially expensive, and their aid is especially poor, this might mean that a parent is borrowing more than $100,000 over the course of four years. And that's just the parent.

Parent PLUS borrowers for bachelor's degrees in 2015–2016, for example, averaged $29,000 in Stafford loans (a type of federal loan); $33,000 in Parent PLUS loans; and $4,000 in private student debt. The family borrowed a total of $66,000 ($80,000 when adjusted for inflation). And these totals don't account for the myriad of other ways families borrow to make college possible that are not tracked: through home equity and credit cards.

Though a borrower with federal loans can qualify for a number of repayment plans that, hypothetically at least, will yield relief, Parent PLUS loans don't qualify for these plans. Parents often have to make impossible choices about how to use their income. Nearly 40 percent of older borrowers—most of whom have gone into debt to pay for their children's education—have chosen not to meet their health-care needs due to their debt. One in eleven Parent PLUS borrowers is in default, and one in five Black Parent PLUS borrowers is. "Parents do not take on Parent PLUS loans in a vacuum," writes Peter Granville in a report from the Century Foundation. "These loans are one factor among many that compounds with the racial wealth gap and forces parents to choose between paying their monthly bills, retiring when they want to, purchasing a home, and putting food on the table."

When a student defaults on a loan, their wages might be garnished or their tax refunds withheld. This withholding also pertains to Social Security payments. In 2015, the Department of Education collected $171 million in student loan payments from Social Security withholding. And one in three borrowers with Parent PLUS loans has experienced one of these Social Security offsets. In many cases, these Social Security payments were not applied to the principal, which means their debt burden didn't decrease. Unless they experienced a financial miracle, it's likely they faced the same financial circumstances and the same withholding the next month as well. Often these offsets reduce Social Security payments to below the poverty guideline. Those wages taken by the federal government—necessary for food or rent or health care—enable the government to make a profit on the Parent PLUS loan program, the only such student lending program that does so.

———

Alana, a freshman I met in the fall of 2023, was set to become one of the million students who rely on Parent PLUS loans each year. When we first spoke, she had just moved to New York City to attend an expensive liberal arts school. She explained to me that her mother raised her and her sisters alone, moving across the west and northwest before settling in Nebraska, where Alana went to high school.

"I don't have a lot of memories of my mother growing up," Alana told me, "because my mother was always working." Her voice was bright and rising. In the past, she told me, her mother had worked at a warehouse and a kidney dialysis center, and now, her mother was employed at a Walmart distribution center, managing incoming and outgoing trucks, and at a doctor's office, scheduling appointments. Alana, too, had worked multiple jobs, beginning with a local movie theater when she was in tenth grade. Later, she was hired at Starbucks, a role she was able to transfer to Manhattan, working almost forty hours a week on top of a full class schedule.

Alana chose her college from an internet search: *What is the best college for becoming a book editor?* Her school was at the top of the list assembled by her search engine algorithm, which she had faith in. Alana applied, was accepted, and decided to attend, even as she remained uncertain about how exactly she would pay for it. At her high school, they'd talked very little about college financing and, other than a cousin, she didn't have any close family who'd gone to college.

When Alana was given her financial aid letter, she googled what all the terms meant, e-mailed briefly with someone from financial aid, and then enrolled, despite some of the details remaining unclear. "I'll just take out loans," she said to me, illustrating how she'd thought about debt at the time. "That's very American."

When I asked her how much she had borrowed, she said, "I'm not sure exactly," which caused my stomach to jump. It was October, and school had already started. She explained that there was a gap in what the school offered her in merit- and need-based aid and federal loans, and her mother was awaiting approval for a Parent PLUS loan for around twenty thousand dollars.

I tried to imagine this number as a "gap" instead of what it was: a canyon. That the school would think that her mother should borrow twenty thousand dollars for just the first year of school pointed to a carelessness with students' lives, as did Alana's matriculation before the financing was finalized. It forced her and her family to fill this "gap" and to internalize it as theirs, which might have been less true had they been in their Nebraska living room, navigating this financing from a distance, before Alana had moved across the country, unpacked her room, enrolled in class, and opened her first course book. There was inertia. She was on the hook for this semester no matter what.

Alana offered to send me a photo of the aid letter. "Apparently my school has the most expensive dorms in the country," she said. Next year, she hoped to save money when she lived off campus. The aid office at her school had not been much help; to each question she asked, she was directed to talk with her "parents," despite Alana sharing that her *parent*, her mother, was not managing this process for her. "If we don't get this loan, I'll be back to square one. And then I don't know what I'll do," Alana said, her voice sinking.

I felt tempted to tell her "It's going to be okay," but I couldn't identify what I meant by "it." I wasn't sure that she and her mother would find the necessary gap money or that their indebtedness would qualify as a positive outcome. Their debt would be shared, and though the origins would be different from the one shared between my mother and me, there was resonance there that I couldn't ignore. "Okay" in this circumstance would mean something else entirely.

She had not been sleeping much, she told me. "I don't think there has been a class this week that I haven't dozed off in." Between working at Starbucks, sometimes seven days a week, her classes, and homework, she had no time for anything else. She did not list the uncertain funding as one of her stressors, though it must have been. Her current situation required a kind of cognitive dissonance: She should participate in her campus life as if it would go on for four more years even though the aid discrepancy might mean she couldn't attend school next semester.

When we hung up, with the promise to talk again once she was further into the semester, I studied her award letter. Despite her school giving her $30,000 in scholarship money, the federal government giving her almost $4,000 in Pell grants, and the school offering another $4,000 in work study money, there was still an enormous cost of attendance that was left unaccounted for. She had already acquired the federal lending maximum of $5,500 and what remained was not $20,000 for the year, as she'd assumed, but $42,000.

That number startled me and I looked at it several times to make sure that I wasn't misunderstanding. When I talked to my partner about it, I cried. "That's an evil amount of money," I said. I was especially moved that she wanted to work with books and authors someday. I didn't see that as naive but hopeful, even as humanities departments collapsed across the country alongside the publishing industry, and editors' wages remained stagnant. Alana believed in a world made more beautiful and interesting by the stories that reflect and expand it.

Her mother had already applied for the loan amount, and if she was approved, would likely need to borrow over $100,000 for four years of college. I wanted to tell Alana that her mother should not take out that loan and that she should not attend this school at all, but I'd known her for only an hour. I told her that she could ask me any questions she wanted, and that I would answer them honestly. I texted her a link to a group of first-generation college students that met on her campus. If I couldn't keep her from joining the nearly 43 million Americans with student loan debt, and her mother from joining the 3.7 million families with Parent PLUS loans, then I could at least facilitate introduction to a group that might trade resources and advice, might make college less lonely.

———

Soon after our first call, Alana texted me that her mother had been denied the Parent PLUS loan because of a bankruptcy on her credit report. "Credit worthiness binds families' possible futures to their collective pasts," Caitlin Zaloom writes in *Indebted*. In thinking about debt's ability to collapse and muddle time, I hadn't considered that a denied application for credit, the very possibility of debt, works in the same way.

A 2011 Department of Education update to the Parent PLUS loan application restricted borrowing almost overnight by lengthening the time frame for parents' credit history from ninety days to five years. This update impacted nearly 400,000 students, who suddenly didn't have access to loans they assumed they'd receive under the previous borrowing terms. More than 128,000 of those students attended majority-Black colleges and universities, and many Black families faced a cost-of-attendance gap without a previously accessible resource to cross it. In response to a crisis for both schools and families, the government walked back the policy change. What remained was a clarity that these harmful financial products are also necessary for many Black students to attend school. As Zaloom considers the implications of the ability to "qualify" for these loans, she notes that to *qualify* is to "invest a subject with particular characteristics, and in the case of PLUS loans, the process of qualifying for a loan identifies families' financial successes and failures as a result of their private actions." While the government is insistent on seeing the student in the context of a certain version of family, they are unwilling to see the family in the context of national history.

After Alana's mother was denied the loan, Alana, who is biracial, briefly considered asking a family friend to cosign on a loan before deciding not to. Lots of lower income students, and especially Black students, are implicitly and even explicitly asked to do this work: to summon resources from extended family and the community to make school possible. And many of their loved ones offer this support with joy and purpose. Although, on average, Black parents have less wealth than white parents, they are more likely to contribute financially to their children's education. This is true at all income levels. I sensed that Alana didn't want to ask her family friend because it felt like a new kind of debt to her—beyond owing the government she would also, in a sense, owe a friend. Instead, she was going to withdraw from her institution.

Over Thanksgiving break, I met her for coffee. We mostly talked about her classes—what she was reading and writing—and what life was like on campus. We talked about the future only a little. As Alana's classmates packed suitcases to travel home, temporarily, for winter break, Alana would pack up everything. After a semester home, her hope was to return to school again, somewhere cheaper. For the next month, she'd concentrate on her limited time in New York City.

"It's been a weird couple of months," Alana said to me when we next talked in February. "I never expected my college experience to go the way that it did." She was trying to accept that her first college experience wasn't what she'd wanted it to be, a process that she thought would take some time. I was hopeful that she included the word "first" because it suggested that she believed there would be another college experience in the future. I'd sent along resources in December that included a list of "no-loan" schools, all of which are competitive, and an organization that works with first-gen students during the application process.

By her last days on campus, her roommates had all gone home already and she was moving through their shared world without them, an inversion of what would come next semester when they moved through the world without her. Just before the holidays, she learned that her creative writing professor had died by suicide, and she carried that loss with her as she looked at her room for the last time. "It wasn't the greatest experience," she said about her semester, but she still thought she was lucky to have it. "At least I had a chance to see what life would be like if it had gone another way."

Though she was imagining a life in which the forces at work on her had converged in another way—if her mother had gotten the loan, perhaps—I think the other life she was imagining was more accurately one in which she had family wealth.

She remembered a day she skipped class to spend time with a friend whose own class had been canceled. That slot felt like an open door, a gift. At that point she already knew she was leaving campus. They wandered around a nearby neighborhood, walking into a bookstore, where her friend found a beloved book from childhood, one her father had read to her growing up. As Alana shared this memory with me, I was aware that we'd never talked about her own father or what events precipitated her mother's choice or her imperative to raise children as a single parent. "It's one of my favorite books now," Alana said. The memory was a layered one. There were fathers, absent and present, friendships—now physically distant. A narrative of intimate knowledge, and somewhere, in the background, a classroom continuing on without Alana. I wondered how it felt to reread that beloved book in Nebraska, away from the friend she bought it with.

Though watching her friends' Instagram stories from far away felt "like a little stab in the heart each time," because she so badly wanted to be back with them on campus, Alana was happy for them. She'd let go of the bitterness she felt at the end of the semester, and what she was left with, she earnestly told me, was gratefulness for the experience. She deserved to make meaning of her life without my intervention, but I had to resist telling her, "You were *not* lucky. You have enormous debt from a school you were, essentially, pushed out of—all because your family doesn't have wealth and inherited knowledge about college financing."

I struggled to balance Alana's right to her own narrative, to the agency to say *this was worth it,* with my sense that the mechanism of debt creates and enforces this kind of thinking. We must "apply" for its kindness in the form of credit, and if we are denied, it is because we don't deserve it. We must make payments toward this debt and are punished if we cannot. If we receive relief someday, through a government program designed to provide it or because our schools have defrauded us, we are "forgiven." These concepts feel weightier when what we want to access with this debt is education, something Zaloom refers to as a "benefit of citizenship." Right now, these benefits are given out unequally, she notes, with the largest share given to those who have historically benefited the most.

I asked Alana if she thought about her debt, to which she responded, "I think about it in that I'm putting money away from my job but also I don't think about it." It was out there, somewhere, she understood, waiting to collect payment from her, which it did the next summer when a collection agency contracted by her school contacted her to begin making $500 monthly payments on her $21,000 of unpaid tuition.

Unlike her federal loans, the unpaid tuition wouldn't qualify for the income-based programs that would minimize interest payments and eventually, after long enough, relieve her of what was left. I didn't say that. What I wanted to believe was—when it's time for you to make payments, when you've graduated and are pursuing a career that brings you happiness and pays you a living wage, it will be different.

Alana didn't know where she would go to school next or when, though she hoped it would be soon. She understood that the time she was away might dull her urge to attend. She wanted to use the momentum of her fall to swing her into a new school. Definitely one with good literature programs, one that offered comprehensive financial counseling, and, hopefully, no more debt.

Chapter 12

"WE WANT TO MAKE sure you have a chance to consider all the ways you can commemorate your father's life and hold him close," someone from the funeral home said to me as we sat in a sunny room on overstuffed furniture a few days after my father died. For several hundred dollars, I could have my father's ashes fashioned into a necklace, earrings, or a bracelet. I could also have them transformed into an obelisk, a vase, or what appeared to be a tiny box for pills. I wondered at the funeral home's decision to sell these expensive and ugly objects even as I understood why a family would purchase them. It wasn't just about holding a piece of the deceased close—on a necklace or looped around your ear—it was about what the purchase was a testament of: your immense, enduring love for someone who had died.

I was not interested in the ash-jewelry or the pill box, or the vase, or the obelisk, I said. I didn't ask them what kind of mark-up was on these items, but I suspected it was high.

"Many people find it helpful to see a body in order to have closure," the woman said to me—tenderly, I thought—when I shared my father's wish to be cremated before the service, with only his immediate family having the chance to see him before cremation. I was unsure what informed his decision to forgo an open casket; he'd only shared his wishes with my mother. It might have been that he was ashamed of his withered figure, or it might have been that he understood that the chance for others to have closure was contingent on an expensive, shiny wooden casket that we couldn't afford. I had no doubt that the sales pitch was true. Some people at the funeral would not have seen my father recently, and his body could offer a transition into a new world without him. First there was my father at work, sitting at his desk, and then my sick father, under blankets, and then my dead father, in a casket, and then no father. To withhold his body disrupted the continuum.

Before the ceremony, our family was invited into a room the size of a large closet where my father had been put in the cheapest coffin that they offered. They'd tried to upsell us on that, too, and I'd held my ground, even as I felt some part of myself bending to their logic: He deserved the best. But I knew better than to believe that one wood type was worthier than another. All of it had been trees. And all of it would burn with him.

I gave a eulogy at his funeral beside a large photograph of him displayed in the place his casket would have been. In the photo, his skin was reddened by the sun, and he was wearing his glasses with transitional lenses, caught in transition, grayish and soupy like they often were, never recovering quickly enough from his introduction to or retreat from sunlight. Afterward, everyone went to the soccer club where he bartended, and I sat outside by myself watching kids play soccer. This was the club my opa had built, in which he found a home after his immigration. It was here that I sang German songs in Christmas performances, that I played indoor soccer every winter, that I sold hot dogs at a boxing match, that my grandparents danced to polka bands, and that my parents, and especially my father, worked at countless weddings, reunions, and anniversaries. I loved this place, and I wished my father had not spent the last years of his life working here every free weekend to pay back my student loans.

In the months after his death, I saw him often in my dreams. In one he came to me rounded and pinkened like he was before his illness. He shuffled his feet when he walked as if he was learning to walk for the first time. In the dream, he lurched toward me mumbling something incomprehensible. "I can't understand you," I said to him. He blurred beneath my tears. The dream version of myself understood that my father had already died and that I was lucky to have this reunion. But I couldn't make out what he said, even as he mumbled in new ways. "It's okay," I said to him, hugging him. "It's okay."

From each dream, I woke up crying. I remained still and urged myself to fall back asleep quickly so that I might reenter the dream world, but I never did.

———

"We call these visitations," a woman from my writing group said to me about my dreams. I'd written a poem about one and the yearning it left with me in the morning. I felt scooped out. Hollow. I was in the poet's living room in Edgewater, along with five other women, most of whom were in their fifties and sixties, who'd been in a writing group together for the last ten years. I'd met one of them at a free library workshop a couple of years earlier, and she'd invited me into the group. They called it the Egg Money Poets Collective in reference to the historical practice of farm wives tending the chickens and selling their eggs, an economic system which they were uniquely responsible for, the proceeds of which they could spend how they liked. I thought the collective name recognized our writing practice as totally and completely ours, one which also had to creatively coexist alongside the rest of our lives. Though some of the poets were retired, many were still engaged in grueling work: as a high school English teacher and a social worker and professor who specialized in trauma care. We met monthly, each sending a single poem to the group that we'd discuss during our meeting.

"We all have them after our loved ones die," the poet said about my dreams. "I think of them as gifts." Most of them had lost their parents by this point, and some had lost siblings and lovers.

That these women had also been visited by their loved ones was a confirmation of something for me, though I wasn't sure what to call it. I'd practiced Christianity as a young person, but I'd become an atheist in college, not in response to a particular text or encounter, but because, almost suddenly, my brain wouldn't allow the alternative. It was heartbreaking and freeing. Rather than a spiritual word or an afterlife, it seemed that my father's visits were an articulation of grief from my own body. It felt comforting to be a part of a community in which our bodies, in their devastation, produced the same language.

———

In my early twenties, a boyfriend told me that my debt, though certainly painful, was also not the end of the world. I was home from New York for the holidays, staying at my grandmother's mobile home because it felt impossible to stay with my parents. The boy, too, was in town for the holidays. He and I lived far apart from one another and were as much pen pals as we were lovers. We wrote letters back and forth, sent each other postcards with scraps of poetry we'd read or found. I pressed the leaves I dried from Central Park onto homemade paper that I made using a flour sieve, hoping what I'd written distracted him from the fact that the paper was ugly, the same color as puke. We'd known one another as young people and reconnected again as emerging adults, both grabbing onto something that reminded us of home.

My grandmother was in Arizona with my aunt, leaving her home empty for the snowiest months, so I performed the Christmas rituals alone, making cookies, watching specials, and listening to the *A Charlie Brown Christmas* album. She'd decorated her house before she left, and her aesthetic was multicolor lights and Christmas humans: a ceramic baby with large eyes dressed as an elf and a plastic dancing Santa who spun his hips to Jingle Bells when I turned him on. She'd given me her bed to sleep in, but most nights I slept on the couch, where I could leave the TV on, falling asleep to the sound of people talking.

"You might not get to shop at fancy clothing stores, but it's going to be okay," he said to me after I told him that I was trapped in this debt and would remain so forever. I was lying on the couch in a nest of Christmas-themed blankets, and he was sitting next to me. Two empty mugs were on the coffee table, their insides red from wine. His prognosis—that I'd live—was meant to be hopeful. If things would be okay, then I might choose to spend time with my parents again. I might not spend another Christmas alone.

He did not have any student debt and couldn't understand the scale of mine. Only a couple of years out of college, my debt burden had grown larger, not smaller. It was not relegated to the realm of consumerism, concerned with the quality and cost of clothing. It had made me physically sick. It had made finding housing difficult. It had made it hard to tell my parents, "I love you."

A different boyfriend, years later, told me that if we were to be together long term, he'd want me to consider prosecuting my mother as part of a strategy to free myself from the debt. We'd only been together a couple of months, and I'd been rehearsing this conversation, which felt like a confession, as I folded laundry and cleaned the kitchen. In the imaginary version of the conversation, I struggled to convey two things, one which I knew to be true and the other that I wanted to be true. 1) I would likely live with this debt for the rest of my life. 2) This debt, if my lover chose a life with me, would not harm him. But as I tried to tell my boyfriend the second fact, I knew it was a lie. I would be unable to add my name to a mortgage application. We would not be able to help children pay for college. But even before that, we would not be able to help them in other ways. We might not have the kind of disposable income that allowed us to pursue joy—not just skipping the kind of vacations unavailable to many, but smaller pleasures, like music lessons for our kids.

When he and I talked, lying in bed one morning, I only told him the first fact. It was not about punishing my mother, he was careful to say after suggesting charges, just that he didn't think it was fair that the debt would circumscribe our lives permanently. "It will affect me, too," he said. "I would want a say in what happens."

Had I been open to it, I might have heard an implied message in his insistence that I consider him: *This debt is shared, which also means, you are not alone.* Instead, I heard: *This debt, which is attached to you, will hurt me.* And because the debt could not be removed, I also heard: *You will hurt me.*

———

Caleb moved around a lot as a child, following his father's military job, before eventually settling in a small town in Washington not far from Seattle. After attending community college for two years, he transferred to the University of Washington, borrowing around $25,000 in student loans, much of which went to the cost of living—basically everything but tuition—since most of his tuition was covered through an equal opportunity grant aimed at expanding access for students of color.

Caleb, who is Black and in his thirties, had been accepted to competitive four-year schools out of high school but understood that his family could not afford them. His mother was still paying off her own student loans from a for-profit school, and these competitive schools would require her to borrow again in the form of Parent PLUS loans. Her alma mater, The University of Phoenix, is one of over 2,270 for-profit schools across the country. According to a report by the Student Borrower Protection Center that maps for-profit schools' exploitation, "instead of providing financial stability to or neighborhood enrichment, for-profit schools are simply new ways of stripping communities of wealth." These schools employ a range of predatory practices that leave students with large debt burdens and without well-paid employment: deceptive advertising, fraudulent financing practices, and misleading reporting on student outcomes. And they target students of color and low-income students, clustering in Black and Latino neighborhoods.

"I ended up really enjoying it," Caleb said about his time at community college, "more than my university experience with the University of Washington." If he'd attended UW straight out of high school, his debt burden would have been twice as much, he noted.

Caleb told me his story over the phone from where he lived in New Orleans, the city in which he was born and where he had family on both sides. After graduation, Caleb stayed in the Seattle area, working at a nonprofit, while making student loan payments and attempting to build an adult life. He wanted to move away but couldn't. "It was hard to leave," he said. "I was hustling to make ends meet and pay bills, helping family when I could and struggling to save." It wasn't until Caleb transitioned out of his nonprofit job to work at a real estate company that he could save up money to do what he'd wanted to do for a long time: leave.

His departure was necessary for him to become who he is today: "In my life you can draw a direct line from the student loan crisis to me being able to explore my true self. Living in the same city, I wasn't able to openly explore my sexuality. When you have been around people for so long there is an expectation of who you are supposed to be." Caleb needed to live somewhere else—somewhere he had not spent most of his life—to be the most complete version of himself. People need to move for all sorts of reasons, including survival. Though Caleb didn't use that word, I thought broadly that it was true. Desire is absolutely a matter of survival.

"Getting out of that environment helped me realize a lot faster," Caleb said about his queer identity, an acknowledgment of a hidden interior landscape, something that had to be revealed to Caleb before he could reveal it to anyone else. In *The Making of the Indebted Man*, sociologist and philosopher Maurizio Lazzarato writes that, "Debt breeds, subdues, manufactures, adapts, and shapes subjectivity." I wonder how often debt, and its avatar, collection, obfuscates and muffles our self-knowledge and desire. It's not just a particular "good" family that the student loan system seems to require and enforce, but a particular individual identity, too.

"I've had so many instances of having to finance my basic needs," Caleb said. In addition to the student loan debt, there were credit cards to cover necessary bills, and a car loan to make it possible for him to get to work, and medical debt to treat an emergency hospital room visit when he was without health insurance because it was too expensive. "Because of this, decisions you make ten years ago affect who you are today," he said, an acknowledgment of debt's ability to bend time itself, a state that scholar Jodi Kim calls "a fatal present tense" in her analysis of debt as a "precarious grammar." Debt, acquired in the past and collected in the present, collapses "then" and "now." A future of relief is always beyond reach.

It had become a day job to learn how to navigate financial institutions just so he could make ends meet. "So I'm not buying into financial despair," he said. "But" implies a contradiction: as in, my financial life is hard and yet I will not feel bad about it. But "so" says I will not feel bad *because* my financial life is hard, because I understand that it is not my fault that it is. The seeds of this understanding began to bloom when he was in his early twenties, just out of college, when he felt like he'd been punished with student loan payments at the exact moment that he was trying to use his education to secure meaningful employment that would allow him to live. "I understood the inequities that young Black graduates had to face, which were immediate. You can't go into the career you want to because you need a job that will help you meet your basic needs," Caleb explained.

As an adult, he didn't see debt as a symptom of a system gone wrong, as well-meaning institutions that were corrupted by capitalism. "These corporations and entities were not looking out for the best interests of working class and poor people," he said, an assertion that seemed to extend beyond student debt to encompass all the creditors who've collected from him.

———

A different borrower, who is white and straight, told me that he was so ashamed of his debt burden that he didn't want to date. It wasn't that his debt meant he couldn't afford to go on dates—to either pay for himself or a date—it was that he was worried about announcing his debt to a potential partner. "What if they don't want to be with me because of it?" he asked.

When we talked over the phone, I felt the urge to tell him *I swear the right person won't care*, but I didn't. He hadn't come to me for comfort. Also, and this part is hard to admit, I might have been wrong. While the "right" person wouldn't blame him for taking out student loans to pursue his engineering degree at a public college, there was no guarantee that he would meet her, instead of one of the many people who would care.

I had stopped dating just before my father died, after breaking up with another boyfriend for reasons that I, again, couldn't articulate. It might have had to do with the debt, or maybe not. The debt was everywhere, and I'd stopped being able to feel its edges long ago. I was brittle, hungry to be touched, and unwilling and unable to be vulnerable with someone whose romantic partnership would facilitate it. I hooked up with a few friends, blurring the boundaries of what had been there, and when one of them whom I deeply and maybe romantically cared for gently tried to understand if we might be something else—something more—I shut him out completely.

The borrower continued, "And then the shitty part of it hit me: What if she has a lot of debt?" The implication was that he would be disappointed. No one wants their partner to have an enormous financial burden, especially one that makes them feel bad. Many people don't want their own wages used to plug the hole in someone else's leaking boat. I appreciated his honesty, his willingness to announce what he surely understood was hypocritical. But I was still annoyed, protective of the hypothetical borrower who he'd decided was not right for him because her financial history mirrored his own. Couldn't that echo be an opportunity for tenderness?

I wanted that for this other, imagined woman, even though I hadn't been able to accept it myself.

The borrower told me that it made him sad: this collision of human connection and the marketplace. And I agreed, but because he'd withdrawn from connection out of fear, I worried that he was left with just the marketplace.

———

I was not the only one being visited by my father. In the six months following my father's death, my sister told me that my mother had recently purchased an expensive car, an old model of a luxury brand. My father's corporation would give my mother a portion of his salary, monthly, for the next two years, along with a small life insurance payout. He had no retirement. Or maybe he had but had cashed it out at some point to cover their debts. We weren't sure. Whatever the source—my mother had funneled a large portion of that money into this car.

The purchase made me uncomfortable. My mother needed an SUV as part of the piecemeal employment she'd created for herself, selling crafts at art fairs. She didn't need *this* SUV, however. The purchase was an intentional *Fuck you* to anyone who thought she should spend moderately in the face of her own debts and recent loss. There was something triumphant in her absolute refusal to consider the social implications of her decisions. But it was also infuriating. I was still trapped in bureaucratic limbo, spending hours each week calling and e-mailing my loan servicers while the collection calls increased, and my debt burden grew. I wanted her to set aside the money to help with the loans. Or to shore up resources in the face of her own uncertain future without home ownership or retirement.

"Why did you have to get this car?" I asked her from my living room in Chicago. I was no longer living in the apartment managed by a bank but on the second floor of a graystone in Logan Square, a few blocks from the Boulevard, the neighborhood's historic tree-lined street. I'd been able to skip the application process because I'd moved into a vacant room in an apartment in which my friend and colleague had already been living for three years. Because of the large trees on each side of the bay window, the living room felt like the inside of a treehouse.

"It wasn't that expensive, and it was really a great deal," she said. She was going to give me $10,000 from the insurance money, she said, to use however I wanted—for a used car, or for anything else.

I was thankful for her passing on a portion of the insurance money, significantly more than most Americans ever receive in inheritance, though it was hard to think of it as inheritance. My debt burden was nearly $400,000. It was not inheritance, but repayment, and it wouldn't mean anything to the loan burden. The interest alone was over $20,000 a year.

"There's no way it was the most affordable option. And it doesn't look good. All of our friends and family just gave us money because we said that we needed it. Was that true? Did we need it? I don't understand." I moved back and forth on the continuum of rage and sorrow.

She said that we did need that money. That every penny and more had gone to my father's medical care.

"But you see how this looks bad, right?" I understood how our country's weak welfare state policed the decisions of poor people, blaming them for their poverty. I did not want to replicate that. I thought people deserving of social provisioning for housing, health care, jobs, and wages should have freedom to buy consumer items that brought them joy. But within the family unit, we could hold each other accountable for our shared resources. She did not need this car. I wanted her to acknowledge that.

"I deserve it." Her voice sharpened.

"None of us deserves a fancy car."

When it was clear that I was not going to accept the logic of her purchase, she changed strategies. "Well, your father came to me in a dream"—something cold and heavy condensed inside me—"and he said that I should buy this car. He wanted me to have it after everything I have been through. He thought I deserved it, too."

I wasn't going to argue with her visitation, her "gift," in the words of my poet-friend. Maybe he had come to her in a dream. It saddened me to think they'd spent their ethereal, fleeting exchange talking about what kind of car she should buy, a replication of the world they'd lived in together—one in which they spent too much time discussing or avoiding discussing their financial predicaments—instead of a new world, in which everything was possible and there were no debts.

I didn't want to talk to him about finances in my dreams. I just wanted to hear "I love you," but I hadn't gotten that either.

Chapter 13

AROUND THE TIME OF our disparate but overlapping dreams, I'd sent in the necessary documentation to assert that the loans were fraudulent, including a notarized handwriting analysis form. The form, titled "Handwriting Exemplar," called to mind the model essays I shared with students and suggested that my handwriting was fixed, rather than evolving as I aged. My signatures were not me but a performance of me. On the second page of the document, I was asked to sign my name in the "usual size" as many times as the thin three lines would allow. I included fifteen signatures.

As I worked through the lines "Kristin Collier" by "Kristin Collier" I kept hesitating about what *usual* meant for me, glancing at the notary to see if she was watching me. She was. Suddenly, I was unsure what it felt like to sign my name or how my hand should feel when holding the pen. All of it felt uncanny and high stakes. Someone from AES would look at these signatures, use a hidden process that wasn't scientific or perhaps even established, and decide if I was lying.

Your own signature, in its usual size, as many times as space allows on the next three lines:

Krist Calr   Krist Calr   Krist Calr   Krist Calr   Krist Calr
Krist Calr   Krist Calr   Krist Call   Krist Calr   Krist Callr
Krist Calr   Krst Calr   Krst Calr   Krsr Callr   Krst Calr

In the months between my handwriting submission and AES's response, the collectors bred and multiplied. I also began to get calls from people looking for my father. Years later, I would read a story about debt collection in nineteenth-century England in which bailiffs, desperate to execute a warrant on a debtor, arrested a corpse on the way to the funeral, forcefully removing the body from the coffin. You cannot "get blood from a stone" or collect debt from a dead person, but you can collect debt from his family. It wasn't clear to me if these calls were scams or real. Was an unpaid debt recorded in a database somewhere that the collectors were, potentially unlawfully, trying to collect?

Around the time I read about the arrested corpse, I requested my mother's file from the county courthouse, wanting to understand more about the theft in hopes that it might tell me more about what happened to me and why. I learned very little, with the exception of a handwritten note on the back of an arrest warrant. "Collier was interviewed," the officer wrote, "and admitted to transferring money into her personal account. She also admitted filing false medical claims."

My mother documented medical procedures that had not taken place, submitted them to insurance, and then paid the insurance money into a personal account rather than that of the practice. I hadn't known the particulars of the fraud but it was basically what I'd imagined. How else could she have stolen so much money undetected? I hadn't understood, though perhaps I might have guessed, that this fraud also involved me and other family members. The warrant states: "Collier sent in claims reporting that her daughter, Kristin Collier, had a root canal and crown procedure done by _____; however, _____ never saw her as a patient." For my missing nerves, sometimes called the tooth's "pulp," a casino probably got a thousand dollars.

When I read this, despite everything I already knew, something sizzled and expanded inside of me. That night, I lay awake, wondering why my body was responding so forcefully. I'd known about the identity theft for many years and had worn its details down as water smooths a stone. There are lots of reasons why one shouldn't submit false insurance claims, but I didn't lose any money from this lie, I told my body as I lay in bed. Nothing has changed, I thought, as I ran my tongue across my teeth. I'd had a real root canal in my twenties after my dentist, someone with frat energy who sang Billy Joel songs while he worked, messed up filling a deep cavity and then had to perform the root canal for free. I wondered which teeth of mine my mother claimed had been hollowed, filled, and capped.

My body seemed to respond to the presence of a secondary self, diffuse and floating out of sight, ghostlike—hiding in databases across the country, emerging sometimes to make its presence known before disappearing again. This other version of me had taken out loan after loan after loan, seeking out new family members to sign their names, tethering their well-being to mine. It acquired credit, and when one of them went to collection, it didn't show up to court. How could it? The ghost? This secondary version, a watery unstable version of myself, didn't have all its teeth, at least not ones with pulp.

I knew my mother's addiction was responsible for her drive for more money, to keep gathering precious resources to feed to the casinos, resources that we needed as a family. And sometimes that knowledge was not enough to soothe me. As I imagined this empty-gummed version of me, she grew pink cheeks and freckles. She wore the mole I had before a doctor had to remove it for its threat, eraser-sized above my lip. But then the mole disappeared. Her brown wavy hair straightened and lightened. She looked like my mother. Had my mother created a second version of me so that she could swallow her up? Had debt first swallowed us both?

———————

In the fall of 2014, I received another e-mail from my lawyer, Todd. "I am at a loss. They have set a new level of incompetence," he writes. "It might be time to file a chapter thirteen and object to their claims in a formal setting. I know we talked about it originally. This is such a catch-22. They won't talk to me without the documents, and they won't give you the documents." Scanning through our correspondence now, I'm not even sure which documents he's referring to. Representatives at AES had received terrified e-mails from a young person in an impossible amount of debt, claiming someone she loved had stolen from her, and begging them to provide her with a *process* that would enable justice and relief, and they'd refused. Each servicer is a large dam, containing and reinforcing an enormous, unnatural system. Each borrower a smaller dam, conscripted to contain the poisonous lake. To help me or any of us would create a leak, the first of many.

Because student loans are protected debts, we would use Chapter 13 to force a conversation with the loan servicers. Once they talked to us, if they still would not agree to release me of the debts, we'd use an adversary proceeding to ask the court to do so. The goal was to avoid using the hardship criteria entirely, because it's very challenging to win.

Throughout and following bankruptcy, my credit would tank. Todd and I didn't talk about this future in much detail, in part because it was also the present I lived within. My credit report had been a con-stant haunting, appearing before me spectral and earthly all at once a few weeks before college graduation. And it had been with me ever since. "People figure this stuff out," he said. "I'll help you."

Around that time, I have a second set of e-mails, which I for-warded to Todd, that contained the details of the default judgment and wage garnishment. Our office manager knew, and so did my principal, whom I'd alerted soon after I learned about it, writing a quick and emotional e-mail, explaining what happened out of fear that he'd think I was irresponsible. Later that same night, I'd sit on my bed looking out my window, and think, "What the fuck? Why did I say anything?" My instinct toward maximum vulnera-bility and exposure was something I'd internalized from the system's demands. I made myself public in response to the debt. As I walked through the halls at work, into and out of meetings, the copy room, our mailbox room, I felt naked and on display.

It's hard for me to read e-mails about the wage garnishment, most of which were from the year the court papers were served to my parents' house and the default judgment was won, when my father was still alive. In one, my uncle's lawyer friend, working on my behalf, wrote to me: "The owner of the debt and com-pany that sued you (Cavalry) will be setting aside the judgment and then dismissing the lawsuit 'with prejudice.' With prejudice means that the lawsuit is terminated in your favor, which means you cannot ever be sued for the debt again and that you owe nothing on that account. Cavalry also will need to fix any damage done to your credit history by deleting anything it has reported against you. So yes, once the paperwork is done, you will be clear of the debt, not obligated in any way to pay anything, and it will not be on your credit."

In subsequent e-mails, I ask him again—just to make sure—"this debt is gone right?" And he becomes annoyed, accuses my family of being messy, and saying, essentially, that he doesn't want to deal with me anymore. Then my uncle, worried on my behalf, also e-mailed me to say that I was approaching it all wrong—the debt was gone and I needed to accept that and stop asking questions that made me look unintelligent and irresponsible. But I'd been right. The debt had not disappeared—it had only laid dormant for several years, before reemerging. It's unclear now whether the collection company illegally sold my debt or something had gone wrong in the process to set aside the judgment. Todd and I added this debt—nearly $14,000—to the list. The bankruptcy filing would stop the wage garnishment and then we'd deal with it along with everything else.

But the lesson in this was hard to disprove, even now, all these years later: The debt is immortal.

———

Under the Higher Education Act of 1965, educational loans could be discharged through bankruptcy proceedings, just like any other unsecured debt, a category that includes credit cards, medical debt, and utility debt. Despite less than 1 percent of government-backed loans being discharged through bankruptcy, 1976 amendments to the Bankruptcy Code tightened the discharge possibility. Critics of the legislation noted that these proposals treated student debtors differently than those with other consumer debt, infusing student debtors with the "criminality" of alimony-dodgers and felons. Proponents of the revision said that the bankruptcy option rewarded those who shirked their responsibility, giving them a free ride. Under the 1976 amendments, students had to wait five years to discharge educational loans, unless they could prove they'd suffered "undue hardship," a criteria that'd hang on through many rounds of bankruptcy code revisions for years to come. Private loans, or loans from nongovernmental lenders, could still be discharged at any point.

Since 1976, bankruptcy provisions related to student loans have been revised five times, each revision protecting a larger group of creditors while narrowing the circumstances under which debtors can receive relief. In 1984, for example, private loans guaranteed by the government or a nonprofit lender were also protected for at least five years. In 1990, the period that students needed to wait to discharge loans was extended from five years to seven years, and in 1998 this waiting period was extended indefinitely. These loans could *never* be discharged, unless hardship was proven. In 2005, all educational loans regardless of private or federal lender were protected from discharge.

In a paper in *The University of Pennsylvania Journal of Business Law*, Brendan Barker writes that critics of this progression toward non-dischargeability argue that it's a response to a phantom student: a high earning doctor or lawyer with hundreds of thousands of dollars in student loan debt that they don't feel like paying, so they decide to declare bankruptcy, keeping the degree that yielded so much wealth while forgoing their obligations. However, this phantom student never materializes. According to a report that Barker cites, in bankruptcies involving student loans in the 1970s, very few filers held those jobs (1.8 percent of debtors were lawyers and 1.3 percent doctors). Our entire approach to bankruptcy legislation for student debtors has been shaped by a debtor who mostly exists in the imaginations of the politicians who proposed these changes and, likely, the lobbyists who depended on this specter to make money from real flesh and blood students.

These days, nearly a quarter of a million debtors with student loans file for bankruptcy each year, and of those, fewer than 300 discharge their student debt. Only .1 percent of bankruptcy filers with student debt get the legal protection entitled to everyone prior to 1976. The lawyer and doctor have been replaced with a different phantom: that of the student receiving relief.

———

Two factors are considered when determining if student loans can be discharged through bankruptcy proceedings. One is whether the debt in question is a qualified educational debt. Though some recent reporting by the Student Borrower Protection Center argues that many private loan debts are *not* qualified educational debts, historically most lawyers and judges have believed that the statute is so complete as to cover every possible type of loan. The second factor is whether the loan will pose an "undue hardship" on the debtor and the debtor's dependents. Though Congress has never defined the parameters for hardship, judges use a test known as the Brunner Test, which uses three prongs that legal scholar Jason Iuliano thinks of as having "three temporary dimensions—present, future, and past, respectively—of a single analysis." Does the debtor have enough income or resources to make payments, while maintaining a minimal standard of living, today? Is the situation likely to improve in the future? Has the debtor attempted to make payments in the past? To receive relief, the judge must decide the answers are "No. No. Yes."

Lawyer Stephen W. Sather, in a paper for the American Bankruptcy Institute, writes that "When Congress originally adopted the undue hardship standard, it provided an alternative path to discharging student loans for those who had been paying on their loans for five years." If debtors did not meet the criteria, they would suffer, but their suffering had an end—a few more years. "Today," he goes on, "it is the sole vehicle for discharge of student loans." Some courts, he writes, have applied the test in such a way that it's impossible to pass it. For example, in one case that Sather describes, a divorced, unemployed debtor, living in a one-room apartment without a kitchen or toilet, failed the second prong of the test, because "he did not present 'a certainty of hopelessness.'" A judge looked at his life and said, it might get easier. Another debtor, Sather includes, failed the third prong: making a good faith effort to pay her loans. This debtor "had nerve damage, bronchitis, and arthritis." Her grandchildren had asthma, her mother had cancer, and her daughter had epilepsy, and the judge said that it was her choice to help her family financially rather than to pay her student loan bills.

Lawmakers revised the bankruptcy codes, ostensibly, because they feared that debtors would behave amorally in relation to their obligations. They also believed that they, the lawmakers, should be the ones to determine which obligations should stand, regardless of circumstance. And yet the codes themselves seem to demand that debtors betray different obligations. The laws suggest that people prioritize their payments to the government or a bank over helping their sick family with rent or medication, making car payments, or finding a home with a toilet.

In January 2015, I took another day off work to travel back to Kalamazoo, my attorney's city, to attend a credit counseling course and debtor education course, a requirement of my bankruptcy—one designed, according to my attorney, to make it harder for people to file for bankruptcy. Following the course, I'd attend a hearing where a judge would approve the bankruptcy plan and the documents we'd submitted. The course was in the basement of the courthouse. It looked identical to many church basements: thin blue carpet, stained from muddy shoes and spilled coffee; fluorescent overhead lights between drop ceiling tiles. As I waited for the course to begin, I poured weak coffee from one of the large brown jugs. Alongside it, the credit counseling man had laid out several blue tins of Dutch cookies, leftovers from the recent holiday, and a few pastries. I took a lot of them. The course would run for three hours.

After choosing a table near the front, I looked around the room quickly, aware that everyone there likely carried some shame for the circumstances that produced this moment. I was the youngest in attendance by what seemed to be twenty years. Many people were there with a spouse. I wished, as we started, that we had a chance to introduce ourselves and share a little about what brought us there—not as an articulation of guilt but of harm.

Years later, I called Todd to ask him about my case and his work more broadly, and he said that most of his clients declare bankruptcy because of a medical crisis, even when they have insurance. "Two days in the emergency room and now they owe twenty thousand dollars." Others are seniors who lost a spouse, or another misfortune found them, and living on their limited social security income, they cannot afford it. "They're just living normal lives, not doing crazy stuff," he said. When he meets with clients for the first time, Todd asks them if they can afford to purchase the monthly medicine they need, and they always say no—whether that price is $100 or significantly higher. The blood pressure or arthritis or dementia or cancer go untreated because they have debts to pay. In the basement of the courthouse, I knew some people were going to lose their homes. Though the mortgage crisis had slowed five years earlier, some of my fellow bankrupters were wrapped up in its wide net anyway. But we were not given name tags, and we did not share our stories.

The credit counseling was focused on two main priorities: 1) making sure that we understood what a budget was and how we should make one; 2) the importance of saving and sticking to the budget that we'd created. The credit man used his wardrobe and his tone to convey his expertise: He was dressed in a black suit with shiny black shoes, and he spoke to us like he was performing a TED Talk, using a slide clicker so that he could circulate the room announcing each new slide as if it was something that would transform our lives.

Occasionally he solicited audience participation, "What *is* a budget? And how *do* you make one?" Despite being a student who'd always raised her hand for her entire educational journey, I refused to participate. While there was certainly information about navigating the financial system that was opaque and confusing, information we might benefit from learning (how can you, for example, secure housing with a bankruptcy on your credit report; how can you refute inaccurate information on said report?) making a budget was not that. *Don't,* I urged my new classmates with my eyes. But many of them were generous and raised their hands, laughing along with his occasional jokes. It was not this man's fault that we were here. And still, I was annoyed.

When he walked us through the mechanics of budget, I wanted to ask: *But what if we have jobs that don't pay us a living wage?* The assumption that guided the lesson was that we had all the money we needed and simply should organize it more thoughtfully. *What if we have student loans that are protected by the federal government? What if the housing shortage means we cannot find a rental unit we can afford? What if collection companies try to illegally collect debt from us despite the bankruptcy?* It was not bankruptcy that I was frustrated with. Bankruptcy is ultimately a process to provide relief, even if its birth was a response to an emerging market economy that encouraged indebtedness, as historian Jill Lepore notes. Todd told me that after the bankruptcy process is initiated, he always asks his client what changes and they tell him, "I can finally sleep." What frustrated me was the presumption that our recklessness had engineered our financial failures and that we should be subjected to this instruction so that we didn't repeat this same reckless behavior.

"Even if you think you don't have any money, you probably have a dollar. Start by just putting a dollar a day into savings. Or if you can't do that, start with a dollar a week. Eventually that adds up to something." A dollar a week adds up to fifty-two dollars a year, I thought. My lenders were asking for nearly two thousand dollars a month for an unresponsive debt that would keep growing anyway.

I don't remember much of the meeting that followed. None of the creditors showed, which often happens. They don't need to—the trustee represents their interests. In place of a complete memory is a desperate urge to smile and present myself as "deserving person," a nod to the poor law morality around poverty and indebtedness that Melinda Cooper studies in *Family Values,* an imposed morality that parses people who are deserving and undeserving of aid and which has shaped our eroding welfare state. *I'm good. I swear.*

On the drive home it would strike me as strange that the class was titled "credit counseling" rather than "budget management." We had already been granted credit—promises we made for our future-self granted and mitigated by lenders—and because of our debt, we would likely not be granted the gift of credit again for a long time. "Counseling" implied that we were taught to be good managers of credit rather than what we were: bad debtors who had broken our promises to the lenders and to our past selves through our inability to repay what we had borrowed.

Through the standardization of the FICO credit score and mass surveillance and information–sharing techniques perfected by credit bureaus, what scholar Joshua Lauer calls our "financial identities" would confirm this broken promise, which everyone would know about: employers, landlords, banks, and people who wanted to sell things to us, sometimes at prices targeted to our credit profiles. "Contemporary credit scoring is the empirical technology that turns persons into numbers," writes Annie McClanahan. Our numbers would narrate our lives, without our consent, reducing the freedom the bankruptcy process had been designed to give us.

Chapter 14

SAIMA, A BENGALI AMERICAN born in the Midwest, had $36,000 in student loans from her nursing degree. She, like many of the borrowers that I'd spoken with over the years, performed work that was primarily about caring for other people, either their bodies or their minds. They were nurses, nursing assistants, therapists, educators. Their financial security fluctuated according to the state and city in which they lived (the average starting salary for a teacher in Michigan was just $40,302 as of 2024) but all of them were made less secure by their loan burdens.

She and I met in a coffee shop. I'd taken a writing class with her years earlier. Though she was much younger than the other students in the class, her writing was sharp, researched, and vibrant. Her essays conveyed an interest in the transformative possibilities of hallucinogenic experiences for people with severe depression, within the context of official therapy and outside of it. We remained loosely in contact after the class was over, occasionally running into one another at literary readings or getting tea. When

I'd last seen her, a couple of years earlier, she'd just begun her program in nursing.

Saima explained that when she first began her undergraduate degree at a selective liberal arts school near her home, her parents were "double unemployed" as they finished school, and their expected family contribution was low. The school offered her an enormous aid package that meant her net price was almost nothing. But Saima took a medical leave her freshman year for a mental-health related disability. "They weren't very accommodating," she said about that experience, though she'd heard that their policies had changed since then. When she was ready to return to school the next year, her family's economic situation had improved and the school was very expensive. So she transferred to a nearby public university, where she majored in psychology and took writing classes on the side.

"I was incredibly lucky that my parents wanted to and did pay for my undergraduate education," she said. Though her parents' income had waxed and waned over the years, especially following the Great Recession when her father was unemployed and her mother supported them on her department store salary, they were able to make it work. But that wasn't possible for graduate school, so Saima borrowed money from the federal government and used a tuition plan offered by her school that, essentially, loaned her another $4,000, interest free, that she would need to pay back in three years following graduation.

Saima was aware that her story is one in which, on the surface, higher education and its attendant lending system seemed to work as it was supposed to. "I was very lucky," she said again and again—a phenomenon that she mostly attributed to her family. She knows people with much larger debt burdens than she has. And yet, the career that she had chosen because she believed in medical care that is responsive to who people are and what they need, informed by how they exist in the world and have been impacted by its harms, didn't pay her enough. After paying her rent, car payment, credit card payment, utilities, etc., she had little left over. When we spoke, student loan payments had not restarted following Biden's moratorium, and under his new plan, she thought she'd need to pay between $300 and $500 a month.

"I do have a gym membership," she said when I asked her about her monthly finances. I wasn't trying to parse if she spent money irresponsibly, only trying to understand what she might have to go without once payments began. She admitted her gym membership as if she had recently purchased a private yacht. The comment suggested she'd read the brand of think-piece that shames young people for small acts of consumerism rather than paying down existing debt burdens. I didn't know if her gym was a sleek, hip one where people wear designer clothes and drink post-workout smoothies with collagen, or the kind I used to belong to, where men often weight-lift in jeans, and there are advertisements for mysterious sandwiches that don't seem to exist. It didn't matter.

"You should be able to go to the gym!" I said. For working class people, there are only so many places from which to draw resources, so the places in which they stop spending money are the same: They don't go to the doctor or the dentist or pay for their medication. They stop buying food for themselves, or at least much of it. They don't care for their bodies.

Recently, Saima had taken another medical leave related to her disabilities, chronic pain and bipolar disorder, and to the work itself. "I'm in a situation now where I feel like I can't go back to the job I took a leave from," she said. Her job at the psychiatric facility made her miserable, spiked what felt painful and impossible about the world in and outside of herself. She'd chosen it, in part, because it offered her the highest salary of the ones she applied to, and as she'd begun to research new jobs, she'd learned that all the places she wanted to work, community clinics serving marginalized people, didn't pay enough.

"When I heard that nurses make $35 an hour right away, I thought it was going to be a whole lot of money," she told me. She thought she'd be able to save for a house and have an emergency fund and build the life that she'd always wanted. But her student debt payments would make that impossible. She'd be able to apply for Public Service Loan Forgiveness, but that relief would be many years away. It also wasn't guaranteed. Even if future relief was certain, it wouldn't change the constraints of her salary and loans in the present.

———

The Public Service Loan Forgiveness program was created and implemented in 2007, in the words of journalist Ryann Liebenthal writing for *Mother Jones*, "to address low salaries in public service jobs where costly degrees are the price of entry but wages often aren't high enough to pay down debts." As of 2022, federal employees with advanced degrees made nearly 30 percent less than workers with similar jobs in the private sector. "The public broadly shares the benefits of a highly educated professional workforce serving in their communities," a report from the Consumer Financial Protection Bureau reminds us. This report notes that public services workers are caught between two "economic cross currents." They need higher education in order to pursue their service-based job, and because of the rising costs of education, they also need debt to acquire their degree even as they face low and stagnated wages that will make repayment challenging.

In what seems like a sinister acknowledgment of the trap public servants are left in, the Arizona Attorney General, suing to end President Biden's broad-based cancellation effort, writes that the cancellation effort will harm the Office of Attorney General because it "relies upon the availability of student debt forgiveness programs to recruit legal talent. Indeed it currently employs dozens of attorneys eligible for relief under the Public Service Loan Forgiveness Program ("PSLF")." They go on to note that it will be harder for them to recruit legal talent if debts are canceled. Rather than paying these lawyers more or making public higher education free, the implication is, we should offer this very specific benefit in an attempt to maintain the system as it is.

As of 2016, 86 percent of borrowers who certified intent to pursue PSLF earned less than $75,000 a year, and over half of them earned under $50,000. If you spent ten years working as a nurse, teacher, in military service, as an EMT, at a library, as a social worker; if you spent all day drawing blood or caring for someone with a disability; if you taught preschool children the alphabet, or if you worked at a nursing home, or were a public defender; and if you did these ten years of work while also making 120 monthly payments toward your student loans, then at the end of the ten years, your remaining debt burden was released, or, as the department phrased it, "forgiven." Successful PSLF applicants often pay back as much as 91 percent of their original loan amount, so the program's appeal, according to Liebenthal, "[is] that it offer[s] a clear path for people who struggled to pay back loans, or struggled to envision how they would ever pay them off without abandoning public service jobs for higher paid positions elsewhere."

In practice, however, the program has not worked as intended. In addition to the basic requirements of the program listed above, borrowers also had to be enrolled in a qualifying repayment plan, and the debt in question had to be in the form of a direct loan, a kind of loan issued from the Department of Education. Students with a government-guaranteed loan had to have their loans consolidated into a direct loan before they began repayments. Private debt would not qualify at all.

In data gathered following the inception of PSLF and the first round of applicants, a host of issues prevented borrowers from receiving relief. After first consulting their servicer, many borrowers spent years believing they were paying toward their PSLF requirement—because they had been *told* that they were—only to learn later that their payments didn't qualify because they hadn't consolidated their loans. A borrower in this circumstance might have made monthly payments of $100 for four years (nearly $5,000) only to be told that not a single one of those payments would count toward their application and that the clock for the 120 payments would be reset starting at zero. For borrowers who did know about the consolidation requirement, the process of loan transfer took longer than it was supposed to, and there were errors: Old servicers misreported balances and qualifying payments to the direct loan program; or, some loans were left out entirely. Other borrowers never knew about the program despite sharing with their servicer what they did for work.

Many borrowers were not enrolled in a qualifying repayment plan even though they specifically asked to be enrolled in this plan. Or their applications to switch to one of these plans were denied without a chance to correct because of minor confusions or errors. Or their return to graduate school kicked them out of the qualifying plan—even though borrowers attempted proactively to manage this very possibility. Sometimes, borrowers were unenrolled from their IDR program because of a delay in certification of family income (some of these borrowers were military personnel stationed overseas who didn't have regular access to the internet). Borrowers had trouble determining whether their employer was eligible, and their servicer was unable to answer their questions about employment certification over the phone (only through the form submission, which was a slow process, and as was true with everything else, there were many errors). If borrowers were lucky enough to work for an employer with loan repayment as a benefit, sometimes the benefits were misapplied in such a way that none of the employer payments counted, setting the borrower back months or years.

The PSLF program failures were as myriad as the borrowers enrolled in it. In 2017, the first round of borrowers became eligible to have their loans forgiven. Millions of borrowers had started the application process for relief, but only fifty-five of them had received it in the spring the following year. The Biden administration attempted to address and correct these enormous failures, and as of June 2024, had approved $62.8 billion in relief for 876,000 borrowers. As is true with the administration's IDR correction, I am buoyed by what this relief means for the people who receive it. "I feel like I have my life back," someone wrote in a borrower's online forum about their approved PSLF. Life as an engine of possibility, as narrative potential, and also, a body. They felt that they'd been returned to themselves.

In an essay for *The Seattle Times*, nurse practitioner Michael Moore explains the way loan relief programs failed him. He works with one of Seattle's most vulnerable populations, those with opioid use disorder. Many of these patients don't have access to housing and traditional health care. He doesn't include all the other ways these patients likely suffer: from estranged relationships with loved ones, over-policing, domestic violence. In his role, he provides quality addiction treatment to his patients and helps them navigate the health-care system. "I love the work that I do," he writes, "and I am great at it, too. I have what most people do not have in their career—direct, unambiguous purpose and meaning." But his student debt makes it impossible to buy a home and he panics whenever he opens his loan servicer's website.

Michael needed this debt to get his advanced degree: His family was poor enough that he qualified for free school lunch as a kid and for a Pell Grant when he began undergrad. He thought that he'd be able to pay these loans off with his salary or that the many relief programs would work as they were intended to. But neither of those things has been true. One program, the Nurse Corps Loan Repayment Program, keeps running out of funds each year. Another nurse-specific program, one with a focus on providers working in substance use disorder, rejected his application because the death rate for opioid use is lower in Seattle than the national average. For Michael's own loans to be discharged, more of his patients would need to die. "I would be lying," he writes at the end of the essay, "if I said I had not thought about flipping out of health care into tech."

I began my career as a teacher because I liked to talk about books, to write, and to spend time with kids, and I wasn't sure what else to do. Like lots of first-generation college students, I didn't have the knowledge or confidence to access campus resources that could help me imagine my life after college, and I worked year-round, making internships hard. I also lacked the kinds of connections that getting many internships hinges on. Had I access to wealth, had I believed graduate school was possible, had I known people with careers that seemed interesting and meaningful and well-paid, maybe I'd have chosen something else.

During my first years of teaching, I was surprised by how physical the experience was. My eighth graders were developing new hormones and new bodies in response to their hormones, and they smelled bad, especially after gym. Girls often bled through their pants. I once turned around from the board to see two newly-in-love students making out in the back of the room. Students hit each other occasionally, though never forcefully. A student in severe distress once blew his nose so hard and so repeatedly that it bled, and then he smeared it on his desk. When I taught sixth grade, my students wanted to hug me every morning. They asked me to lace up their skates when I took them to the ice rink in Central Park. A student who puked on herself asked for my help wiping off her shirt and hair. When students were feverish, I felt their foreheads and gave them tissues and water. I sat next to them when they cried with my hand on their shoulder. Over the years, I watched them sprout facial hair, watched one of their bellies swell for nine months before she left and never came back. Rarely had I felt so attuned to so many bodies and to the influence of the world on those bodies in the hours I didn't see them.

An awareness of the forces that shape us, either kindly or cruelly, is at the core of public service work, as is the hope to augment what is kind and counteract what is cruel. My friend who works as a public defender spent years working seventy hours a week to help sex workers combat unjust policing practices that threatened their ability to house themselves and care for their children. My friend who works in tribal law regularly helps Native people keep their homes as landlords find reasons to kick them out, into a city with no housing in a state with no housing. Another friend, an early childhood educator, teaches students the alphabet, holds open picture books so that students can track the illustrations as she reads, calms them for naps. After a flu turned to pneumonia turned to sepsis and nearly killed her years ago, she might have decided to leave her grueling classroom work once she healed but didn't.

Though I've been teaching for sixteen years now and spent most of those years teaching at schools in which the majority of students qualified for free and reduced lunch, which is what we said instead of "poor"; though most of my students came from families with adults who had not been to college—and who wanted, more than anything for their own kids to go; though many of my students lived in public housing and faced all sorts of structural insecurities, the government has yet to grant me relief for my federal loans through the PSLF program, which I have been enrolled in since I moved to Chicago. Signatures and applications have suddenly gone "missing." I've been asked for different signatures from different people. Once, I was told my school did not actually exist before, later, it suddenly did. Sometimes payments were forgotten or miscounted. For a while no one could tell me if I was still enrolled in the program. Like everyone else, I'm waiting.

Eleni Schirmer notes that "While the nation has faced an acute K–12 teacher shortage for almost a decade, less than 5 percent of all college graduates have majored in education since 2015—an alarming reversal from 1970, when 20 percent of college graduates studied education." There are already overcrowded classes and shuttered schools, especially in poor districts, across the country. This swelling and constriction pushes students into conditions in which they cannot learn, in which a single teacher cannot meet an entire class's needs. What happens to our students and their futures when the crowding and emptying continues? Service work, including teaching, is always about caring for people's physical selves alongside their many other selves—artistic, intellectual, spiritual. The work is tender, intimate, funny, interesting, devastating, and sometimes humiliating. In its attention to the bodies of hundreds of millions of people—indeed, all of us—it animates the country itself, creating and sustaining our collective, national body. We can't exist without it.

———

"I'm in pain every day," Saima said toward the end of our meeting, speaking slowly, enunciating each word, as if she was thinking about it as she said it. She added, "and in so many ways the world has been my oyster." Though her parents' income was stretched thin to support other family members, especially family living in poverty in Bangladesh, they'd been able to offer Saima consistent financial support. She'd had stable housing, attended a good high school, and had the chance to go to graduate school.

The contrast between the opportunities she'd been given and the pain she was in—bodily and financially—illuminated something true, and rarely acknowledged, about the higher education lending system: It often doesn't work even for the people it should work for. Below the surface, there is unrevealed suffering, made worse by debt. And even in the rare cases where that's not true, debt's presence makes the work of caregiving precarious, diverting public servants into new jobs with higher wages and more security.

"We need people like you in medicine," I said after she shared her wish to be a psychiatric nurse practitioner, a job that would require more school and more loans. Over the years, I would have benefited from a practitioner like Saima who chose to cultivate empathy and who had her own experiences navigating mental and physical distress and medication.

When I got up to leave, I told her that I hoped she started writing again, which I meant, but seemed to be a naive thing to say when I thought about it later. She was on medical leave and struggling to find employment that she believed in and that would also pay her well—how would she ever have time to write?

Chapter 15

IN SEPTEMBER 2016, TODD e-mailed me a case update. "Where do you want to go from here? I think the next step is hiring our own handwriting expert." A year before, I'd moved to Minnesota to start a fully funded graduate program, which meant that my tuition was covered by the university, and I was given a small living stipend in exchange for teaching undergraduate writing courses.

I understood the risk of leaving my full-time employment in the middle of an ongoing bankruptcy, after which I might still have hundreds of thousands of dollars in student loans. Unlike many of my classmates, I'd have to take on a second job to make the three-hundred-dollar bankruptcy payments each month. But it felt impossible to stay where I was. My relationship with my mother was inconsistent and painful, my father was gone, many of my colleagues had moved to new jobs, and I was beginning to feel bitter and distant, toxic and cut off from the world around me. I'd worked fifty hours a week for the last eight years, and I wanted to reshape my relationship to time. There would be work still, but there would also be opportunities to read, write, and think. The debt would follow me, I knew, but I hoped when it found me again, something would be different.

My Minneapolis apartment was on the first floor of a medium-sized rental building, adjacent to the sidewalk entrance. My proximity to the front door meant that I could hear folks standing outside to smoke or to talk. The walls felt porous and open. But I could afford it, and the landlord had agreed to rent to me after I offered a larger-than-normal deposit and passed on an official letter from my attorney, promising him that I was a very responsible renter "in spite" of what my credit history suggested. The implication was unavoidable: I was not like other renters with bankruptcies, which I didn't think was true. I was like everyone else—caught up in differing and overlapping systems of hardship—and we all deserved places to live.

Todd had passed on my fraud paperwork to the attorneys representing the lenders sometime in early 2016, and they had written back requesting more writing. They needed writing from the time the loans were taken out, not writing from nearly ten years later when I had completed the notarized fraud paperwork. I e-mailed him three documents as my handwriting samples, offering him these notes:

Journal entries from 2004 to 2008, twelve pages, dates marked in the text.

Journal entries + college notes; two pages of journal entries from 2005; five pages of notes from my Introduction to Poetry class, which I took in the winter of 2006.

Notes from my Modern Poetry Class. These are eighteen separate flash cards I made myself to study for my modern poetry class, which I took during the fall of 2006.

In my e-mail, I explained to him that I also included a college transcript, so that I could prove to their handwriting expert that I did in fact take these classes, as if I might go through the elaborate effort of forging flash cards and anthology annotations to pretend I was an eighteen-year-old fraud victim who was very interested in poetry.

Cyriack,[1] Whose Grandsire

Cyriack, whose grandsire on the royal bench
Of British Themis, ...

- This *herental sect* was killed by the duke in honor of the pope/church on Easter Day.
- he was a militant protestant. uses [sonnet] for political purposes
- apostrophe, when the the poem addresses someone/thing. Here it is God.
- refers to the way in which Catholics worshipped relics (stock & stone). Milton wanted to get rid of this superstition and was part of a purist sect.
- Milton relies enjambment
- Babylon: children of Israel taken into captivity by Babylonians, god's chosen ppl are enslaved by tyrant. Here god's chosen ppl are the whid ensigns & protestants. Encourages ppl to join this cause. A sort of propaganda.

pope, whose tiara has three crowns.
9. Babylon, as a city of luxury and vice, was often linked with the Papal Court by Protestants, who

he had been married less than two years (hence "late espousèd") when she died, in 1658; since Milton had become blind in 1652, he almost certainly

The first journal entry is dated July 2004, one month before I started school and around the time my mother acquired the first fraudulent loan in my name. My childhood dog has just died, and I am worried that no one will love me like the dog did again. In the next entry, partially cut off, I've seen my high school crush, who is dating someone else, at open mic night. In yet another, I mull over the sadness I experience each year on my birthday. The journal entries switch to college and evolve to include ideas for short stories: "Two old men sit in tiny plastic chairs selling books to college kids who just don't care. They fall asleep on the sidewalk reading." And, in what I guess is meant to be a sort of a lesson or surprise, "Then someone steals a book."

These handwriting samples placed me in direct contact with an earlier version of myself, one unaware of what awaits her four years later. At the bottom of the e-mail to Todd, I acknowledged this vulnerability: "Some of this stuff is really embarrassing to read, but I know that it's necessary." The lenders had already taken so much: hours spent waiting to speak with someone, hours navigating a bureaucratic paperwork maze with mostly dead ends, so much of my money, my sense of a secure future. They'd also taken my ability to trust my parents, my belief that our family was committed to love and generosity, honesty, and care. My parents were part of that of course, but the lenders were, too.

And now they required I share something I'd written just for myself, which someone was going to scan through, matching it word by word, letter by letter, searching for a reason that they could tell me, again, that this debt was mine. Which they did, when they rejected the newest batch of handwriting samples in September. The lawyer representing the lender wrote, simply: "The client reviewed the additional handwriting samples sent by your client and denied the fraud claim."

When Todd passed on this finding it did not include any details about this rejection or which method they used to study twenty pages of writing and eighteen flash cards. In my response, I see now that what began as painful curiosity many years earlier (why is it so hard to get the necessary paperwork?) had transitioned to rage at a world in which loan companies have this much power, in which their loyalty is not to the students they claim to support but to the act of collection.

They did not care if the debt was actually mine. They cared about whether I could prove it. "I don't understand how banks can continually supply loans to a forty-year-old woman who is signing an eighteen-year-old child's name again and again," I write to Todd, "especially once they saw the mounting debt which was obvious from my credit report. Especially when she is signing alone, without me, hours away from where I was at school. I don't understand how these people cannot be accountable for that."

I thought, again, about all the other borrowers—all the frauds and the misunderstandings that undergirded the entire system. The misplaced hopes of students, who were promised that their education would lead to a free life, with access to medical care, affordable housing, and a well-paid job. They lived with these harmful debt burdens, and perhaps this feral growing rage, sometimes forever.

I told him, yes, let's hire a writing expert, which I noted would be hard for me to afford, but I would do whatever was necessary. It was not just that I wanted to wrestle my future back, one that was kind and open: I wanted the loan companies to be held accountable. I wanted a future that contained justice.

———

The rental home that my parents moved to following their bankruptcy was twenty minutes north of our old home along a highway that lined the edge of Michigan. Behind the house was an enormous empty field that sometimes flooded into a pond following a winter of heavy snow, releasing a swarm of mosquitos into the humid air by mid-June. On the other side of the marshy field was more field and then a steep bluff leading down to a strip of beach and the wide mouth of Lake Michigan. When my father was still alive, he built steps to the beach, using salvaged plywood and rope, and my parents climbed down to the lake where they walked the beach and celebrated their great fortune. Despite everything, they'd ended up somewhere beautiful.

During these walks, my mother began to pick up rocks from the shoreline: sandstones, Favosites, crinoids, Petoskey stones. The Petoskey stones are my favorite; they look like small dinosaur eggs, spotted with a hundred brown milky eyes around which are spindly halos. These stones are the remains of an enormous coral reef, dredged up and dragged across the earth during glaciation—when large sheets of ice moved across the Midwest, flattening its mountains. My mother first collected these and other rocks, showing family and friends, and then began to glue them to decorative items: picture frames, doormats, lamps, wall clocks. To make the rocks appear as they do on the beach, just as the water has receded, she coated them with a veneer. So their shine was eternal, the lake's lasting resonance.

While she experimented with this art, something she hoped to sell, she earned money cleaning homes and businesses in town. This work was hard, and I imagine, strange. While the homeowners were at work or on vacations, she was there, scrubbing sinks and bathtubs, scooping out the bits and pieces of them left behind—their hair, a film of olive oil on the counter, a stain of makeup on the bathroom sink. Sometimes, she cleaned a dentist office, not the one she had worked at, and at the dentist's urging, brought home spare toothbrushes and toothpastes. In her home today, there is a drawer in her bathroom filled with these items, ready to be used if my sister and I stay there long enough to need them.

―――――

"Would your mom be willing to testify?" Todd e-mailed me to ask nearly three years into the bankruptcy process. "Would your grandparents?" We had ultimately decided not to hire the handwriting expert following the lender's rejection, because it would be expensive and seemed unlikely to matter, and Todd was now hoping to bring our case before a judge to argue in person about what had happened to me. There were no guarantees about what the lenders would do if the judge decided for us, if they would prosecute my mother, but it seemed unlikely. The statute of limitations had passed for criminal prosecution, and the resources they'd need to put toward a civil charge would probably not be worth what they could collect. My mother was a single, low-wage worker already burdened with existing debts.

The online payment system for my bankruptcy did not work, so each month when I wrote my check to my "Chapter 13 Trustee," I tried to hide it between other pieces of outgoing mail in my apartment entrance. That I understood I should not be ashamed of this bankruptcy, that no one should, didn't affect the actual shame that I felt. Because the private loans were being disputed, the monthly payments went toward my federal debt, afforded through a combination of tutoring and bartending on top of my graduate student teaching.

"I think my mother would," I write back. Being back in a courtroom again would terrify my mother, even if it provided her an opportunity for restitution. Her last court experience had not yielded the chance to attend a recovery program or engage in any restorative justice process: She'd been removed from the world—briefly, luckily—and then thrust back into it with a legal financial obligation that rivaled the cost of an undergraduate education and no meaningful pathway to well-paid work given her record. She'd also have to announce to a judge and to a team of lawyers something she'd never been able to say to me: the exact mechanisms by which she stole from me. I didn't know if most of the process had occurred online or over the phone or in person or how long it took. I'm not sure if I hadn't asked because she could not bear the answer or because I couldn't.

Testifying would also be destabilizing for my grandparents, not because of language barriers but because of the shift it would require in their understanding of themselves as parents. My oma and I talked on the phone sometimes, and she knew that I had not consented to these loans, but she was steadfast in her belief that everything my mother did, she did, somehow, for me and my sister. She saw my mother's gambling dependency as a "blip" in her life rather than an addiction. My oma begged me to forgive my mother, saying that my mother needed my forgiveness to be happy, to survive. At first, I asked, "What about me?" and when her response was "You're strong. You'll get through it," I stopped resisting. My distance from home allowed me to tolerate, however uncomfortably, my oma's painful assertion: that it was me who was committing harm in my unwillingness to move forward as if this debt did not exist and in my inability to summon and implement a universe with a different timeline, the one our lives might be playing out on had none of this happened.

———

Recently, I'd learned that my kidney was dying. At the beginning of graduate school, just after I moved to Minneapolis, I began to feel pressure on the left side of my body, just below my rib cage, as if a small fist had suddenly sprouted inside my body and was trying to get out. I'd seen several doctors who'd suggested that it might be a pulled muscle, or less helpfully, "nothing," so I'd managed it, sleeping on my left side to dull the impact of the pressure and occasionally wrapping a bandage around my ribs when it felt hard to be still with the pressure.

Finally, I insisted that a doctor look for *something* to explain the sensation and an ultrasound and renal scan enabled them to see that the right kidney was doing 90 percent of the work, and the left one was atrophying, no longer the size of a plum but a fig. "You didn't know you had one kidney that didn't work?" the doctor asked, startled.

They were unsure of the cause. Its dysfunction might have been connected to the many kidney infections I'd had in my early twenties, or it might have been because of an error in its genetic implementation. Maybe I was born with a single good kidney. But I didn't believe that. I knew that the pressure I felt was its swan song. "We can remove the kidney," the doctor said, "but I don't recommend a surgery if it stops bothering you." The "if" pointed toward the organ's eventual death. Today, the pressure is gone, and after several more scans and new doctors, I know that the kidney died from a prolonged urinary stricture. I carry with me a small corpse.

Debt demands a body. That was true in ancient civilizations and true today, as these systems of punishment and collection become reincarnated in new forms that echo the ancient ones. Debt demands, regardless of what we can give. When I couldn't pay in my twenties, I was collected upon anyway.

———

In the end, my mother didn't need to testify. We had a hearing date, which the judge rescheduled for six months later, following his family emergency. In the interim, the lenders made a calculation—surely financial—about what this process was worth to them and decided they didn't need a hearing, that an affidavit signed by myself and my mother about the debt's origins would suffice. After which, I'd be released from the debt. At that point, they'd have the option to collect from her, but my lawyer thought they likely wouldn't. "If they do, I'll help her," he said.

Everything we'd done—all the e-mails and unreturned phone calls, the handwriting samples, and the rest of the bankruptcy process—had led here. Each dead end the lenders erected forced us to find a new pathway. And yet, we didn't actually need to do any of it. Had the lenders been open to my initial request to release me of the debt, we could have negotiated without the bankruptcy, skipping all of it, and signing the same affidavit. I would have saved hundreds of hours e-mailing and calling lenders and driving to meet my lawyer; I would have saved money in bankruptcy fees; but more significantly, I would have been spared the constant terror of not knowing what would happen to me.

My mother finished signing the settlement in the days preceding Thanksgiving in 2018. I was visiting my new boyfriend's family in New Mexico. Mike and I had met in my graduate school program. In our first extended conversation at a program party, I tipsily told him an abbreviated version of the last ten years, softening the low points with humor. Already, I sensed that I might love him someday, and, though I had not planned to say any of it, some unthinking part of me wanted him to know all the ways the debt extended and blurred me. I don't know if my confession was invitation or warning. He laughed when he was supposed to and seemed warmly interested, rather than alarmed, and I understood that I wanted to keep talking to him, not just about this but about everything.

Just before the holiday break, we had rushed our collective signatures—mine, my mother's, and a lawyer representing the lenders. An earlier copy had been lost in the mail, and a new one had to be overnighted so that it was completed on a decided date.

"What will happen to me?" my mother texted me before she signed the document. Mike and I were driving into the Sandia Mountains to the east of Albuquerque, named for the red hue they turn at sunset. Her question was not just about the debt, I sensed, but about the rest of her life. What she was also asking was, will you forgive me now? And I texted her back truthfully: "I don't know."

After we finalized the settlement, I kept waiting to experience the relief it promised. I wasn't debt free yet—I had around $9,000 left to pay as part of my bankruptcy agreement—but I was free of the largest portion of the debt, the part that had made it feel as if my life was impossible. I'd been living with this enormous debt burden for so long that the debt existed somewhere inside of me, had fused with me. After a post-Thanksgiving hike, standing in the shower at Mike's parents' house, I willed my body to feel differently. I turned the water hotter and hotter as if challenging the debt to stay put. In the weeks that followed, I periodically asked myself, Is this the moment when I'll feel different?

I felt haunted by the debt even though the collectors had stopped calling and the loan correspondence for my federal loans had been paused for bankruptcy. Sociologist Avery F. Gordon argues that ghost stories and stories of hauntings are meaningful frameworks with which to consider trauma. In her book *Ghostly Matters: Haunting and the Sociological Imagination*, she writes, "the ghost or the apparition is one form by which something lost, or barely visible, or seemingly not there to our supposedly well-trained eyes, makes itself known or apparent to us, in its own way, of course. The way of the ghost is haunting, and haunting is a very particular way of knowing what has happened or is happening."

Sometimes the ghosts gripped my neck, lightly, when I used my debit card at a grocery store checkout, as I worried, for a brief, strong second that it would be rejected, regardless of how much money I had in checking. They showed up in every phone number that I didn't know, when my body tensed, ready to be told a new debt had gone to collections. And they appeared in the specter of a different life, the one I might have had without debt. If I had been able to take out loans for graduate school, if I had been able to work only a single job while teaching in my twenties, if I had been able to pursue different, uncertain jobs, if I hadn't paid seven hundred dollars each month, if I had entered into romantic partnerships with less debt, without the betrayals that gave me the debt—who would I be? This different life haunts many of the debtors I talk to, who imagine body doubles who own homes, take vacations, and move away from situations that harm them. They look at the other version and think: What if?

I wanted my mother and me to be free, but we weren't, not really. I had not forgiven her and she had not created the conditions for forgiveness, but I still maintained a relationship with her, a connection that I hoped would someday generate a real reconciliation. In the brief windows in which I was home, for a few days over summer break or a week at Christmas, the debt was all around us, shouting at us. I wanted my mother to know the particular and strange way I engaged with the world—the dumb shit that made me laugh, images that moved me, new and acute pains that pricked me as I grew older ten hours from home—but I couldn't share any of that with her.

On each trip home from Minneapolis, I said to myself: This time will be different. I'll offer more of myself. I'll laugh more. I'll tell her a story about my students or about me that really reveals some-thing. But it was never different. Seated at our backyard table, before grilled corn and potato salad, I felt myself withdraw and retreat. The severing of our identities in the eyes of the lenders had not released me to come to her again, new and wanting to be known.

———————

Once, cleaning an office late at night with a close friend, my mother heard her friend yell from the next room. Later, she'd recall that it was not out of pain, but what sounded like surprise. When she got to her on the other side of the office, she was dead, and my mother sat with her body until the ambulance and her family arrived. For months afterward, my father came with her to clean that office, and my mother cleaned other spaces with trepidation. She must have felt like she'd become a ghost, like she'd been reborn into a quiet and lonely world in someone else's home. I used to think it was shame that drove her to quit the work, but these days, I think it was the eerie sense of trespassing, the look at domestic life she now felt shut off from.

Eventually, the rock art became enough of a business that she took it on the road, driving across southwest Michigan, setting up booths at art fairs and craft markets, selling to tourists looking to remember their vacations on the lake. When my father died, the work became harder. Coastal erosion, expedited by a new subdivision next door to them, washed out the stairs and the rope. It was harder to get to the beach. And it was harder to carry the stones back to her house when she did. First, she used backpacks, and then she used a beach wagon with sand tires that my sister and I got her for Christmas. The rocks were too heavy for one person, but she kept at it anyway. Each day, a new shoreline, the bones of the past, ready and waiting.

In the fall of 2020, as a new wave of the pandemic crested, I began, for the first time in many years, collecting new student loan bills and piling them on the desk at which I graded student essays. The specter of my loans had recently taken a familiar, material shape: collection.

Seated in an office at the St. Paul high school where I taught, I'd been alerted of the new loan's existence when an e-mail appeared in my in-box from AES with the subject line "The results of your request are now available in your paperless in-box." I had not requested anything from AES in nearly five years. I did not want to click on the e-mail because I sensed, already, that my debt had returned. The message informed me that my loan had new terms that would require me to begin making repayments in December. Private loans, unlike federal loans, were not paused under the pandemic moratorium. This loan's total was $30,000.

As I taught that day, the loan hovered around me. When I facilitated discussion in my classroom, I felt the loan's pull on me. *How can a loan for $30,000 appear out of nowhere? Why wasn't this loan included with the bankruptcy? How will I afford monthly payments?*

When I spoke with Todd, he was surprised. It was AES who had provided us with the list of debts that guided the settlement, so there shouldn't have been anything unaccounted for. He was not worried. "Just send AES a copy of the settlement," he told me over the phone.

"But what if AES didn't own the loan then?" I ask.

"It doesn't matter," he said.

After we hung up, I thought of the eight months I spent on the phone with AES representatives begging them to send me the paperwork that they never sent despite their insistence that they had actually sent it and would again in the future. When I spoke with them again, I asked them why this debt was not adhering to the settlement, as my lawyer had instructed me to.

"What settlement?" the representative responded. "We have nothing about any settlement here. We had you paused for bankruptcy which recently ended, according to our records, so now you are set to begin payments again."

"How can you not have details about the settlement?" My voice sounded thin, almost carbonated. "It was the lawyers representing AES who signed it." But there was nothing in my supposedly big, long complex file that noted anything about the settlement. When I asked her the name of someone I could send it to, she was baffled. That would be "hard" to do. I could send a copy in the mail to AES or I could fill out a special online form that would trigger someone to eventually contact me over e-mail and then I could send *that* anonymous person a copy of the settlement so that they would hopefully pass it on to someone else, someone that mattered.

"Thank you," I said, in spite of myself. I was not thankful. She had not done anything for me. But my drive to participate in the system as it asked me to was hard to shake. For a long time, it seemed to me, that's all I had. Our conversation was an echo of all the conversations where I desperately asserted that the debt was not mine, which was a way of asserting that I existed, that I was my own person and not my mother.

When I cross-checked the debts following the phone call, the account numbers didn't match up with any of the listed debts. This new resurrected debt was a reminder of how the lending system's infrastructure protects creditors. Even when I managed a victory within a legal system hostile to student debtors, it was incomplete. The lenders still tried to collect from me, even when the courts said they could not.

This zombie debt reminded me of what my body already knew. Regardless of what happened with this new loan, it would be hard to be truly free. Annie McClanahan captures this experience: "This feeling of being haunted explains what might feel uncanny about being in personal debt: It is the experience of being followed by something we left behind, of carrying our past with us like dead weight." After the conversation with the AES representative, I stopped opening the envelopes but kept them, moving them from the mail pile to the desk pile.

A friend of mine, Alex, told me about his experience with these collection notes. He had enrolled in a glass-blowing program at a small college, taking out an enormous aid package at the urging of his school. His program disbanded his senior year, and Alex left school without the degree he had been working toward for four years, a few credits short of his bachelor's degree, a degree that because of department dysfunction would require him to enroll for another semester, which he could not afford.

He received the loan bills at his apartment in Louisville. At first, he opened them and then he stopped, instead chopping them into tiny pieces like confetti. Instead of throwing them into the air in celebration, he blew them into glass. "I have a dream of selling these for the price of my debt," he told me, a price which he didn't name. We lost touch, but I remember seeing his artwork years earlier. It looked like something from the future: bulbous and alien. I wonder if transforming the loan shreds was a way of cauterizing them, rendering them visually and emotionally neutral. I don't doubt the power of such acts, even as I understand the debt keeps growing, fed by interest rates and a legal system that protects it.

Chapter 16

I ONLY HAVE TWO small stories about my mother's time in jail. She couldn't shave, she'd complained to my father, because they were not given razors. I imagine this fact was followed up by a characterization: It made her feel like an animal, alienated from herself and the small routines that structured her old life. In the second story, my father received a call from her one afternoon requesting that he make up the guest room for a visitor. "Why?" he wanted to know. Her friend was going to be released the next day, and she had no money and nowhere to go. My mother wanted to offer her a warm shower, a queen-sized bed, and some food for a few days as she got on her feet. I don't think the woman ever came, perhaps she'd found somewhere else to stay, but my mother had found connection in prison, another person she wanted to care for.

Years later, while I waited for the security check on my first day teaching writing in a women's prison in Minnesota, I saw a sign that said in order for visitors to take photos with their loved ones they had to buy tickets. Each photo cost a couple of dollars, purchased with loose change and dollar bills at a machine near the entrance. Why was it necessary for the correctional facility to make money off of these women and families, desperate for photo evidence of their reunions, something to hold on to when their brief visits lapsed, and they were separated again? They could just offer these photos for free.

I was there because I thought the women I'd be teaching were worthy of interesting classes and rich educational experiences just because they were human. But I also taught them because my mother had been ensnared in the criminal legal system and I wanted to understand something about its impact that I'd never been able to ask her, even after all those years. Though she might have served up to nineteen years in prison—had she not agreed to a plea bargain and had she had a record and had her life circumstances been different—she ultimately didn't. Her sentence was brief. And, still, I sensed something from that experience stayed with her, some internal mark at having been caged, made external in the record and the criminal legal debt that followed her, more than many teachers' salaries, and one she'd struggle to pay back. The question I couldn't ask her: What was it like?

Looking at the ticket machine, I imagined there must be some ambivalence on the part of the incarcerated women during these visits with family. Of course they must want documentation of themselves with the people they love most—often their children. Yet, while their kids probably dressed in their very best clothes for the visit, the women wore the uniform of their institutionalization. The same handful of outfits in each photo, the same colors: lots of gray, muted greens, and blues. Like my research on debtors' prisons suggested, to be in prison was still to be without time. The world around them moved forward, and they, to some degree, remained frozen.

———————

"The United States has a long history of both formal and informal practices linking the punishment of its marginalized populations to processes of debt," according to sociologist Alexes Harris in her study of debt and the criminal legal system, *A Pound of Flesh: Monetary Sanctions as Punishment for the Poor.* Though debtors' prisons were officially shuttered across the United States in the 1830s, they've continued to reemerge in new forms in the century since, shadows of their former selves, still acting upon our bodies.

The Thirteenth Amendment abolished slavery and involuntary servitude "except as punishment for crime," an exception that allowed for debt peonage and convict leasing. African Americans could be charged for quitting a job, walking at night, loitering, talking too loudly in public, or being homeless, generating enormous court fines that white employers paid off, forcing the debtor to work off this debt for years in horrifying conditions that resulted in tens of thousands of African Americans dying between the 1870s and the 1940s. Under this regime of reenslavement, new layers of debt were added to the existing debt when white employers charged their employees for land usage, seeds, food, livestock—the ingredients of survival. "The result," writes historian Donna Murch, "was a newly freed population ensnared in an endless cycle of debt, forced labor, and worker abuse." It was, she quotes writer Douglas Blackmon, "slavery by another name."

———————

The classroom I taught in at the prison looked, for the most part, like my classrooms in the public schools. At the front of the room was a smart board. Tables were arranged in rows—which we always moved into a circle—and on the walls were posters with mostly unattributed quotes, some handwritten by students and some printed off by education staff. I read them in class in the minutes I waited for students to arrive. *The Whole Purpose of Education is to Turn Mirrors into Windows. Education is the Most Powerful Weapon You Can Use to Change the World. Education is the Key Which Will Unlock the Door of Opportunity for You. Dream Big.* Around one half of the room was a thick line of tape on the floor—separating students from staff workstations—with reminders for students not to cross it. I always stood on the student-side of the tape, but there were some parts of the classroom that I could cross that they could not. I thought of that line every evening as I exited the prison and drove an hour home.

My students, like incarcerated people across the state and country, were employed by the prison in a variety of positions that the prison's basic functioning depended on—such as working in the kitchen or in the laundry facility. I didn't ask them how much they were paid, but reporting suggests they earned, on average, less than a dollar an hour. As of 2022, some incarcerated workers for the Department of Corrections earned as low as twenty-five cents.

They relied on that salary—and if they were lucky, the wages of family and friends on the outside—to buy everything: lotion, Q-tips, medication, ChapStick, soap, deodorant, batteries, microwave bowls, e-mails, photos of their daughters, and until July 2023 in the prison at which I taught, every single phone call with a family member. A federal prison in Michigan charges its residents $2.15 for a serving of Advil—two hours' worth of work for four to six hours of headache relief. A hairbrush was worth three hours of work.

———

Today, debt that ensnares borrowers in the criminal legal system falls under two categories: private debt and criminal-justice debt. In the first category are car payments, payday loans, credit card debt, medical bills, and short-term cash advances. When borrowers struggle to repay these debts, because they don't have steady work or housing or because a major or minor catastrophe has befallen them, the creditor might bypass bankruptcy proceedings and take the debtor to civil court. If the debtor doesn't show up or the judge decides that the debtor can pay but is choosing not to, they might charge them with "contempt of court" and issue a warrant for their arrest. They'll stay in jail until they can post bond or pay down the debt, a threat known as "pay or stay." Sometimes people don't show up to court when summoned because they can't find childcare or miss work. Sometimes they don't show up because they are scared.

Journalist Eli Hager, writing for *The Marshall Project*, explains that judges have a lot of discretion in deciding whether someone can pay, whether they are "indigent" or simply unwilling. They might assess whether they are authentically poor through an interview or questionnaire, or they might decide through a visual assessment of the debtor themselves. Judges have, in the past, decided that a debtor was not actually indigent because they had what appeared to be a very expensive tattoo or were wearing a nice jacket. Judges want to see that the debtor has used all possible forms of fund-raising— that they have quit smoking, asked family and friends for help, and returned soda cans, which in Michigan, would yield ten cents each.

It seems to me they are not assessing financial ability so much as whether they are a good debtor or a bad one. A good debtor makes their effort and their suffering legible—they have garage sales and scour empty parking lots after tailgating for sticky cans. They ask their poor families to give up money they need so that they can pay the court at a rate that confirms they are good.

During an early class, we read Sylvia Plath's "Morning Song," a poem about the alternating haze and sharpness of postpartum. The students had requested a class about motherhood, and I'd altered the course so that it would be about all sorts of caregiving, within and beyond biological families. It would be about receiving care, not just giving it. There was something selfish in my revision: Though I anticipated that some students were not mothers, mostly I was working out something for myself. I was not just seeking to understand what my mother had gone through but also what mothering meant. Perhaps I could expand it and make it more porous, not to negate what each of us already had or hadn't received from our own mothers but to create new possibilities for the future.

I'm no more your mother / Than the cloud that distills a mirror to reflect its own slow / Effacement at the wind's hand. One of the students I spoke with thought perhaps the speaker had lost her child. This student had had twelve miscarriages before having her son, from whom she was now removed. She was worried he was embarrassed to have a mother in prison. She'd be getting out soon, and unlike many of my students, had a supportive and financially stable family ready to receive her, but because of the particulars of her incarceration, connected to her addiction, she would be unable to stay with her parents right away and her son was unable to stay in the transitional housing she qualified for, which was also incredibly expensive. She didn't talk about the outstanding debts connected to all of it, but I knew they existed. And I knew that finding meaningful work to help pay them would be challenging. The punishment would not end in prison.

And now you try / Your handful of notes; The clear vowels rise like balloons. "The baby's alive," another student said. "It cries at the end. I think the mother was just depressed after childbirth." This student was a mother of several kids. She was enrolled in a few college courses, and her handwriting was tiny and perfect: squarish and evenly spaced. One of her poems was about the quiet in the morning just before her children woke, the smell of her coffee as she tipped the cup toward her mouth.

My favorite student poem of the semester was about two mothers: one that existed—violent, alcoholic, standing over her child with a knife—and a different one, a kind of shadow mother, that didn't. This other mother—kind, patient, and nurturing—was the sort of mother my students tried to be, separated by physical barriers and costs. More than one of them had been let down by friends whom they'd sent precious funds to buy their children gifts, only for their money to evaporate. Most recently, a student had trusted someone to buy her daughter an Easter basket, which never came.

When I told them about my own writing interest—debt—they all shared that they had it, from the carceral system, from credit cards, and some of them from the student loans they acquired before prison, though they didn't offer the particulars of their burdens. They seemed numerous and overlapping, infinite and impossible to repay.

Once arrested, criminal defendants begin to accrue a new kind of debt that is especially vicious, one *produced by* the justice system, known as monetary sanctions or legal financial obligations (LFOs). These sanctions fall into three subcategories: penalties that are part of the sentence (like a traffic ticket); fees, which could include those for jail booking, a public defender, drug testing, DNA testing, court costs, and per diem for pretrial detention; and restitution, which is a payment to the victim(s) for personal or property damage. According to Murch, low-income populations make up 80 percent of criminal legal defendants, and this criminal legal debt becomes a drag on their lives, creating obstacles to housing, employment, education, and transportation, a reinforcing cycle of debt. In some towns it is impossible to get to work without a car, and it is hard to get a car with a bleak credit report. It is hard to get work without a home to live in. Murch writes: "Poor people face debt, jail for minor infractions, and further debt to pay for their punishment. The well of poverty grows deeper as extractive states, municipalities, and private companies seize the income of vulnerable populations." In most states, people cannot be released from court supervision—itself an enormous cost—until all fees have been paid, and in many states, people are unable to vote while these debts remain.

The cycle of extractive punishment and debt creation is also one of deepening unfreedom, borne out on individual lives, families, landscapes, and bodies over generations. The wages that a woman gives over to a private company for her electronic monitoring are wages she cannot give to her child to buy books or art supplies, wages she cannot give to her brother to help with medical treatment, wages she cannot give herself for dental care. This is true for student loans, too. What's lost in one generation is rarely found in the next. The collection continues, even when it officially doesn't, even when the collective architecture has invisible walls instead of real ones.

On the drives home from prison, I often thought of my mother. I wanted to believe that her incarceration was not a confirmation of what she believed—that she was bad—but the opposite: She was a good person who had made a harmful choice, and she didn't need to be jailed to understand that. I don't know if my mother walked around the facility's yard, alone, burrowed deep in her own thoughts or with the friend she'd made, telling old stories as a form of intimate exchange, a form of care. Maybe my mother remembered the one vacation she took with her family as a child: a road trip along the exterior of Michigan, with a stop at each of the Great Lakes.

My mother never called me or my sister when she was incarcerated. Surely, she missed us. Her silence was caused by her shame, but also, I think, a belief about the bounds of motherhood, some sense that it has borders that can't be crossed or that I wouldn't have wanted her to cross them. To an extent she was right, though she'd misdiagnosed the borders' origins. I was embarrassed that she'd been to jail. But I had been, and despite my best efforts still was, devastated that she'd left me alone with the debt. Debt erects and reduces borders all at once, necessitates and negates intimacy. It reconfigures the feeling and space of family. Though I wasn't completely sure, I didn't think the changes were irrevocable. *It can still get better*, I'd think on the darkened highway, miles from home.

Chapter 17

IN THE YATES GALLERY on the fourth floor of the Chicago Cultural Center I stood before 1,065 ceramic vessels. The size and shape of salad bowls, they were arranged in long rows that extended across the hall's floor. The exhibition, by artist kelli rae adams, was titled "Forever in Your Debt." The vessels were an attempt at translation, helping viewers to make material sense of the average student debt burden of $37,000. She first conceptualized this work in 2016 when she was living in France, helping a friend to establish an artist residency. She'd been making wood-fired pottery to help fund her stay— usable items like cups and bowls—and she and her collaborator had just fired up the kiln when she went inside to check her e-mail. In her in-box was a message from her loan servicer alerting her to the new student loan total after the previous year's interest had capitalized. She wondered, she explained to me over the phone when we first spoke in the winter of 2024, "If I were to repay this debt by making these vessels, what would that look like? How many would I need to make?" She did a quick calculation, and the number was mind-blowing. She thought, "What if someone could actually stand in the presence of all those vessels? What would it be like to then see those vessels filled with money?"

From there, the work began to take shape. Rather than using her own student debt total, which was approaching six figures, for the installation, she chose to use the average debt burden. Because an average bowl of mixed change totals about $40, she'd need to make 925 bowls. By the time I saw the project, several years into its run, she'd added another 150 bowls, offset from the rest, to acknowledge the applied interest. Visitors who added enough change to fill a bowl—whether online or in person—would receive one of the vessels from the project at its conclusion.

I sat in front of the bowls, so that I could watch them and watch people watching them. From this angle, the vessels looked like a field of open mouths. To my right, kelli sat at a school desk where she spoke with museumgoers for hours at a time, a few days a week. A crowd was around her, and someone asked, "Is this just *one* person's debt?" Another person entered the room, looked around, and then began to walk the length of the bowls, slowly, at a pace that acknowledged the scale. It took several minutes. Someone else crouched near the interest bowls, arranged in a flattened diamond, to take a photo of a bowl with change in it.

kelli spent a year's worth of weekends, and sometimes weekdays, seated at the elementary school desk talking to visitors. At first, she'd been on site to record any full-bowl contributions to the project ledger, but then, she explained to me, "it very quickly became clear to me the value in making myself available to talk with people and to receive their reactions and hold space for what is often a very emotional experience." Viewers had been, for the most part, overwhelmingly empathetic and compassionate. People had cried.

Others had expressed their luck at not having to take out student debt but had acknowledged the huge issue it is for others.

The interior of the bowls was glazed licorice red and because of the way the glaze fired, at first glance, it looked like the bottoms of the bowls were sparkling. The exteriors were white—the color of milk. Each bowl had one or several indentations, which kelli called dimples, that she pressed into the vessels. If you were to pick the bowls up, you might place your fingers here—their presence made the bowls less strictly utilitarian and more bodily, stranger. They struck me as intimate and alien.

At the conclusion of the installation's previous run at MASS MoCA, the combination of in-person and online donations totaled more than $37,000—and adams emptied the bowls. Half of the proceeds were used to pay down her debt and the other half donated to organizations working to reimagine higher education financing or to alleviate student debt. The bowls I saw at the Cultural Center, with the exception of ten or so, were empty. They were expectant, waiting to be filled by something. The vessels might be used to feed someone or to make a portion of a student loan payment. It occurred to me that this duality is always true with debt: Money used to pay the servicer is money not used for something else, often something essential. There's always a pretense of choice. I liked to imagine the bowls as retired, in someone's kitchen cabinet or holding keys near the front door.

When we spoke in the winter, I told kelli how interesting I found the use of second person in the show's title. "The 'your' could be a reference to the institutions that we are in debt to or it could be the people who've donated change to the exhibition or donated their time and presence," I said.

kelli had also been thinking of the multiplicity of the second person—your—as well as the complexity of this expression.

"Forever in your debt is typically used to express gratitude," she said, "and inherent in this project is a layer of gratitude, while also a recognition that these structures are deeply problematic and predatory. I needed the debt to be able to attend school. But to access that opportunity, one should not have to be in debt forever to balance the scales."

During a lull in the crowd, I approached two of the museum staff who were joking around while looking out over the bowls. I asked them what they thought. Rather than giving their observations, they said something else. "It's the debt you can never pay down," the man said. "They can take everything; take your social security; take your wages, go after it and you forever."

The woman he was speaking to paused before replying. "I didn't know that," she said. I'd wanted to tell her that he had it wrong, but I couldn't. He left to check in with another staff member, and I asked the woman if she had any student debt. "Yeah, I do," she said. "I got my associate's in criminal justice at MacCormac College, now Generations College. I want to go back to get my full degree, but I can't afford to." She was busy making payments on the debt she already had. When I looked up the school later, I learned that it's a private not-for-profit two-year school with a tuition of about $13,000 a year.

The second time I spoke with kelli, in late spring, I asked her about her own student debt, the catalyst for the project. She'd attended Duke University for undergrad on a 75 percent merit scholarship, which meant that it was more affordable than the state schools where she'd been accepted, which did not offer competitive aid. After graduation, she owed $35,000, the equivalent of about one year of tuition. kelli wanted to live abroad, and her school counselor recommended that she teach English in Japan. She recalled what the counselor told her: "You know, as someone who has student loan debt, Japan is a good option because you will earn a reasonable salary." She was accepted to a competitive program that placed her in a rural area, and she stayed in faculty housing that lacked hot water and heat for $150 a month, sending $1,000 to her loan servicers each month from her $30,000 salary. At the end of three years, she'd paid off her debt and had begun an in-depth study of ceramics with a local artist with whom she'd begin an official apprenticeship a year later. "It's interesting to think about the debt," kelli said, "because if my undergrad debt had not fully been eliminated by then, I would not have had the flexibility or freedom to take the apprenticeship."

kelli could not "escape the grasp of art-making," she told me. "It grabbed me by the sleeve every time I tried to pursue a different path." She was accepted to the Rhode Island School of Design (RISD) for graduate school after her return to the United States, and she delayed the final enrollment decision as she contemplated what it would mean to take on so much debt again. Tuition in 2006 was about $40,000 a year, after the stipend she'd receive for teaching while in school, and would thus require taking out a significant amount of student loans. She sought the counsel of mentors who told her that this was how the system worked. She'd paid so much debt off quickly before and was relying on the fact that an MFA would make her competitive for well-paid academic jobs, so she enrolled. Though kelli had applied to a number of those jobs since graduation, because of higher education's increasing reliance on adjunct labor, she'd been unable to secure a tenure-track position. Her debt, despite regular payments, had risen significantly since graduation, though she did not want to share the exact number. I sensed it was high. It obviously made her feel bad.

"It's a leap of faith," kelli said about the Save As You Earn (SAVE) repayment plan she'd recently enrolled in. kelli's plan was one of a handful under a bucket called income-driven repayment (IDR), but which have a host of names (Income Based Repayment Plan, Income Contingent Repayment Plan, Pay As You Earn, SAVE). The basic idea was engineered by Milton Friedman in 1955 in his engagement with the idea of "human capital." Eleni Schirmer summarizes his thinking: "As a kind of capital, education counted as private property, and its cost should be shouldered by the individual beneficiary, not the public." In his paper on the "Role of Government in Education," Friedman argues that the government should loan individuals money for their secondary education or professional training, with a contract to buy a share of their future earnings. The cost of the education is ultimately borne by the individual through the mechanism of debt. In 1992, when Congress noticed that borrowers were suffering, often for long periods, under large debt burdens that were required to be paid with fixed monthly payments, they returned to the discussion started by Friedman, developing the first of the IDR plans known as Income-Contingent Repayment. Between 1992 and today, the plans have been adjusted to be more generous and reach more borrowers. What's considered "protected income" has increased, the portion of discretionary income that borrowers pay has dropped from 20 percent to 10 percent, and more borrowers qualify for enrollment, each of these adjustments executed because borrowers have continued to struggle and their debt burdens have continued to climb. The shifting math decides how much borrowers can and should pay and for how long—the government choosing what kind of suffering is ultimately tolerable.

Borrowers who enroll and stay in one of these plans do well. According to the Student Borrower Protection Center, these borrowers "have more success keeping up with their loan payments, pay down their non-student loan debts more quickly, and enjoy improved access to other forms of credit." The plans are meant to help students, and sometimes they do.

But historically, IDR has not worked well enough. Despite its availability, delinquency and default rates soared in the ten years preceding the 2021 SBPC report. Just before the pandemic, a little over half of borrowers who were in repayment were current on their loan payments, and the rest of borrowers were in some combination of default, deferment, or forbearance. In the year directly before the pandemic, someone defaulted on a federal loan every twenty-six seconds. SBCP rightly notes that this default rate should have been impossible given the fact that $0 payments are available under IDR. Yet, the defaults happen anyway. Many people who need IDR the most are not accessing it. They miss reenrollment requirements or deadlines, sometimes because of an error by their loan servicer.

As of 2021, only thirty-two federal student loan borrowers had received relief out of the millions who should have qualified. Though the Biden-Harris administration corrected for some of the past failures of IDR, offering over $54 billion in relief for 1.3 million IDR participants as of April 2024, there still must be a financial and psychic toll of waiting, seemingly indefinitely, for relief that didn't come and didn't come and didn't come—before, eventually, it did. Had the reprieve been available when the plan said it would be, those borrowers might have purchased homes; they might have changed jobs; they might have had children.

In part, IDR was created because it was easier for Congress to negotiate than expanding the grant program to make college more affordable for students or funding schools directly to make college cheaper.

————

kelli's use of the word "faith" in her assessment of what her payment plan required of her acknowledged the power dynamic between borrowers and the government. To keep paying off our loans using the myriad of shifting available programs, we have to believe—often without evidence—that our government will care for us, our health, and our futures. A couple of months after our call, the Eighth Circuit Court of Appeals issued a temporary injunction on that SAVE plan in response to one of two lawsuits, prohibiting the Department of Education from executing the plan's promises—that payments are lowered and long-term borrowers receive forgiveness—until the court makes its final ruling. In the meantime, the eight million people enrolled in the program and the four hundred thousand who've already had their debts erased are in limbo.

As part of kelli's research into loan consolidation so that she could enroll in SAVE, she cross-checked her debt total on her servicer account with what the federal government had listed and noticed that the numbers were off by $30,000. The government account listed one loan as being paid in full that was still in repayment on her servicer account. She was certain that the larger of the two was the correct total, but, still, there was a moment of possibility. Eventually, she located someone who could confirm the correct amounts and the person, without warmth or apology, told her that there had been a mistake. The $30,000 still existed even though it was not showing up, even though they told her that she had paid it off.

"I had a kind of out-of-body experience while I was having the conversation," kelli told me, "because it was really bizarre; the whole ecosystem is incredibly odd and rather dehumanized." The faith the system requires of us is one often reserved for humans or for other intimate, trusting relationships—like one someone has with their god. And, yet, the system does not respond to us as if we are human. I could imagine another borrower only checking the government account, certain that their information is accurate. Perhaps, realizing their loan was nearly half as much as they thought, they offer to help their sibling or parent buy a car, or they decide to have a child, or go back to school to complete their undergraduate degree. What would it feel like to learn that you'd made an important, perhaps irreversible, decision based on a lie?

———

"Debt, I have since understood, is also a time tax—it seizes the future, and corrodes the present, wearing down health, wealth, and pursuits of happiness," Eleni Schirmer writes in her profile of aging debtors for *The New Yorker*. Of the forty-five million borrowers who held debt in 2022, 20 percent of them were over fifty years old, comprising the fastest-growing demographic of student borrowers. In my regular outreach, it's often this group of borrowers who responds most quickly, offering me their stories. Out of hope or out of exhaustion, I'm not sure. The demographic growth of this group of borrowers is in part, Schirmer thinks, because policy makers have misdiagnosed debt's impact as circumscribed to the primarily upwardly mobile and young, believing like the lawyers who advised me on my own debt burden that "time itself will solve the problem." But these policymakers have been wrong, she writes. "Americans are not aging out of their student loans—they are aging into them."

Sher, a sixty-seven-year-old borrower from Louisiana, experienced this evolution deeper into debt, rather than out of it. "I've been teaching since in vitro," she said, when we met online in 2023. Both her mother and grandparents were teachers, a career that, Sher reminds me, used to be a reliable pathway to the middle class for Black women. Though she initially didn't think she wanted to join in the family business, she changed her mind when she saw a need for strong educators in her community. The rest of her professional arc followed a similar trajectory—she identified an absence, or an ache, and became an expert in that area, transitioning to a new role before she identified the next thing that students and educators needed. Sher had been an elementary special education classroom teacher, an assistant director of education at a hospital, a conflict-resolution-mediation specialist in the Orleans Parish school system, a senior program advisor and consultant for Educators for Social Responsibility, and most recently, a graduate school adjunct professor, supporting students in their certification and master's education courses. She had pursued meaningful and often incredibly hard work, work that could only be done out of an abundance of love for people and belief in their futures. "Through my work, I knew that all children can learn," she said to me, "and I kept learning that there were institutional and system barriers keeping that from happening. And I wanted to be part of the change, using my schools and tools and abilities to help families."

Because her tuition at the University of New Orleans was affordable when she attended thirty years ago, Sher was able to pay for her undergraduate and master's degrees through a combination of scholarships and work, leaving her debt-free. However, she needed to borrow for her PhD program in education, a credential that was a requirement of her university employers. Either she got her PhD or she could no longer teach with them. What started as an $85,000 loan burden (almost all of which were federal student loans) in 2004, spanning the entirety of her graduate coursework that began at the for-profit Capella University before she transferred to Lesley University, had grown into something unrecognizable: $165,000, despite Sher's regular loan payments since 2007.

"That's an incredible amount of money," I told Sher after she detailed the numerical dimensions of her debt. There was never a way for me to properly account for with language what these numbers meant in borrowers' lives. I often found myself struggling to convey two seemingly disparate ideas: that millions of people have student debt, and they should not be ashamed of it, and, their debt, each debt, was startling and unique in its harm. "I'm sorry," I said to all the borrowers I spoke with, a sentiment that felt like offering a hug after a catastrophic car accident, instead of what was needed: emergency surgery. Sher nodded and smiled.

Though Sher had made consistent loan payments in the past twenty years, there had been necessary pauses. Her home was destroyed in Hurricane Katrina like those of thousands of New Orleanians; during this time, she took a break in her coursework and placed her loans in deferment while she rebuilt her home and her life. When Sher told me that one of the items she took with her during evacuation was a small box that held loan information and correspondence, I imagined her at home, sirens ringing, rain thick, wind grabbing and throwing trees. She had to decide what she could carry with her, knowing that what she left behind she might not see again. This loan data was as essential as family photos and heirlooms, an essentiality born not out of love but out of fear. Without this data, payments might be misapplied or lost, and she might pay for it in the future.

Years later, following months of intense pain and medical appointments in which doctors told her she was fine, she nearly died of acute pancreatitis, an illness whose treatment led to liver failure and diabetes. For a year she was unable to work, and she spent the savings she'd carefully built draining the account she might have used instead to pay off a loan. Again, she needed a deferment on the payments, but at the time, she didn't care, because she was focused on saving her life.

Under the current Income-Driven Repayment program, Sher should receive relief, but, because of the loan deferments, it won't be until 2036, when she is seventy-nine years old. She had good insurance through her husband, a blessing she acknowledged as transformative, but her medications were expensive, and if her liver failure eventually awarded her a spot on the transplant list, there would be the associated expenses of a transplant and recovery. These loans— the payments of which were $717 a month—might complicate her health care in the future.

Beyond her medical fears, Sher, like the borrower Jim who returned to nursing school, noted that the loans have stolen opportunities for joy and pleasure. "Without loans, I would be able to do my dream thing and go to Paris or Istanbul," she said, her smile expanding in proportion to this dream. Then she added, laughing, "I could expose my blue-collar guy to more things," referring to her husband, whom she met and married in her fifties. They fell in love on the deck of a neighbor's home when they were rebuilding after Katrina. Their neighbor set out a cooler—beer for him and sodas for her—and two chairs and said, "ya'll talk." When she spoke about him, she laughed and smiled.

I started to tell her that this dream was beautiful, not indulgent, but necessarily hopeful, but she continued telling me additional ways her world would be different without debt. Often borrowers' stories were so big that they spilled into the spaces where I might have responded. Sher didn't say that in her eighties, when she finally had disposable income, she might not be able to travel to these dream-spaces anymore, or that she might not receive the transplant that she'd eventually need and live long enough to be debt-free. Or that her husband might die, that any number of surprising or predictable losses might befall them.

I wanted to ask, If we only imagine happiness and pleasure for our future selves, what does that say about what we deserve in the present? But we ran out of time.

———

The faith our repayment plans demand of us reminds me of the faith many of us offered to our schools and our teachers when we first encountered the education system as children. I remember what it felt like each fall to gather my class supplies into a backpack, board the bus, and greet my teacher while she—and in elementary school it was always a she—waited for me at the classroom door. It felt like anything was possible. I believed that my teachers were loving and powerful and they could open doors to language, to stories, and to the rest of the world. I was right. Even students who have a painful relationship to school, often due to structural inequalities, still want badly to learn.

"One of the things that always packs an emotional punch is when children run up and instantly want to drop in coins," kelli told me. Their first instinct, without understanding anything about the exhibit, is to give something of theirs away. It's an act of faith and curiosity. That contribution transforms their relationship to the art-work into one of participation.

I couldn't help but imagine those kids as older. I couldn't help but think of what awaits them. How can we as a country agree that what those kids deserve, ten or fifteen or thirty years later, is the contract that they are offered: either be born wealthy or take out loans that may someday make your life unlivable. Every kid at the start of their educational journey wants to know: Am I smart? Am I good? Am I special? Am I worth it? What we are saying, right now, with our higher education funding model, is an unequivocal "no."

When kelli and I had coffee the morning following my first museum visit, we talked about the experience of having her work in this enormous public venue. Nearly five hundred people a day wander through some part of the Cultural Center. Every day, she met people from all over the country and the world. When I returned to the exhibit after coffee, no one else was in the gallery. For a few minutes, I was alone with the work, except for the museum staff. It felt as if the mouths of the bowls were trying to articulate something to me—a whisper gaining volume. I looked down at my notebook to try to record their language before I was interrupted with a sharp comment from the museum staff: "You cannot be there."

I looked up, worried he was talking to me. A woman in her early twenties had somehow walked into the center of the exhibit without me noticing and was standing in the middle of 925 bowls. And now, aware that she was in the wrong place, and that she misinterpreted the engagement expectation, she was glancing left and right to trace a pathway out. She was wearing thick-soled heavy boots and was carrying a large purse, and she seemed suddenly conscious of the bowls' fragility. "I'm so sorry," she said to the museum staff, quietly. More people had entered, and everyone was watching her. I wondered if the long rows of the vessels made her feel as if she was in a precious, fragile garden. She carefully picked her way out, wobbling and stepping around the rare flowers—lovely, cruel monuments to an immortal debt.

Chapter 18

ON THE CLASSROOM SMARTBOARD was Wong Kar-wai's *In the Mood for Love*, my students in desks fanned around the screen. The film was part of a writing studies course I was teaching in which my high school students watched movies and responded to them, offering analysis, criticism, and connection. We sat in the darkened classroom as the onscreen lovers moved into and out of shadows, lingered under streetlamps, and crossed one another in apartment stairwells.

My collection letters from AES had slowed and then stopped entirely months earlier, and recently I'd gotten notice from my bank that my credit score had spiked, after plummeting in the wake of AES's reporting to the credit bureaus about my delinquent debt. In addition to sending them the settlement paperwork over e mail and mail, I'd filed a complaint with the Consumer Financial Protection Bureau about AES's attempt to illegally collect the debt. According to public complaints, thousands of other people reported they had been harmed by AES. In one complaint on the CFPB's Complaint

Database, a borrower said that AES would not release their cosigner despite them meeting the conditions of the original lender. AES's stated reason was that the borrower requested a brief forbearance when Hurricane Irma struck their region of Florida. At the time, an AES representative assured them they could apply for this forbearance without impact, and now, despite making monthly payments on time for six years, AES has not kept their word.

Another borrower told the database that over the course of ten years of repayments, they've paid extra each month, assuming that extra would go toward the principal. Instead, they found out that AES had been applying it to interest, never disclosing this fact to the borrower. "I only became aware of it after noticing that, despite my efforts to pay down the loan aggressively, the principal balance had barely decreased," the borrower wrote. Another entry: "American Education Services is harassing me. They call me constantly. They sent me a letter telling me my father was dead and they needed new contact information for someone else to drive insane. Today, I got a message from a friend saying their husband received a call from AES asking for me." Borrowers said that AES has stopped them, inexplicably, from being able to pay online; they rejected appeals for forbearance while borrowers negotiated around fraudulent schools that had closed; they included debts that did not belong to the borrower on their credit report; they continued to collect on debt that qualified for bankruptcy after the borrower met the undue hardship criteria. Despite nearly a thousand complaints, AES remains in business.

I'd stopped logging in to my AES account soon after being notified of the debt, worried that I might accidentally trigger a process that would reset the statute of limitations on private debt collection and imply that the debt was mine. But in the back of the classroom, perhaps cushioned by the dark, a movie I love, and students I cared about, I decided to log on again. Something, mysteriously, had changed, and I wanted to understand why.

I clicked on the "loan details" tab and looked at the "balance overview." Nothing was due. The loan balance was zero. I refreshed the page and then scanned through the listed loans, eight in total, all labeled as in default but none of which had balances next to them. The last time I'd been on this tab, one of these loan balances, the zombie loan, was approaching $40,000.

Though my lawyer had contacted them several times, and I contacted them even more, no one from AES got in touch with me to explain how they were handling the contested debt. Rather than notifying me that they were honoring the terms of the settlement or explaining that they'd made an enormous, terrifying mistake, they'd simply deleted the loan—or perhaps done something else that I could not find record of.

I checked the message in-box. Nothing. I clicked through each tab. Nothing, nothing, nothing. I hadn't slept well for months over this zombie debt, couldn't focus on what I read or sometimes what conversation I was having. That no one had taken five minutes to tell me this debt was cleared confirmed what I already knew to be true about every lever of the loan system: They are reckless with borrowers' lives.

In May 2024 the Consumer Financial Protection Bureau sued AES for allegedly illegally collecting on student loans that had been discharged through bankruptcy proceedings. The CFPB also alleges that AES falsely reported these debts to credit reporting agencies and sent borrowers dishonest paperwork about them. According to research by the Student Borrower Protection Center, tens of billions of dollars of private student loans may qualify for bankruptcy discharge, a fact that they say AES has known to be true (their investment arm notified investors about this very possibility) but has deliberately lied to students about. Had I known this in 2008, my entire life would be different.

———

Steph's decision to have a child was the most considered decision of her adult life, she told me. This deliberation was not just about the kind of family she and her husband wanted to create; it was also about her debt. She and her husband were both working; their combined salaries at the time were about $55,000, and they'd run out of deferments and forbearances for her private loans. Her private debts, like many others, didn't offer an income-driven repayment program. "We can keep paying my private loans or we can have a baby. We can't do both," Steph said, illustrating her thinking at the time.

So, she did something that had once seemed impossible: She defaulted on her private loans. Because her mother had cosigned on these debts, this decision impacted her. "You don't want to tell your parents that you are about to wreck their credit and that they'll be receiving even more harassing calls and letters," she said. Her mother was supportive. Steph and her husband stopped paying and diverted their resources toward a child, and a year after giving birth, she was sued by two private lenders. With the help of an attorney her mother paid for, Steph settled the $42,000 outstanding balance for $12,000—she'd make $100 monthly payments until the debt was paid off. "A great deal," she said. When another lender came after her a year later—this time from National Collegiate Loan Trust, the owner of my zombie debt—she got a new lawyer in Florida, where the lawsuit was filed. They tried to settle but were unable to and ultimately the judge dismissed the lawsuit because NCLT could not provide proof of ownership.

In May of 2024, The Consumer Financial Protection Bureau took action against NCLT and its servicer Pennsylvania Higher Education Assistance Agency, commonly known as American Education Services (yes, *my* servicer, AES). The lawsuit concerns their alleged failure to respond to borrowers begging for relief during the COVID-19 pandemic. Borrowers waited months and even years to hear back. Sometimes NCLT allegedly promised that requests would be granted that were not. An earlier CFPB lawsuit was aimed at NCLT collection lawsuits for private debt that they could not prove they owned or debt that was too old to be collected on and they filed collection lawsuits on anyway.

Steph's debt, now on the other side of the statute of limitations that applies to private loan collection, was out there still, but it was ghostlike. It lacked teeth. AES could no longer collect on it, and it had disappeared from her credit report. The combination of the student loan moratorium, her husband's larger income, and the settlement of her private loans had allowed Steph and her family to consistently save money for the first time in their entire lives. "Having a cushion is a totally different way of living," she said. Before this cushion, she lived in a constant present tense. When their bed frame broke, they could not get a new one. When her mother visited, she filled their cabinets with groceries. When Steph needed to see family, they had to buy the tickets for her. She felt unable to achieve markers of independence and adulthood because she could not care for herself the way she wanted to.

Even with her savings account, Steph told me, "I'm learning where the walls are all the time." She and her husband were still paying off their federal debt and her husband's private debt, and though they were making larger payments, they were unable to save much for retirement. Without debt, she and her husband would have moved to New York City, which had been their dream, and they would certainly have had more children, and she would likely be teaching college writing like she'd wanted to. Though the job would still be underpaid, without the loans, she'd make it work.

Steph said that while her experience with debt has been awful, she found value in understanding what it means to live in a kind of poverty. "If you haven't experienced it yourself, it's impossible to know what it feels like for your body to be on edge and constantly under threat, to never be able to rely on anything, to know that if one thing goes wrong, your whole life might shatter." This experience of instability, and as she phrased it "danger," had informed her politics.

This turn came when her understanding about debt was no longer grounded in shame, but in a belief that she deserved better. That we all do. It started with the default, her refusal to pay. "It was the first decision I made in defiance of my debt rather than borrowing down to it," she said. "If I could go back and do it differently, I would," she said about her decision to attend two expensive schools for which she needed loans. I thought that her decision not to pay was an acknowledgment that relief should not be contingent on a borrower having made perfect decisions about higher education.

The pandemic moratorium, during which all loan payments were halted on federal student loans, continued the work the default had started for Steph. She'd never imagined a nationwide pause in collection, but it happened and continued to happen year after year. "Once you open the door of possibility, it won't be shut," she told me. "We won't close the door till there's full cancellation."

———

"I have around $40,000 in private student loan debt and a few thousand in federal school student loan debt," I told a stranger standing beside me outside of the Department of Education in Washington, DC, in the spring of 2022. It was sunny and warm, not yet humid, and the trees wore milky pink plumes. *Should I have included the zombie debt in the total?* I wondered in the pause before the man beside me spoke. Though the debt no longer registered on my credit report, I was not convinced that it was truly gone. Rather, it felt diffuse and atmospheric, as if it might someday gather into a material form when it was ready.

"I don't have any debt. I'm lucky. And I don't think anyone else should have it either. That's why I'm here," the stranger said to me.

He and I were part of a crowd of a couple of hundred people who'd gathered the month before the student loan moratorium was set to expire, to demand that President Biden make the pause in collection permanent. We'd just articulated our debt burdens because one of the speakers had asked us to. "We have nothing to be ashamed of," she said. In the back of the crowd, people stood on top of benches so that they could see. One of the signs I took a photo of read: "I graduated in 2012 with $90,000 in student loan debt. Paid $600 a month for ten years and I still owe $90,000." Student loans are insatiable. You can feed them all that you have, and they remain hungry.

It benefits the systems that indebt us when we are ashamed, certain that we have done something wrong in our acquisitions, that *we* are wrong, and because we are wrong, remain committed to the act of repayment. To name the debts publicly, to strangers or to anyone, is to rob them of their moralizing power. "You are not in debt because you have lived beyond your means," the Debt Collective, one of the groups that organized the action, often says, "but because you have been denied the means to live."

I'd joined the Debt Collective a couple of years earlier as I watched my stack of AES bills take up increasingly large amounts of desk space and psychic space. After living with my debt for fifteen years, I sought a community of people who understood the experience and responded to it as I saw and felt it: as a crisis. The Debt Collective is a union of debtors who, in their own words, fight "against predatory financial contracts and for the universal provision of public goods, including health care, education, housing, retirement and so that people don't have to go into debt to access them." When I spoke to one of their organizers soon after signing up, they asked me: "What's your debt story?" It was the first time that someone had asked me that. Though my response was shaky and hurried, after speaking, I felt different, as if something had loosened inside of me.

After more speakers, we began to march in loops around the Department of Education. Organizers handed out bright yellow vuvuzelas, and the collection of them, floating above the crowd, looked like a waving sea anemone. In the video I took, the noise of the horns is animal and mournful even as the crowd is angry and jubilant. On another sign, written in thick black marker: "I worked two jobs in college and have $21,278 in student loan debt. How about you, Biden?" We walked around the department thirteen times in total to represent the Israelites marching around the walls of Jericho to bring the walls down.

I noticed one man marching with us wearing an UberEats backpack, and I wondered if he was on the way back from a scheduled route when he saw us or if he'd head out soon, either coming from or going to his underpaid job without health care and labor protections.

It didn't matter if he had debt—the demand for cancellation was only the beginning. In the video, I pan my phone over to one of my best friends who came to DC with me from Minneapolis. We'd booked the cheapest hotel in walking distance, one that'd never changed out its carpet or drapes after the smoking ban in the early aughts. Her smile is wide and glowing. She's cheering along with the crowd.

After the march, more people from the crowd took turns using a microphone to tell their own debt stories. In one testimony, someone shared: "I am over a hundred thousand dollars in debt. I had such grief and shame for having so much student loan debt. And, yet I am doing amazing things in the community. It's not right or just. It's abusive. It's shameful. The Department of Ed should be ashamed." The voice seemed to get larger as the woman continued, taking on mass and moving outward into the crowd. "I am burning this debt for myself and for the other women of color that I know who are burdened by these debilitating debts that are making it hard for us to live normal lives. Thank you. We love you."

As she spoke, she held a thin piece of paper, on which she'd recorded her debt total, an echo of the ledger kept by the servicers who tracked her and collected from her. The crowd chanted, "Burn it burn it burn it burn it." Someone leaned forward with a lighter and then the entire paper was on fire. She released it, and the paper was white-orange in midair before it burned into nothing. We all clapped, and then someone else shared. A new debt total, more flames, a disappeared ledger. Palm-sized bonfires again and again, extinguishing the record—the number—that had been used to hurt us.

This action reflected a realignment of exterior and interior worlds. Debtors understood that their debt had harmed them, that their desire to go to school had harmed them, and that they did not deserve to suffer. But the messages they received from servicers, collection agencies, their schools, and the federal government were that they, the borrowers, were the cause of that suffering. If their harm had occurred in documented and circumscribed ways—such as evidence that a for-profit institution had lied to them—they *might* get relief. Otherwise, it was their duty to pay and pay and pay, maybe forever. These testimonies collapsed the space between what they knew and what they were told, and I wondered what these collisions of interior and exterior worlds would produce.

———————

"I am thirty-one years old and seventy-three thousand dollars in debt," Cassie, the writer and server from *Writers & Lovers* tells an auditorium of students at the end of the novel—evidence of her own collision of worlds. She's on the precipice of selling her book, she's recently found a teaching job that makes her happy, and she's just shared—for the first time—the exact contours of her debt burden. Over the course of the novel, she's revealed so much: all her fears and desires and shames and yet she has not said this number to anyone, including us. I wonder how many other readers were thinking about it, waiting for it, like I was.

The speech is a kick-off to a writing workshop, and the announcement of her debt burden is a way of making particular what has destabilized her life. Though her mother has died, and she's been estranged from her father since high school, though she's moved six times, writing has remained a constant for her. "This has been my home, the place I could always retreat to," she says. She can only make this proclamation surrounded by a community of people in whom she finds hope. She's not worried about what debt burdens might meet her students on their journeys into higher education. She's reminding them that writing is a kind of protection. Through writing, we can imagine homes for ourselves, shelters from the most harmful parts of the world. Her testimony acknowledges that she did not deserve to suffer, that there are reasons to be hopeful. People and language are two of them.

———

Soon after the protest, the moratorium on loan collection was extended, and a few months later, in August 2022, President Biden issued an executive action using the authority provided under the Higher Education Relief Opportunities for Students (HEROES) Act—the same act that President Trump first used to pause debt collection during the pandemic—to cancel between $10,000 and $20,000 in federal student debt for borrowers. The cancellation was means-tested: $10,000 would be "forgiven" for individuals earning less than $125,000 and married couples earning less than $250,000. Borrowers who'd received a Pell Grant would be "forgiven" for up to $20,000. Organizers who demanded complete and immediate cancellation pointed out to me that this means-testing was immoral, but just as importantly: It was not strategic. It took nearly six weeks for the application to be released, during which a handful of right-wing lawsuits were filed. Had the executive action worked, nearly forty-three million borrowers would have been impacted. "It would be," in the words of Debt Collective press secretary Braxton Brewington, "the largest transfer of household wealth in recent American history." About $430 billion could have disappeared. "Nearly twenty million people would have their debt completely zeroed out, disproportionately lifting Black, Hispanic, and low-income Americans out of financial despair," according to Brewington.

I spent the afternoon following Biden's press release refreshing my Twitter page, allowing debtors' comments to float up and around me. *I can finally save for a house. I can help my mother pay for medical treatment. I can help my son pay for school. I can afford a root canal. I never thought this would be possible.* Neither did I. Some people would keep on living because of the cancellation—I knew that for sure. And it was also true that some people would keep suffering. *This won't mean anything for my debt total*, other borrowers shared.

A right-wing effort to overturn the plan ultimately succeeded, and the Supreme Court ruled the executive action unconstitutional. Chief Justice John Roberts, writing for the majority, said: "The authority to 'modify' statutes and regulations allows the Secretary to make modest adjustments and additions to existing provisions, not transform them." The action was, in short, too significant. Mike Pierce, the Executive Director of the Student Borrower Protection Center, told me in a phone call that one way to make sense of the ruling is to "think about this Supreme Court as an appendage of the conservative movement." He said, "You have six Republican-appointed judges taking the language of the law and throwing it in the trash can and reaching for a political outcome." The sneering tone Justice Roberts used when asking questions of the Solicitor General during oral arguments conveyed that the ruling was about "disciplining people for having the audacity to ask their government to help them," according to Pierce. An organizer from the Debt Collective told me that the Biden White House lacked an effective execution strategy to realize their hopes for students. It's not enough to want relief, they said, "You actually need to fight tooth and nail to win it."

Certainly, the second Trump administration will be hostile to student borrowers. As I write this in early 2025, it seems the likely first outcome is that monthly student loan bills will increase,

significantly for some students, because the many relief initiatives
that have already been struck down by the courts will not be revived
under the new administration. The SAVE plan—which lowered
payments for more than eight million borrowers and created a pathway for eventual full cancellation—remains blocked by a legal challenge and will either be overturned by an appeals court or repealed
by congressional Republicans. The payment plans that borrowers
will be left to choose from are more expensive. Journalist and attorney Adam S. Minsky, writing for *Forbes*, investigates a range of
scenarios for borrowers moving forward. Some borrowers might
expect to see their payments double or even quadruple. A Parent
PLUS borrower earning $100,000 a year could see their payments
skyrocket from $540 a month to $1,400.

"I say it all the time, I'm dying to get back to do this: We will
ultimately eliminate the federal Department of Education," Trump
said during a campaign rally in September 2024. In early February 2025, Republican lawmakers took the first step to realizing that
vision, introducing a bill that would eliminate the federal agency,
terminating its operations at the end of 2026. In late March, Trump
issued an executive order, with few details, calling for the disman-
tling of the department so that, according to his press release, "tax-
payers will no longer be burdened with tens of billions of dollars of
waste on progressive social experiments and obsolete programs."

The Education Department manages the Pell Grants and work
study program, funding for students with disabilities and early childhood education, and the enormous federal student loan portfolio
and the repayment plans that comprise it. In the department's own
words, it "promotes student achievement and preparation for global
competitiveness by fostering educational excellence and ensur-
ing equal access." It seems clear that the access, achievement, and

preparation Trump wants is for some students, not all students—just the ones whose families can afford to pay for it. Stephanie Hall, the senior director for higher education policy at the Center for American Progress, writes that "Students need to recognize this as a direct attack on their future."

If the department is shuttered, some of those responsibilities will be passed on to states, some to other departments (possibly the Small Business Administration as Trump has ordered). And some, it seems likely, will dissolve entirely. The management of loan disbursement and collection, a process already riddled with errors, will not become more equitable and streamlined under the supervision of a new agency with no experience and no mandate from the administration to *protect* students.

Meanwhile, an agency that has done meaningful work to protect students, the Consumer Financial Protection Bureau, is also facing significant changes. These changes, the Debt Collecive wrote in a message to its members, mean that borrowers have fewer opportunities to get support with problems in their loan accounts. If you are accidentally billed for ten times the amount that you should be, the infrastructure you would have relied on to help you has been gutted, dissolved, or is under attack. In response to Trump's firing of the bureau's director, Rohit Chopra, Mike Pierce noted that it was "a dark sign of things to come," and an illustration of Trump's focus on "doing the bidding of oligarchs who ushered him back into power."

———

Despite an uncertain and challenging future for borrowers and students, Steph, the borrower who'd stopped paying her debts, was right. A door had been opened, and nothing the Supreme Court or President Trump can do will close it entirely.

In another photo I have from that day, my friend Emily leans over a large book of blank pages, where borrowers and allies have written messages in colored pens to be delivered to President Biden. On the page opposite her, someone has written in neat, small handwriting: "Protect students, not the rich!" And on the same page, near the bottom: "We also want a part of your American Dream." I'm touched that the primary demand is for inclusion in a future currently reserved for some Americans, but not others. We are all inherently deserving. What if our government saw us this way?

In the image, Emily hasn't finished her message yet; she's holding a neon green marker, its tip pressed against the paper. I've caught her in movement, in the act of creation. She's started her sentence with a *C*, and I can imagine the rest of the word—*Cancel*—from here. She wasn't asking for forgiveness. None of us were. There was nothing we'd done that warranted absolution.

Chapter 19

I SPOKE WITH MY father for the first time since he died in the fall of 2022, or, rather, he spoke with me in the form of a letter sent by my mother out of nowhere, along with some holiday decorations from my childhood. "I'm sorry," she wrote on a note affixed to the envelope, "for waiting so long to send this." I did not know what "this" was but the handwriting on the front looked familiar.

When I received the package, I was about five months pregnant. Mike and I had married a year and a half earlier at a courthouse. In the vows we offered to one another in our bedroom before we departed for the courthouse, we promised one another that our love would link us to the world, rather than making us an island, that it would be grounded in commitment, care, and freedom, and that we'd always share a politics aimed toward creating freedom for everyone.

Though we did not care about marriage as an institution, it offered us a chance to blend our lives in new ways, and our legitimacy in the eyes of the state made it easier to be cared for by one another. Though not much remained of the original debt—just a few thousand dollars in federal loans—it also meant that my debt would become our debt. In Mike's vows to me, he told me that in any version of any life he could ever have, he would always choose this one, he would always choose me. I'd spent a large portion of my adult life trying to outrun the debt. Even today, there are moments when it's hard to imagine anyone choosing me, walking toward what I have fled.

This pregnancy was the second pregnancy I had. The first began in late January the winter before. Overwhelmed with work at the start of the new semester, I didn't research anything about pregnancy other than which days you were supposed to have sex. So I mistook the symptoms as period symptoms, only taking the test after my period was several days late. I was pregnant for eight weeks before I miscarried, which means, practically, that I experienced my pregnancy for a month. Because my body held on to the fetus instead of finishing the miscarriage and releasing it, I underwent a procedure to remove it under anesthesia that left me alert enough to keep asking my doctor if I was talking too much.

To be unpregnant after being pregnant was a relief, which I felt guilty for experiencing, and which I only fully identified after becoming pregnant for the second time in mid-June. When I read the test results, I cried and then cried more because the first cry wasn't one of joy but of fear. I recognized the sensation, increasing in the weeks that followed, that my body was no longer fully my own, that my needs and the fetus's needs would sometimes be in conflict, and that in the case of conflict, it would likely be the fetus's needs which would take precedence over my own. This feeling was confirmed when a week after learning of the pregnancy, *Roe v. Wade* was repealed, and people with a uterus became second-class citizens with fewer rights than a fetus.

Beyond the legal confirmation that my own desires no longer mattered was an echo of shared personhood, which I couldn't avoid. Once I was of my mother, growing for nine months inside her, and then I was of my own for eighteen years. And then from eighteen to twenty-one, I was of my mother again, or, rather, she was of me. We shared my personhood: my Social Security number, my signature, my birthdate, my aim, which was to go to college, the aim she co-opted to secure the loans. We did not share a home anymore, but in databases across the country, we were nearly indistinguishable, a confusion that was replicated across my twenties and thirties when I begged lenders to separate us. To share my body again, even with a fetus who was too small to have a heartbeat—just cardiac activity—felt terrifying. Having spent much of my life searching for borders, for confirmation that I was a person all on my own, pregnancy felt like the removal of all borders, starting with the ones closest to me.

The letter my father wrote to me has been ripped out of a notebook, and sentences are crossed off and rewritten. The handwriting is unmistakably his but shakier. He's written the date, March 11, the day following his birthday and a month before he would die. The title, at the top, is "Kristin's Wedding Day!!" and he begins the note by saying how sorry he is not to be present. "You are my child," he tells me, "and you bring light into any room you enter." When I read it the first time, seated on the floor just inside our front door, I had to keep setting it down because I couldn't bear to hear his voice. Before he died, I'd saved a series of voice mails on my phone, aware that they might be the last, and then never listened to them again. When I'd gotten a new phone, I'd kept the old one in a small box that I stored in the back of my desk. The letter is poetic and effusive, more so than anything he'd ever written or said to me when he was alive. He has no doubt that I will choose someone with the same qualities he values in me. At the end of the letter he writes, "Kristin, no matter where I am, I will always be your dad. I will love you forever." Love is not bound by body or time.

I don't know why my mother didn't send the letter to me before my wedding or give it to me when I returned with Mike to Michigan soon after to celebrate with our friends and families. I'm not sure if it was because she could not part with this piece of him, just as I'm unsure why she sent it to me when she did. I could ask, but I won't. It doesn't matter.

Recently, I reread the note for the first time in years, and noticed that my father, perhaps accidentally, included an early draft of the letter in the envelope. At the top of the rough draft is a partial list of my friends who donated to the medical fund-raiser, along with the total, which he has crossed out and updated. A reminder of debt's presence in a moment of intimate, familial exchange. *Here?! Even here?* I think. I recall the borrower who used her inheritance to pay off a large debt burden and the one who spent the last day of her mother's life talking about student debt. *You're not welcome here,* I think seriously before smiling at its absurdity; it sounds like something out of an exorcism prayer, which, in a way it is.

––––––

In *Mother Country,* not long after Shannon eats her loan notices, she's in a harrowing car accident that nearly kills her, forcing doctors to rearrange her insides twice, and leaving her with $147,000 in medical debt, which, added to her student loans, brings her total debt to $258,000. She marries a rich engineer whom she does not love because he is beautiful, has health insurance and money, and offers her a stability that's out of reach for her without him.

Shannon wishes to flee her life of precarity into a new life of abundance and motherhood. She and her husband try to have a baby and cannot. Shannon's desire to be a mother seems to stem from an absence of power and an excess of tenderness that she's unable to offer anyone, not her parents, her new husband, or even herself. Her barrenness is a confirmation of the powerlessness she's experienced first as a daughter and then as an adult who cannot care for herself because of her enormous debt burdens.

Her indebtedness confers and confirms her American-ness, and being a mother will offer a new and better confirmation of a different kind of American citizenship. Early in the novel, she reflects on the differing lives of wealthy women: "When she saw them at the coffee shop wearing upscale leather shoes and unpacking chic strollers from Range Rovers, she knew they'd come from a different place to begin with. No student loans. Wealthy husbands, helpful parents: places Shannon had never been. A baby was the ultimate American symbol of success. And one more thing she'd never have."

On a trip with her husband to Morocco, Shannon steals the three-year-old child of a Mauritanian teenager who's survived trafficking and enslavement and protected her daughter in spite of so much violence, creating a home for her in the coastal Moroccan vacation town in Souria. As an undocumented person facing deportation, the child's mother has no recourse to reclaim her child, who soon departs to the United States with her kidnapper while the child's grieving mother wanders the streets searching for her.

This theft transforms Shannon's world, which now looks more like that of the wealthy women she envied than the one she lived in before. It transforms her body's aims, which cease to be punishing and become, instead, nourishing: She needs to care for and keep alive a young child who does not want to be there, who screams for hours because she misses her home and her mother, the one Shannon attempts to wash from her memory.

The novel's coupling of debt and motherhood, the belief that both are part of what it means to live in this country, is striking. One of them is of extraction and the other is of growth, both of a kind of presence, a collection against the body. At the end of the novel, Shannon reaffirms her identity as mother and citizen: "It was the highest sign of American success, and she'd acquired it. A hundred forty-seven thousand dollars in medical debt, a student loan balance the size of a mortgage, but she'd jumped the gameboard spaces over *debt* and slid straight into the *parenthood* safe spot at the board's center. She was, at long last, an American adult."

The night my daughter was born in February 2023, Mike and I passed a red fox on our way to the hospital. It was sitting directly beneath a streetlamp, the light spread around it like a gauzy skirt. "A good omen," Mike said. As I tried to sleep through the contractions—and could not—I was cared for by a young and skilled nurse who brought me lemonade and water, expertly inserted an IV, and prepared me for what lay ahead. She was gentle and kind, and I felt so attached to her and so scared about my labor that I cried when she said good-bye to me in the morning.

Sometime in the pre-dawn, when the nurse came to check my blood pressure, I asked her why she was working the night shift. My sister had worked this shift for a long time, and I knew the way it destroyed her sleep cycles and made it hard for her to see friends. "I have too many student loans not to," she said to me. Because these overnight shifts paid her more, she was going to keep working them until her debt was paid off. Here was an intersection of a topic I'd been wrestling with for years and a person who was tasked with caring for my body as it entered a wild, feral process and the land of motherhood that waited for me on the other side. I wanted to ask her *How much? When did she expect to pay it off? How had this debt shaped her?* But I didn't. "I'm sorry about the loans," I said. "I have them, too. You're an excellent nurse and your patients are lucky to have you."

I could not get Frances out of my body until 6:00 p.m. the next night—she was stuck—and eventually the midwife I'd chosen had to be substituted out for a doctor who told me that because of my daughter's dropping heart rate, they would need to either use a giant suction to pull her out or perform an emergency C-section which would require her to be pushed back up into my body. "If she's not out by the time I return, you will have to tell me which one you want to do and both have risks," she said. I'd been awake for two days straight and my pain and fear meant that I heard Mike, the nurses, and the doctor as if plunged to the bottom of a lake. When the doctor returned, Frances was close enough for the doctor to try a move in which she essentially yanked her out, ripping a painful third-degree tear in me.

She was handed to me from within a thick fog; I could hardly see anymore. They placed her on my chest, screaming, and covered in shit and blood—she'd pooped in the womb—which they were wiping off as I held her. She was completely alien and of my body all at once—the most familiar, terrifying, and wonderful sight I'd ever seen. *Frances, Frances, Frances,* I chanted to her, *I love you.* Because there was so much work to do stitching me up, and the nurses were worried that I was not strong enough to hold her during the procedure, Mike cradled her on the room's sofa while I lay by myself on the bed. From my position, I was unable to see them, so I turned my head to watch the highway, which glittered and shook beside me. We'd forgotten to close the blinds. I couldn't stop crying. It was the first time I'd been apart from her in nearly a year.

In *Luster,* Edie has health problems: a debilitating illness affecting her stomach and depression and anxiety which she doesn't name but articulates through her isolation and her sense of alienation from the art that she loves and from herself. At one point, like Cassie from *Writers & Lovers,* she cannot recognize her own face in the mirror. Some of the loveliest images of the entire book are those of dead people, whom her boyfriend Eric's wife dissects for autopsies and whom Edie begins to paint. This anatomical study and the uncertain relationship that facilitates it—Edie's romantically charged friendship with Eric's wife—animates Edie's art and offers some of the only tenderness of the entire book, at least between adults. The dead people she operates on can't tell their stories anymore, but their bodies say something nonetheless.

At the end of the novel, after Edie becomes pregnant accidentally and then loses the baby following an incident of police violence, she remembers her brief experience with motherhood as a sunlit dream and a sunlit seizure. She wanted the baby, or she sort of did. I wonder if Edie believes her body to be infertile ground, in part, because it is a body under the siege of collection. I wonder if motherhood, like her artwork and the violent sex she yearns for, is part of a record, the proof she seeks that she was there.

The shift from being pregnant to being a mother was startling and otherworldly and overwhelming. And in the hormone plummet following birth, I had to fight my tendency to believe that I was not worthy of this new baby. Mike's sister flew in from New Mexico to stay with us for ten days. A former pediatric nurse, she showed us how to bathe Frances, recommending that we wet small cloth towels, each no bigger than my hand, to drape them over her to keep her warm. She showed us how to swaddle her using muslin blankets and how to pick her up while supporting her neck. Mike's sister went grocery shopping, cooked for us, warmed the generous meals our friends had prepared for us, and showed me how to help Frances latch.

I spent a lot of time sitting in the bathtub soaking my wounds in epsom salt and crying. Worried about my own abilities as a mother, I was not alone with Frances except for once, when Mike and his sister dropped off doughnuts and thank you cards to our care team at the hospital. In our quiet living room, I held my sleeping daughter. Outside, there were several feet of snow and more on the way. The sky was slate. She made small animal sounds and opened her eyes.

We stared at each other for a long time. "You were inside my body," I said to her. I read somewhere that she could smell me, that she remembered me from our nine months together, and I wondered if that were true. If she remembered me at all, I thought, it was as an impression—as sound and smell and nourishment—not as an individual, discernible human. I liked the idea of mother as experience. Not a person, or not only a person, but movement, the swirl of the world around you, the many ways you can offer and receive care. It was expansive and ever growing.

"I love you," I said to her and knew that it was true.

Chapter 20

FINANCING COLLEGE HAS ALWAYS been stressful for poor and working-class families "since the early days of the republic," writes historian Elizabeth Tandy Shermer. While there has never been, universally, fully funded higher education, college was, for a long time, much cheaper than it is today. In inflation-adjusted dollars for the year 2021, the average price of tuition for four- and two-year schools in the 1963–1964 school year was $4,336. When the Pell Grant program was born as part of the piecemeal affordability measures created under the Higher Education Act of 1965, it "subsidized more than 80 percent of the cost of attending the average public university and all of the costs of attending community college," according to higher education scholar Sara Goldrick-Rab. In the 2022–2023 school year, the average price of tuition for all schools was $14,688 and the Pell Grant covered less than a third of tuition and fees, which, with room and board, were $27,673.

Scholars note the movement away from publicly financed public education to debt-financed education coincided with the conservative campaign to shrink comprehensive social wages that were part of President Johnson's Great Society programs. "Reagan's election in many ways ended the post–World War consensus that higher education should be liberal in outlook and accessible to everyone," writes journalist Will Bunch in *After the Ivory Tower Falls*. Once in the California governor's office, Reagan got to work punishing the "small minority of beatniks, radicals, and filthy speech advocates" he'd campaigned against. He depicted, according to scholar Christopher Newfield in *Unmaking the Public University*, "The University of California as a threat to social order and even national security." While Reagan was unable to end California's pledge for free tuition at its public universities while he was governor, he laid the foundation, imposing a series of increasingly punishing fees and shaping the national conversation about what the government owes its people and which people. Students protesting unjust wars or asking more of their university or government, or studying poetry or Chicano studies, or existing in racialized and gendered bodies that Reagan didn't like were not deserving of a free education, so they should take on debt. In the words of scholar Ruth Wilson Gilmore, "Debt robs. But debt also disciplines."

"Privatization has systemically diminished the public university's distinctive features," writes Newfield. One such feature was a meaningful education for free or close to free, which enabled students to choose a field of study because they were interested in it or good at it rather than believing that it would help them to pay back their loans. Without the presence of student debt, Newfield points out, graduates from low-income backgrounds had the same opportunity to take work that they wanted—sometimes poorly paid—travel internationally, or become artists. "The boom in student debt has reduced these freedoms, and likely reduced the socially valuable innovation that comes with them," Newfield writes.

How would the future be different for everyone I've spoken to if they were debt free? Had free college always existed, how would that have shaped the entire higher education landscape, the messages of their peers and teachers and high schools? What would it have felt like to never have received a collection notice, spoken to a debt collector, checked a servicer account, signed a promissory note, filled out FAFSA, or asked a parent what they could afford?

In a writing class I'm teaching to high school students, we recently ended the hour with a generative writing exercise. One of the prompt options was about a time they'd felt estranged from their bodies, for reasons as simple as having a broken bone or the flu, or for more complex reasons. It was winter in Minneapolis, and the classroom was on the first floor with a hill rising upward to a different level of the building just beyond my window. Outside, we could not see the city or classmates cutting across the quad, just the hunched lawn, covered in snow, so we were cocooned together in the classroom, jazz playing quietly from the smartboard speakers.

Something happens when we write together all at once—our brains and our hands moving in a kind of loosely synchronous dance. It feels to me like magic, and I think it feels that way to students, too. If not magic, then at least a quiet relief. The writing is an affirmation all its own; it might turn into an essay or a story, or it might not. It's not valuable because it will become something else that can be given away, or transformed, or measured, but because it's movement and record of movement all at once, learning in motion.

These exercises are not handed in and are not graded—though there are opportunities to share them, play with them, and extend them. They are confirmation, I hope, that what my students think and how they think matters, in a completely unqualified, unmeasured way. I cannot rip educational experience from its context: College applications, letters of recommendation, the financial aid process, tuition payments, and student debt awaits them. But I can show them that deep, sustained engagement with the world and with themselves, in the form of writing, can make them feel free.

————————

Not every borrower I've spoken with believes that all borrowers should receive wide-scale relief. One borrower, Zoe, wished, instead, that her interest would be lowered to make repayment possible.

Zoe, who was white and in her mid-thirties, grew up in a small Midwestern town and attended college at a state school a few hours from her home. Based on her family's income and her academic history, her school awarded her need- and merit-based aid, including the opportunity to apply for work study. What remained in cost, around $6,000 a year, her father paid for in cash. "Education was a big point of pride in my family," she told me via our virtual meeting. "My dad was so proud to be able to pay for it." Zoe's wire-rimmed glasses sat large across her face. Behind her was her work desk, which featured a statue of the scales of justice and a blue paper lamp with fuchsia birds in flight. The only debt she had leaving undergrad was about $7,000 from a semester of study abroad during her senior year, she said.

Her father's cash payments came from a different kind of labor. He grew and sold marijuana before it was medically or recreationally legal. And for that work, he pled guilty to a felony at the end of her senior year of college. This detail about her father recalls Caitlin Zaloom's research: The families she interviews do everything they possibly can to help their students go to college, neglecting saving for retirement or meeting their own needs, exchanging one stability for another. They hope they'll create good lives for their children even if their own lives become harder.

"My dad used to pay taxes on what he sold," Zoe told me, joking that's how Al Capone was caught. I'm not sure how her father was. His tax payments confirmed his belief in government and perhaps a hope that those taxes would translate to care. Her father died in 2020, and it was clear that Zoe missed him a lot.

Following his conviction, Zoe enrolled in a regional law school and had to borrow the total cost of attendance, which amounted to about $50,000. During her second year, she was able to find a paid internship, which eased her burden, but there was a cost to that, too. "The most prestigious internships seemed to be unpaid," she said, "and unpaid work wasn't an option for me." The principal for her law school debt was $158,000, and the last time she looked at the exact number was before the start of the pandemic. At the time it was $217,000.

She'd been enrolled in an Income Driven Repayment plan since graduation, after which she worked at a law office that focused on medical malpractice, worker's compensation, and Social Security Disability before recently transitioning to this federal job. "For the longest time, the balance stayed the same. Because of the way IDR worked out, I was paying interest on them every month. And then when it was transferred, because I got a new servicer during COVID, it went up," she said. "And I don't know, it's one of those things where I probably should pay attention and try to do the math and figure out if they charged me interest in months they weren't supposed to." She trailed off. Zoe was obviously incredibly smart and detail-oriented, and yet, she did not have an explanation for this change. In part it might be because it ultimately didn't matter. Even with her $530 monthly loan payments, she'd never be able to pay off the loan burden.

"You should qualify for PSLF," I told her after she described her new job to me, but she was certain that wasn't true. Later, I looked it up, and I was right. Her servicer with whom she registers her employment should have told her, as should the government. Beyond her misconception about the bounds of PSLF was a real fear that if she made a misstep—put her hope into the wrong program—she would be kicked out of her IDR plan and the nearly $60,000 of payments she'd made in the last nine years would be for nothing. That fear was not unfounded. This has happened, and these errors have meant that borrowers lost years of payments. (When we checked in seven months later, Zoe had clarity on PSLF but didn't think it was worth the risk of switching as it would amount to about a year's difference in relief).

Zoe was ebullient in our conversation, joking and laughing, even as she shared events that were destabilizing: her father's conviction and death and the closing of her law school, which happened a few years after she graduated. Her school was forced to close because it wasn't meeting students' needs. It took on too many students too quickly and "got greedy," in Zoe's words. A friend who researches higher education wondered, when I spoke with her about the closed school, if it's possible that Zoe's school had its own debts to pay. "It's another cost of not having free college," she noted. "Students go into debt and institutions do," forcing them to be disciplined and sanctioned by creditors.

According to Zoe, the influx of new students were unable to pass the bar, an indication that they might not have been ready for law school to begin with. It also suggests, to me, that the school was not preparing them to become lawyers. Though the law school's closure had not impacted Zoe, she acknowledged that it had hurt many of her former classmates, some of whom have a lot of debt now with a worthless degree to show for it. It's hard to get a job with a degree from a school that no longer exists.

I asked her if the available relief options feel like the right ones, and she said, "I'm not going to say the loans should be forgiven because I am getting value. I have no issue paying it back. Because of these loans I was able to go to law school, which had been my dream since I was in fifth grade. It kills me that I can't pay them off." But for her, she said, "there's no light at the end of the tunnel because of the interest rates." Some of her loans had interest rates of 7.9 percent and the rest had rates of 6.8 percent. "If the rates were reasonable, I could pay off my loans sooner, and more of my money would be freed up to spend in the economy."

———

Today, there are nearly three hundred programs known as "promise programs," implemented at state and local levels across the country, which aim to bridge the gap between existing grants, scholarships, tuition waivers, and stipends and the cost of college. These are collectively known as "last dollar" programs. Minnesota's version, "North Star Promise," which began in the fall of 2024, impacted nearly 17,000 students, benefiting Minnesota residents whose household incomes are under $80,000. Notably, students cannot access this promise if they are in default on existing state and federal student loans. This of course disqualifies some students who are suffering the most, those who left college because of structural reasons and then, likely because of the same structural reasons, could not make payments on their loans.

The most comprehensive of college funding proposals has been Senator Bernie Sanders and Representative Pramila Jayapal's 2021 College for All Act, which aimed to eliminate tuition and fees at public two- and four-year schools for any family making under $125,000 (about 80 percent of the population) and required states to reaffirm their own financial commitments to education and reduce their use of low-paid adjunct faculty. It also earmarked over a billion dollars to support tuition reduction at historically Black colleges and Universities and minority serving institutions, which are not public colleges, but serve the country's most marginalized students. The cost of this program would not be borne by taxpayers, but by Wall Street in the form of a small tax on stock trades, bonds, and derivatives, requiring an industry that has profited off of other people's debt to help eliminate some for students. The bill is currently in committee.

All these existing and proposed programs rely on means-testing, the bureaucratic sorting of who gets the benefit and who doesn't. Any kind of means testing will inevitably leave people out who desperately need the benefit, and those people will either not go to college or take on debt burdens that will likely shape the rest of their lives.

In her argument for free college for all, writer Meagan Day points out that in a universal college funding model that uses progressive taxation, "the people paying the most for free public college for everyone are the rich." Unlike our current model of differentiated tuition, this payment "takes the form of collective taxes over the course of a lifetime, not individual tuition costs over the course of a few years." She notes that the wealthiest children across the country are very unlikely to attend a public school. She also recognizes that that's not the point.

This is the college model that I believe in—one in which any kid can go to public school for free. Rather than reinforcing historical inequalities, college should be part of repairing them. And it should open pathways to the sort of public service work that our country relies on, generating nurses, social workers, teachers, public defenders, and EMTs. As Day writes, "Where a meager means-tested welfare-state model breeds alienation and competition, a robust universal welfare-state breeds trust and cooperation." Alongside free college, health care, housing, jobs, good wages, and retirement are required. College should not be and cannot be the *only* pathway to a free life.

"There has never been a middle class in history that was not created by public infrastructure—by facilities offering rough equality regardless of personal means," writes Newfield. "As the middle-class cuts public education, it cuts the conditions of its own existence." To create rather than cut the conditions for its existence, Newfield believes that a university must prioritize racial equality and maximum access to schools for everyone who wants to attend while maintaining the highest possible quality. "The university needs to be understood as engaged in forms of individual and collective development that cannot be captured in economic terms. Education cannot pay in this way. It must not be expected to," according to Newfield. There must be time for discovery, curiosity, experimentation, elaboration, introspection, and play—and these experiences are sometimes necessarily at odds with economic return.

It is not the political system or business system that is going to save us, Newfield writes, because neither of these has been able to "confront the core problem of our time: In a world of six billion people, and four to five billion poor, how do we develop the whole of society and not just the protected minority?"

Years ago, when I first began to wonder about student debt's impact, I posted a call on my social media for people to share their debt stories with me. Someone—I'll call him Ian—from my hometown reached out. We had attended elementary, middle, and high school together though we hadn't been friends. I tried to remember who he spent time with and could not, unsure if that was because our social lives didn't intersect or because he was lonely and disconnected. "It all started in elementary school," he began in his first message to me. "I had a 504-learning plan for reading, writing, and language arts. I remember our fifth-grade end-of-year assembly, thinking, *I want to be like them, winning academic awards.* It never happened. In fact, my grades fell. You might remember that I always use to leave class for a few hours." After his introduction, the rest of his message was vague; he acknowledged that he had student debt now and that he wanted to check in with his wife to clarify some of the details of his debt burden. He said that he'd likely put the whole story in a Word doc, that it would be "therapeutic" and possibly "too long" but that he was looking forward to it. He apologized that the story he'd write me would be poorly written because he was not a strong writer. I thanked him in my reply, offering encouragement, and reminding him that I'd love to talk whenever he was ready. He never was.

Ian located the origins of his debt in the way that he *learned.* I don't have the rest of his narrative, but I can infer that his journey might have included a departure from college, that it likely didn't include a merit scholarship, and that he didn't feel he had the options he might have had had he been more academically competitive. Even if none of that is true, what is true is that Ian believes he has debt, in part, because of who he was, even as a child, when all he wanted to do was be acknowledged for being special and capable. Like many borrowers I've spoken with, he's internalized the messages of the system, the sense we have received what we have *earned*.

I love watching Frances learn, her understanding of the world coming to her in flickers, sharpening as she acquires language and draws new connections. When she learned the color "orange," for example, she suddenly saw it everywhere, a whole landscape aflame with meaning. "Gurt," the word she says for *yogurt*, delivers to her the exact thing she wants, not just any food that I have chosen. It gives her power; autonomy. That she would ever believe that the way her mind works is not good enough enrages me. I want her to believe that if she has to take out student loans someday, it is not her fault. She would not be any more deserving of education if she were "gifted and talented," more creative, a better programmer, more advanced in math, read at a higher level, were more entrepreneurial, or an actual genius. This is also what I want people to understand who've paid back their loans and are critical of debt relief or free college for others. Their debt should not have existed for them, and they should have had a better option. But someone's survival in the system doesn't justify its existence.

Zoe and I spoke again a few weeks after our first conversation, and she said that she had looked at the numbers and despite meeting all the requirements of her payment plan, her debt burden was growing. The plan she was enrolled in didn't even cover interest, she noted. She was in the same home office as last time, the same scales of justice behind her, but she sounded less buoyant. Zoe worried that the IDR plan would be subject to the whims of whatever administration is in power when she meets the twenty-five-year mark, the time at which her loans should be canceled. "If for some reason it doesn't work out, then the choices I've made for the twenty-five years leading up to it are really poor," she said. I understood what she meant—that her faith will have been misplaced—but even so, I hated to hear her frame even her imagined future around poor choices.

"I think you qualify for borrower defense to repayment," I said. Borrower defense is a provision of the Higher Education Act that allows borrowers to seek relief if their college misled them or engaged in misconduct. If, for example, their college advertised employment numbers or bar pass rates that were inaccurate, then students can make the case that they took out these loans under fraudulent circumstances and should not pay them back. This defense has been especially important for students who attended for-profit schools and as of April 2024, the Biden administration approved 17.2 billion in federal student loans for 974,820 borrowers under borrowers' defense. These numbers are a victory for borrowers, many of whom led the organizing efforts for relief, but people still had to live with staggering amounts of debts from schools that coerced them into enrolling or lied to them about the value of their education or closed, sometimes while students were currently enrolled.

Zoe nodded along as I said this. Some of her classmates had completed the borrower defense application, but she didn't want to because to her, it would feel like a lie. "The lawyer brain in me knows I'm going to need to make a case that I didn't get value from my degree. And that's not true. I did," she said. That's not what the law requires claimants to prove, but the application for her seemed to imply that. It reminded me of my conversations with Alana, the borrower who was forced out of school in New York. It was important to Zoe to say that while some people might frame what happened to her as harm, she believed it was worth it. "I have been working as a lawyer so it would feel disingenuous." The price was inflated, she thought, but ultimately, she got the job she wanted.

I paused for a moment, considering how I wanted to respond. I was trying earnestly to learn about Zoe. And still. I wondered if anyone had offered her another perspective: that it was not dishonest for this debt to be relieved, that her loans in particular were acquired under unjust circumstances, and that I thought, in fact, all student loans were. "I can see how you are making decisions according to your values," I said, "and I can imagine in your shoes, I might think, this is bullshit. The school that charged me a ton of money has closed, so I don't need to pay this back."

Later in the conversation I asked her, "How would your life be different without debt?"

She would still live in the same Midwestern town, she thought, doing the same work she is doing now. "I do think my retirement would be significantly higher. That's where I've really been behind. I can't contribute as much as I need to because of my loan payments," she said. She also said that the way she spent time outside of work would be different. She sat on a community disability nonprofit board and volunteered for a land conservation organization. Zoe also offered free legal advice to folks in her community, as long as it didn't conflict with her job. "I would have done more of that over the years if I wasn't so tied to these debt payments," she said.

Then she offered something that surprised me. "I also have a second job that does come down to some of the debt and income stuff." She worked for a small business, on and off, sometimes picking up shifts during the summer busy season or on weekends. She loved and believed in the business, part of her hometown, so it was not just about the money. Even so, it was notable that a lawyer working for the federal government picked up shifts of any kind.

"I can't stress about my debt," she said as we were wrapping up the call. "It's not ignorance—maybe a little bit of denial. I don't ignore it but I can't give it too much power either."

Zoe was not the first borrower who told me they would like to pay back all of their debt. Sher, the borrower who wanted to show her "blue collar man the world," also voiced that goal. Even if all the debt were canceled, I think borrowers should be given the right to make payments if it feels important to them. Why not? Pay back as much as you want even if the government tells you you don't need to.

But it seems that borrowers who'd like to repay their debt— and most people I talk to desperately want their debt payments to end entirely—want to because they want to keep a promise they made. For them, repayment is not about money, per se, but a belief that repayment makes them trustworthy and good. I, too, want that, and I think that a promise which you were forced to make to have access to education—the possibility of a life in which you can get a well-paying job and benefits—a promise made under dishonest and unequal circumstances, doesn't need to be honored. It's the government that has broken its promises to us, not the other way around.

Chapter 21

MY MOTHER MET FRANCES when she was seven weeks old, scheduling her visit for the same time as my sister. The overlap was intentional. Some homing mechanism deep inside me was calling my family back to me, in the closest version of the original form. Also, I was worried about my complex dynamics with my mother and wanted my sister there as a buffer.

The seven weeks before had been challenging. Frances struggled to sleep in her bassinet, so Mike and I slept very little, especially in the first month. On my night shifts, I dressed so that I was cold, sat myself uncomfortably on the couch, and got lost in strange TikTok algorithms to keep myself awake. I was worried about accidentally falling asleep holding my daughter, who would herself not sleep unless she was held.

On top of the sleeplessness, my body would not produce enough milk to feed her, and I was told by lactation consultants that in order to produce more, I should breastfeed her every two hours and then pump breast milk for fifteen to twenty minutes afterward to stimulate my lactation hormone, prolactin, and to offer my daughter at least some of the benefits of human milk with the little I could extract. By the time of my mother's visit, I had not slept more than two and a half hours in a row since before my daughter was born, and I was brittle.

That winter I'd been reading about gambling addiction, not the physiological mechanisms that made people vulnerable to addiction but the casino mechanisms that created addicts. I wanted to understand something about my mother that she had been unwilling or unable to tell me: why the woman I'd known as one kind of mother—patient and generous and responsible—suddenly became another kind. Everything I'd read about the lending system had led me to believe she was preyed upon, and I sensed the predation did not begin and end there. Perhaps the research was not just an attempt at distillation and reflection but of prevention. I was a new mother, and I did not want to hurt my daughter.

Since I'd learned of my mother's gambling addiction, I'd thought of it as a disease, not a weakness or character fault. I had not, however, also understood it as a response to carefully designed objects and the environment they're embedded in. In *Addiction by Design*, anthropologist Natasha D. Schüll uses fifteen years of research, mostly conducted in Las Vegas, to understand pathological and problem gamblers' relationships to the machines themselves. While slot machines were once thought of as companion spaces to engage women while their husbands played table games, by the early 1990s, they'd been moved to occupy key spaces in casinos and were generating twice as much revenue as all the other live games combined. As of 2003, industry experts who talked to Schüll thought that 85 percent of revenue came from machines.

Because these machines are so lucrative, casinos use every available tool to guide patrons toward them and then keep them playing until the patrons' funds, or sometimes bodies, give out. Designers choose carpet, lighting, ceiling height, scent, and sound to reflect what players articulate—and the data confirm—keeps them on machines. The more users play, and the more quickly that they play, the more the casino makes money. To enable rapid gambling, handle pulls have been exchanged for buttons, allowing twice as many games per hour. New methods of money transfer have allowed patrons to insert larger bills or use loyalty cards which connect to their bank account—all to keep players from having to pause their play to make a trip to an ATM or to stop a game by forcing them to load more coins. Near misses have been programmed into the machines to give players the sensation of winning even when they have not, and when individual player data—which is triangulated and surveilled by casino programs—suggests that players are reaching a pain point and might soon quit, casinos' hosts are dispatched to their machine to give them coupons and other casino rewards. The entire casino ecosystem is designed to extract the maximum amount of revenue out of players.

It's not just that this extraction's accidental by-product is addiction, which would be bad enough, it's that addiction is the fuel of this extraction: This extraction depends on it. Once players are addicted—which happens rapidly in machine play, three to four times more quickly than in live games—they are no longer playing to win, but to achieve the zone state, in which their bodies blend with the machine and the world outside of this symbiosis dissolves into nothingness. Schüll writes, "Repeat machine gamblers experience a flow that is depleting, entrapping, and associated with a loss of autonomy." The zone state is a total obliteration of self. One gambler she spoke to recalled being so entrapped by this zone state that she vomited on herself. Another time, she wet her pants. A different gambler, a diabetic, felt his blood sugar crashing but physically could not leave the machine, even as, eventually, he began to fall into a diabetic coma. It's "not the case that gambling addicts are beyond choice," according to Schüll, "but that choice itself formatted by machines becomes the medium of compulsion."

I called one of the casinos I thought my mother had gambled at, to ask them about their machines. I wanted to know what informed the placement and type of machine games they have, and more importantly, I wondered how they responded to clear patterns of harm in their players. I doubted that they would offer me anything beyond the industry equivalent of "guns don't kill people." And still, I wanted to ask. I left long voice mails in the in-boxes of people that reception routed me to. But no one called me back.

A beautiful writer I met when teaching the class in the state prison passed on wisdom from another teacher: An essay is a slice of pie. You, the writer, need to choose how big to make the slice, which also means deciding how much of the rest of the pie goes unseen and uneaten. I was trying to expand the slice of my mother's story.

The night before my mother's visit, I texted her to ask that she not use her vape pen in the house. Sleep-deprived and grappling with postpartum depression, I saw threats everywhere. My mother had smoked her pen around me while I was pregnant and while I knew she would not smoke it near Frances, I was worried about her using it in other rooms in our house. I didn't have the brain power to research how long the chemicals lingered in the air. It seemed easiest for her just to go outside. I understood that there might be undercurrents to this request, and I tried to neutralize them, writing a message that I hoped was kind and nonjudgmental.

But my mother felt those currents anyway. She felt I accused her of wanting to harm her granddaughter. She told me that I'd hurt her. Did I even want her to come? Maybe this once, I told her, she could keep her feelings to herself instead of making it about her. If she felt hurt, maybe she could just absorb it. I did that all the time. Our interaction tapped into a vibration within me. I didn't sleep for the entire night—free-falling through the gaps of time between nursing and pumping. When dawn came, it felt like I'd survived a drowning.

I had wanted her to visit before the exchange, but afterward I was not so sure. Whether I wanted her to or not was beside the point. I knew that we needed, or at least I needed, help. When my mother and sister arrived, they cleaned and grocery shopped and organized parts of the house. They took turns holding Frances, whose evening fussiness was cresting. The only thing that would soothe her when she cried was swaddling her and swaying with her. Some friends who understood my relationship with my mother wondered if seeing her with Frances would be healing. Would intergenerational care made material—right in front of my very eyes—unlock what all my research and therapy had been unable to achieve?

While I understood on a cognitive level that I needed the help my family could provide me, my body had its own narrative. I stopped producing milk almost entirely. Desperate to make breastfeeding work, I began to pump alone in the bedroom, hoping that a peaceful, solitary environment might release my sympathetic nervous system's hold on my body. During one of these solo pumping sessions, I researched milk production cessation under times of extreme stress, and concluded that, evolutionarily, it made sense. You do not want to stop to breastfeed when stalked by a predator. Later, I felt less convinced. Women would not need their milk to dry up to know that they should not stop to feed their baby when stalked by an animal that wants to eat them. Still, parental guidance messaging drove me against all biological hurdles and every instinct of self-protection to give up basically all sleep and free time so that I could breastfeed.

Because I was pumping so much, my sister and my mom were often alone with Frances, holding her and talking to her. In my bedroom, away from them, I was glad that they were with my daughter. While the debt and its wide-reaching tentacles had made a close relationship with my mother, for the time anyway, impossible, I understood that Frances could choose to have whatever relationship she wanted to have with her grandmother. I hoped it would be replete with trust, joy, curiosity, and love. I wanted that for them both.

———

Schüll notes that gambling addiction, officially called "disordered gambling" and formally named "pathological gambling," concentrates on players' motivations and psychiatric profiles rather than the games that they play. Of the listed ten DSM-V criteria, all of which my mother meets, I'm most moved by this one: "often gambles when feeling distressed (e.g., helpless, guilty, anxious, depressed)." My mother struggled when I went to college—with my departure and with understanding herself as an adult and individual apart from me. I remember watching her break down into sobs in my dorm room when she said good-bye, sensing that her departure was also a rupture. Much later, she confirmed that to me, though she could not articulate why beyond that she missed me. "I just had a really really hard time after you moved away," she said. Because she had me at twenty-one, I think, her adult identity was fused with mine, even before she codified that fusion through the theft. I know she gambled, in part at least, because she was suffering, because she was scared, because she did not know who she was, and the machine allowed her to disappear entirely.

Gambling addiction's inclusion in the DSM was a useful one for the industry: Now they could point to a particular class of people for which gambling was a problem. For everyone else, it was harmless. Just fun. That mentality has guided the industry's engagement—or lack of engagement—with the destruction they cause. While between 1 and 2 percent of the *general* population meet the criteria for disordered gambling, 3–4 percent meet the criteria for its lesser diagnosis, problem gambling. But of the *repeat gambling* population, upward of 20 percent meet the criteria. Schüll writes: "Between 30 percent and a staggering 60 percent of total gambling revenues have been found to derive from problem gamblers."

Casinos are not the only ones invested in understanding addiction as an unfortunate and inevitable by-product of an individual's freedom to choose. The spread of commercialized gambling in the 1980s and 1990s was a response to the Reagan-era tax cuts and the recession they engendered: States wanted to raise money without reimposing taxes. While the majority of state gambling revenue comes from the lottery, as of 2021 eleven states collected the majority of their gambling revenue from casinos. How much of this profit came from people who lost their homes? Who indebted themselves? Who destroyed important relationships? Who tried to, or did, die?

———

If I felt abandoned by my mother at times, I also felt that the state had abandoned us both. Before my mother's visit, I wondered if there might be a way to share some of this with her. In addition to welcoming my daughter, we might welcome a more complex way to engage with what had happened to us both, we might widen the slice of the pie.

What I wanted to say to her, what I did say to her in my head while I sorted through hand-me-down baby clothes before my daughter was born and while she napped on me after her birth, was this: *I know you believe that what you did makes you bad, but that's not true. There were interventions that could have happened and didn't, at the casino, at the banks, from your own family. If you can see the harm as shared, rather than only yours, maybe it will help you heal.* I'd begun to think that maybe I needed her healing for my own. But I did not say any of this to her. Between our argument about vaping and the breast-feeding challenges, that kind of intimacy did not feel possible.

Halfway through the weekend, my mother and I were with Frances in our living room. Outside, the world had begun to transition from winter to spring. We'd gone for a walk in the neighborhood earlier that day, and the edges of everything were green, just barely. Frances was cooing on the floor, and my mother bent to pick her up. "Come to Mama," she said, and we both, for a moment, froze. I waited for the aftershock, to understand the slip as confusing and painful, layered, and fraught, but the aftershock never came. "I'm not your mother!" my mother said, laughing. "Your mama's right there." When she left to drive the nine hours home, I knew that she felt sad and relieved to go, a feeling I shared.

Though my milk supply had dwindled, I waited another week before I began to wean. I had already known the journey was over long before the visit. "The breast milk is yours, not Frances's," my therapist said to me, helpfully, on one of our calls, in which I was crying, again, about not being able to give enough of it to her. That framework changed everything. I could choose to keep torturing myself to offer her a few ounces, or I could not. It was my choice on how to use my body. So much of new motherhood is about an absolute explosion of boundaries between you and your child. But I can love us both in relation to each other, and I can love us separately, as unique, discrete people. And I do.

———

Recently, I've been moved by the idea that we, debtors, might challenge what it means to be in debt, that we might flip the script on our creditors entirely. Why should we adhere to their terms? "Credit is a means of privatization and debt a means of socialization," scholars Fred Moten and Stefano Harney write in *The Undercommons: Fugitive Planning & Black Study*, a poetic reimagining of indebtedness, among other theories. Credit refers to capitalism's marketplace: the credit extended to us in the form of loans—mortgage, payday, student, etc.—and credit cards. It also refers to the marketplace's wide net: the institutions that track and benefit from our participation in the economic system. Debt, on the other hand, a debt which they go on to define as "bad debt," is social and includes all the nonmarket things that we give to one another because we genuinely care for one another and want to make each other's lives better and easier. "Debt is mutual," they explain. "Credit runs only one way."

Bad debt is acquired when you make your sick friend soup, when you pick your aunt up from the airport, when you participate in a local mutual aid network—driving food to folks in an unhoused camp. It's acquired when you bathe your sick husband because he can no longer stand. It's earned in the sixteen-hour road trip your friend takes with you from New York City, steering the U-Haul at 3:00 a.m. while you sleep against the seat beside her. Or when you help your embarrassed student wipe the puke off her shirt because she's come down with the flu in class. These debts to one another are not recorded any-where and will never be paid back. Unlike credit, which keeps track of exactly how much you owe, to the cent, and will use force if nec-essary to collect from you, the debt that Moten and Harney are wit-ness to "forgets." These debts are "bad" because they are outstanding and always will be—a forgetting that contradicts a marketplace that doesn't believe that anything should be free.

"The debtor seeks refuge among other debtors, acquires debt from them, offers debt to them. This place of refuge is the place to which you can only owe more and more because there is no cred-itor, no payment possible," according to Moten and Harney. Here, you give to and receive from one another freely over and over again. Anthropologist David Graeber defines debt as a promise corrupted by math and violence, but in this refuge of bad debt, scholar Jodi Kim points out, the promise has not yet been corrupted. It "refuses quid pro quo calculations of reciprocity." I like thinking of a place with other debtors as a place not of shame but uncorrupted promise. Not just a place where we willingly and joyfully owe one another but where our futures hold *promise*. Everything is possible for us.

We, the bad debtors, are also bad because we are accumulat-ing these debts in nonmarket, non-commodified ways that creditors can't track or earn from. Our time with one another is unproductive for *them*. Bad debt, therefore, is realized in not only what we do *for* one another, but *with* one another. It's in the late-night dance parties I had in my second Chicago apartment—swaying and dipping and spinning with friends and neighbors as we passed one another the phone to DJ. It's in the park down the street, where my roommates and I set up picnics and lawn games and invited passersby to join us. It's in the late night walk I took across a frozen lake in Minneapolis with new friends, stoned, singing and talking about what poems we loved the most. Bad debt is in the classroom in the state prison when a student read a poem to the class about the jar of basil her mother had kept in a cool dark place, the earthy bright scent of it she can still smell now.

"It is not credit we seek," write Harney and Moten, but "... bad debt which is to say real debt, the debt that cannot be repaid, the debt at a distance, the debt without creditor, the black debt, the queer debt, the criminal debt. Excessive debt, incalculable debt, debt for no reason, debt broken from credit, debt as its own principal." Fuck credit; we deserve something so much greater.

———

Frances is a year and a half now, as I write this, and she has transitioned from the chubby, warm, milk-breath of baby life into a toddler. While she's responded to music since she was born, recently she's begun to dance—not just bob her head to the rhythm but move her whole body in ways that feel at once patterned and wild. I caught her in such a dance this summer, when we were visiting family. Across the living room—a halo of lake-light all around her—"Old McDonald" played from a toy's small speaker. At first she moved her head around in a half circle and then she stomped both of her feet, raising her knees high, before shaking her hips back and forth and then moving her whole body sideways. It was staccato and liquid, beautiful and chaotic. She kept going, repeating that whole sequence but more quickly and soon doing each of the moves all at once, so that energy radiated out of her in every direction.

She had never seen me or, as far as I know, anyone else dance. It was not like her desire to brush her own teeth for the first time or when she has tried to put on her own shoes. Frances's movements emerged from inside her—a joyful, buzzing, unselfconscious expression. To be a good mother to her, I thought as I watched her dance, was not just to help her tune in to the messages of the world, listening to those that are informative, protective, interesting, loving, and necessary, and identifying those that should be resisted. To be a good mother is also to help her attune to the messages already inside of her.

"We saw it in a step yesterday, some hips, a smile, the way a hand moved," Harney and Moten write of bad debt. I imagine this movement, the people doing these movements, all across the country, and the world, people different from me, but assembled in this shifting space of refuge beyond the institutions that wish to harm us. I think about Frances stomping her feet in unfettered delight. I do not want Frances or any of us to be wrapped up in predatory debt, kept alive through credit and collection. But I hope she comes to understand herself as someone having bad debt. I want that for my mother, too, and for everyone I've spoken with about their debt and for everyone I haven't.

At Debt Collective meetings, we talk regularly about the power that comes from so many of us owing so much money. Organizers repeat a quote from oil baron J. Paul Getty: "If you owe the bank $100, the bank owns you. If you owe the bank $100 million, you own the bank"—meaning, of course, that despite what credit tells us, we have power. I've believed in the potential of organized debtors and celebrated the material victories that we've won for borrowers—billions of dollars, in fact—but it's only recently that I've really felt this belief after speaking with so many borrowers and after tracing debt's antecedents, consequences, and limitations. "We owe our creditors nothing and we owe one another everything," we say at our meetings. We debtors, bad debtors, are everywhere. I can't believe I didn't see it before.

In ancient Mesopotamia, massive debt cancellations were called jubilees. They were issued by kings in hopes of restoring the social order that had collapsed and fragmented under systems of debt bondage that scattered family members. *In Debt: The First Five Thousand Years*, David Graeber reminds us that the earliest word for freedom came from the Sumerian word *amargi*, which means "return to mother." It was only when debts were canceled that debt peons could drop their sickles, pack their small bags, and return to the place where they were not an engine of labor, of repayment, but a daughter.

If we return to one another, if we find one another in this cosmic expanse, if we work toward a future in which love structures our relationships, in which the needs of everyone are met, if we choose a future that is just, reparative, and kind, a future in which education is free, then we can conjure our own jubilees. It's happening already, I think. There have been real victories—such as the $62.5 billion canceled through the reanimated PSLF program and another $51 billion in Income Driven Repayment and $17.2 billion in Borrowers Defense. None of that relief or near-relief has been as quick, complete, and permanent as it could have been had Biden canceled all $1.7 trillion of student debt using the "compromise and settle" authority that the Higher Education Act afforded him. Maybe the courts would have blocked that, too. Maybe not. "Cancel it all, immediately, and dare the court to reimpose life-destroying debts on forty-five million people," writer and Debt Collective cofounder Astra Taylor once said.

There are ways to give us free college. There are ways to abolish our debts, to give us free lives. In *Abolition Geography* Ruth Wilson Gilmore writes: "One must live a life of relative privilege these days to be so dour about domination, so suspicious of resistance, so enchained by commodification, so helpless before the ideological state apparatuses to conclude there's no conceivable end to late capitalism's daily sacrifice of human life to the singular freedom of the market." Of course there can be an end. Of course we must engineer it ourselves.

Once, in elementary school, annoyed by a minor injustice that I can't remember anymore, I briefly ran away from home—though not far. Just across the street from my house through my neighbors' backyard to the nearest park, where I crouched below a multi-level playground gym and slide. I did not want to be away from home, but I wanted to be found, and to be found, I thought that I had to leave. I wanted someone to look for me because the act of looking was confirmation of love and belonging. My family searched for me, but they could not find me, and eventually I went home.

Let us return to each other—from all across the country and the world, from across geographies of isolation and suffering and heartache and exploitation. Because our returns are generative and energetic. They are productive and powerful.

Let us return to each other again and again and again.

Acknowledgments

This book would not have been possible without the generosity, vulnerability, and bravery of all the borrowers who gave me their stories, most of which never made it into the book. I want to give an additional thanks to Ahavah, Bianca, and Maria—three of my former students—whom I spoke to several times about their experiences with secondary and higher education and debt, none of which are featured directly in the text but influenced my thinking nonetheless.

I've been fortunate to find a publishing home in Grand Central Publishing. Thank you to Rachel Rodriguez, Jim Datz, Marie Mundaca, Rebecca Holland, Jeff Holt, Emily Baker, Estefania Acquaviva, and Brant Rumble. Thank you, Morgan Spehar, for responding to so many e-mails. Maddie Caldwell, thank you for being attuned to and supportive of my vision for the project and for your warm, clear, and detailed feedback. You pushed me to think in larger, weirder ways about the book's structure and threading of materials. I wish every writer the experience I had working with you.

Thank you to my agent and friend, Sarah Fuentes, for your advocacy, vision, and brilliant edits, and for finding me before I knew I was ready to write a book. You've made the unfamiliar publishing landscape feel more knowable and kind. I have thought more deeply about debt, and the world, through our exchanges.

To Julie Schwietert Collazo, for fact-checking the entire manuscript with grace and thoroughness; what an enormous gift that afforded me the confidence to keep working on new rounds of revisions and edits. Much gratitude to Emily Oliver, Connor Stratton, Anna Rasmussen, Amanda Minoff, and Will Harris for reading portions of the manuscript; your insights helped to shape thorny sections of the book. Thank you to Eleni Schirmer for reading a draft with an eye toward the student lending landscape and higher education; the resources and thinking you provided were invaluable additions to the project.

I'm lucky to live in a state that supports its artists; thank you to the Minnesota State Arts Board for funding that allowed me the chance to work on the project, instead of hustling for more income, and to Yaddo Artist Residency for giving me two perfect weeks of uninterrupted work, a lovely desk with a window, exceptional food, and meaningful conversation with other artists. Thank you to New Literary Project and the Jack Hazard Fellowship for supporting the book in its final stages and for recognizing the unique challenge of being an artist and a high school educator.

Thank you to *Longreads* for publishing the essay from which this book sprung, Carolyn Wells for such thoughtful edits, and Seward Darby for grabbing me out of a slushpile and passing me on to the right editor. Thank you to the editors of *American Precariat* for including my work in your moving anthology and pushing me to expand and sharpen my thinking on debt and the body.

The University of Minnesota offered me three years of funding, collaboration, and mentorship; thank you to my entire cohort, who were generous, funny, smart, and great people to share food and drinks with: Anessa, Alexis, Joe, Liam, Miriam, Connor, Hannah, Will, and

Erica. To Charlie Baxter, for the conversation and play readings; Patricia Hampl and Julie Schumacher, for the necessary thesis guidance; Sugi Ganeshananthan, for mentorship across classes; Eric Daigre, for shaping my teaching pedagogy; and to Kim Todd for being such a dear friend and advocate of my work, for pushing me to be more ambitious and to believe my writing could have a life in the world.

One of my life's greatest fortunes has been to experience trusting, joyful, vulnerable, and sustaining friendships across the country, and to rack up "bad debt" with people, on whom I had to depend, especially during my earliest years navigating my loans. Thank you to my community in New York City—the crew from study abroad, especially Marc and Jill, and my best buds during my second year living there, Phil and Dave. And to all my colleagues at my Chicago teaching home, Chicago Bulls College Prep. The conversations I shared with my English team, Bri and Elsie, grounded me and challenged me, nourishing me so that I could love my students and myself more completely. They were perhaps the first people to tell me I should write a book about debt. To the rest of my Chicago and southwest Michigan family, some of whom I've known since grade school: Katie, Kristin, Michelle, Jenna, Jacky, Linnea, Adam, France, Bleeker, Julie, Amber, Nate, and Trent. There are few memories that you don't touch, and the community we've created makes me hopeful for a better future.

St. Paul Academy and Summit School has been a wonderful teaching and learning community; here, I've been lucky to collaborate with students, to have some of the richest discussions I've ever had about texts, and to consider what I think education—at its best—can offer individuals and the world. Thank you to Tom and Carrie for helping to facilitate a year away from the classroom so that I could work on this book.

Acknowledgments

The Debt Collective has transformed and radicalized my understanding of indebtedness. It's also affirmed my belief in the strength of unions and collective storytelling. I am incredibly grateful to organize beside collective members in our shared struggle for the world we deserve. We are not in debt because we have lived beyond our means but because we have been denied the means to live.

Thank you to the students, faculty, and staff of Minnesota Prison Writing Workshop for offering me the gift of teaching with you, and for believing in and creating an education that extends beyond bars. And to my long-time Minnesota community—those who have been mentioned, along with Sarita, Allie, Josh, and Dylan—thank you for making Minneapolis my home, for watching our child, helping us move, feeding us, talking leftist politics, and participating in all the rituals of caregiving and celebration that make life, and writing, possible and worthwhile.

Thank you to the Alberti and Weinstein families who have offered love, support, and encouragement. Thank you, Uncle Juergen, for cosigning on all the documents that allowed me access to the adult world. Kelsey, I was so lucky to grow up with you and to now share an adult life with you; thank you for your faith in me and your longtime support of this project. Thanks to my father for a childhood grounded in discovery and play, and to my mother for believing, from the first letters I recorded, that I would become a writer. For navigating complex barriers and continuing to wrestle with the past for the sake of our future. I love you all.

To my best friend, editor, advocate, and partner, Mike: I love you with my whole heart. To Frances, for the responsibility and gift of motherhood; your existence is a clarion call to keep fighting.

Recommendations for Further Reading

The first book I read about debt was David Graeber's *Debt: The First 5,000 Years*. My roommate in graduate school loaned me his copy, and when it became clear that I had grown attached to it because I kept rereading it and adding Post-its that became unwieldy, he generously gave it to me. It was this copy I read again and again as I began to research the book. It offers a complete overview of the history and concept of debt, an argument against popular origin theories of money, documentation of debt's relationship to morality, story, and language, and is, despite the violence it documents, actually funny at times. It was the first book that addressed ongoing questions I had about my own debt. RIP David Graeber.

Annie McClanahan's *Dead Pledges: Debt, Crisis, and Twenty-First-Century Culture* is incisive, enraging, and beautiful in its cultural unpacking of the way debt has shaped literature and art, with attention to the subprime mortgage crisis. Like Graeber, she sees a world beyond debt or at least a world in which we significantly confront its coercive power in our lives. She proposes meaningful resistance in her cataloging of "sabotage"—as a political framework and material imperative.

Maurizio Lazzarato's *The Making of the Indebted Man* and Stefano Harney and Fred Moten's *The Undercommons: Fugitive Planning and Black Study* both pushed my theoretical thinking as well as my sense of possibility when I considered my own aesthetics writing about debt. Moten and Harney are wonderful to listen to in discussion. I recommend every podcast that interviewed them about this book. Melinda Cooper's *Family Values* shaped my larger understanding of how neoliberal forces have responded to and defined the family and undercut social wages.

I also recommend the Debt Collective's *Can't Pay Won't Pay*. Co-written by longtime organizers and scholars, it connects student debt to other forms of extraction—racial capitalism, settler-colonialism, municipal debt, and health-care debt, to name a few. The work is especially meaningful because it argues for union organizing as a counter-force to this violence.

For deep dives into the student loan landscape, I recommend Elizabeth Tandy Shermer's *Indentured Students*, Caitlin Zaloom's *Indebted*, and Sara Goldrick-Rab's *Paying the Price*. The first of these books offers a detailed historical overview of the inception and development of the loan program, and the latter two research on the existing piecemeal funding architecture, relying on student interviews over a series of years. Zaloom movingly argues that the presence of student loans is now a definitive feature of the middle class. *Burdened*, by Ryann Liebenthal, also covers the history of student loans with special attention to the manufactured choices made by Congress to tie funding to the individual student rather than creating more universal models.

Women's Study Quarterly Spring/Summer 2014 magazine is entirely focused on debt, and I recommend reading all of it.

The Student Borrower Protection Center, in its work as a fierce borrower advocate, contains a treasure trove of reports on everything you could ever research connected to student debt, the programs managing it, or its wide-reaching harm.

As I began my literary research into debt, I chose to focus on "student debt" to help narrow an enormous reading list and hopefully sharpen my analysis. The books I chose for the manuscript were the ones in which student debt most significantly impacted the characters or plot. Send me your recommendations on literature that engages with student debt. I want to read them. If you're thinking about writing such books, please do.

References

I underwent an extensive fact-checking process on the entire manuscript. Below are the sources referenced in the book.

"Academic Competitiveness Grant (ACG) | Library | Knowledge Center." Accessed September 10, 2024. https://fsapartners.ed.gov/knowledge-center/library/program/Academic%20Competitiveness%20Grant%20%28ACG%29.

Account, Admin. "Driving Down Distress? The Principles & Incomplete History of Income-Driven Repayment." Student Borrower Protection Center, September 10, 2021. https://protectborrowers.org/idr-history-report/.

Administration, Substance Abuse and Mental Health Services. "Table 3.38, DSM-IV to DSM-5 Gambling Disorder Comparison." Text. Substance Abuse and Mental Health Services Administration (US), June 2016. https://www.ncbi.nlm.nih.gov/books/NBK519704/table/ch3.t39/.

Argys, Laura M., Andrew Friedson, and Melina M. Pitts. "Killer Debt: The Impact of Debt on Mortality." FRB Atlanta Working Paper, no. 2016-2014 (2016).

Association, National Education. "Starting Teacher Pay | NEA." Accessed September 8, 2024. https://www.nea.org/resource-library/educator-pay-and-student-spending-how-does-your-state-rank/starting-teacher.

Baker, Brendan. "Deeper Debt, Denial of Discharge: The Harsh Treatment of Student Loan Debt in Bankruptcy, Recent Developments, and Proposed Reforms." *University of Pennsylvania Journal of Business Law* 14, no. 4 (n.d.): 2012.

Barbone, F., M. Bovenzi, F. Cavallieri, and G. Stanta. "Cigarette Smoking and Histologic Type of Lung Cancer in Men." *Chest* 112, no. 6 (December 1997): 1474–79. https://doi.org/10.1378/chest.112.6.1474.

"Biden-Harris Administration Announces Additional $7.4 Billion in Approved Student Debt Relief for 277,000 Borrowers | US Department of Education." Accessed

September 4, 2024. https://www.ed.gov/news/press-releases/biden-harris
-administration-announces-additional-74-billion-approved-student-debt-relief
-277000-borrowers.

Blagg, Kristin, Jung Hyun Choi, Sandy Baum, et al. "Student Loan Debt and Access to
Homeownership for Borrowers of Color." Urban Institute and Federal Home
Loan Bank San Francisco, 2022.

Brookings. "Income-Driven Repayment of Student Loans: Problems and Options for Addressing Them." Accessed February 24, 2025. https://www.brookings.edu
/articles/income-driven-repayment-of-student-loans-problems-and-options
-for-addressing-them/.

Bunch, Will. *After the Ivory Tower Falls: How College Broke the American Dream and Blew Up
Our Politics—And How to Fix It.* William Morrow, 2022.

Castellani, Brian. *Pathological Gambling: The Making of a Medical Problem.* State University of
New York Press, 2000.

Center for American Progress. "The Continued Student Loan Crisis for Black Borrowers,"
December 2, 2019. https://www.americanprogress.org/article/continued
-student-loan-crisis-black-borrowers/.

"Collections | Federal Student Aid." Accessed September 4, 2024. https://studentaid.gov
/manage-loans/default/collections.

Collins, Sara R., Shreya Roy, Relebohile Masitha. "Paying for It: How Health Care Costs
and Medical Debt Are Making Americans Sicker and Poorer." The Common-
wealth Fund, October 26, 2023. https://doi.org/10.26099/bf08-3735.

"Comparing the Compensation of Federal and Private-Sector Employees in 2022 | Con-
gressional Budget Office," April 25, 2024. https://www.cbo.gov/publication
/60235.

Consumer Financial Protection Bureau. "CFPB Sues Student Loan Servicer PHEAA for
Pursuing Borrowers for Loans Discharged in Bankruptcy," May 31, 2024. https:
//www.consumerfinance.gov/about-us/newsroom/cfpb-sues-student-loan
-servicer-pheaa-for-pursuing-borrowers-for-loans-discharged-in-bankruptcy/.

Consumer Financial Protection Bureau. "CFPB Takes Action Against Student Loan Debt
Collector Performant Recovery for Illegal Fee Generating Scheme That Cost
Borrowers Thousands of Dollars," December 9, 2024. https://www.consumer
finance.gov/about-us/newsroom/cfpb-takes-action-against-student-loan-debt
-collector-performant-recovery-for-illegal-fee-generating-scheme-that-cost
-borrowers-thousands-of-dollars/.

Consumer Financial Protection Bureau. "CFPB Takes Action to Require National Colle-
giate Student Loan Trusts and Pennsylvania Higher Education Assistance Agency
to Pay More than $5 Million for Student Loan Servicing Failures," May 6, 2024.
https://www.consumerfinance.gov/about-us/newsroom/cfpb-takes-action-to
-require-national-collegiate-student-loan-trusts-and-pennsylvania-higher
-education-assistance-agency-to-pay-more-than-5-million-for-student-loan
-servicing-failures/.

References

Consumer Financial Protection Bureau. "Conduent Education Services, LLC," May 1, 2019. https://www.consumerfinance.gov/enforcement/actions/conduent -education-services-llc/.

Consumer Financial Protection Bureau. "Performant Recovery, Inc.," December 9, 2024. https://www.consumerfinance.gov/enforcement/actions/performant-recovery-inc/.

Consumer Financial Protection Bureau. "Search the Consumer Complaint Database." Accessed February 24, 2025. https://www.consumerfinance.gov/data-research /consumer-complaints/search/detail/10257192.

Consumer Financial Protection Bureau. "Search the Consumer Complaint Database." Accessed February 24, 2025. https://www.consumerfinance.gov/data-research /consumer-complaints/search/detail/10130312.

Consumer Financial Protection Bureau. "Staying on Track While Giving Back: The Cost of Student Loan Servicing Breakdowns for People Serving Their Communities," June 22, 2017. https://www.consumerfinance.gov/data-research/research-reports /staying-track-while-giving-back-cost-student-loan-servicing-breakdowns -people-serving-their-communities/.

Cooper, Melinda. *Family Values: Between Neoliberalism and the New Social Conservatism*. Near Future Series. Zone Books, 2019.

Day, Meagan. "Why We Need Free College for Everyone—Even Rich People." Jacobin, 2019.

Debt Collective. *Can't Pay Won't Pay: The Case for Economic Disobedience and Debt Abolition*. Haymarket Books, 2020.

"Debtors' Prisons, Explained | Teen Vogue." Accessed August 3, 2024. https://www .teenvogue.com/story/debtors-prison.

DeFusco, Anthony A., Brandon Enriquez, and Maggie Yellen. "Wage Garnishment in the United States: New Facts from Administrative Payroll Records." *American Economic Review: Insights* 6, no. 1 (March 2024): 38–54.

DeSilver, Drew. "For Most US Workers, Real Wages Have Barely Budged in Decades." Pew Research Center (blog), August 7, 2018. https://www.pewresearch.org/short -reads/2018/08/07/for-most-us-workers-real-wages-have-barely-budged-for -decades/.

"Digest of Education Statistics, 2021." National Center for Education Statistics. Accessed September 12, 2024. https://nces.ed.gov/programs/digest/d21/tables/dt21 _330.10.asp.

Dissent Magazine. "Modern Family." Accessed September 8, 2024. https://www .dissentmagazine.org/article/family-values-melinda-cooper-review/.

Education Data Initiative. "Student Loan Debt Statistics [2024]: Average + Total Debt." Accessed September 1, 2024. https://educationdata.org/student-loan-debt-statistics.

"FAFSA® Application | Federal Student Aid." Accessed September 10, 2024. https: //studentaid.gov/h/apply-for-aid/fafsa.

"Federal Family Education Loan (FFEL) | Library | Knowledge Center." Accessed September 1, 2024. https://fsapartners.ed.gov/knowledge-center/library/program /Federal%20Family%20Education%20Loan%20%28FFEL%29.

References

"Federal Pell Grant Program." Program Home Page. US Department of Education (ED), August 30, 2022. https://www2.ed.gov/programs/fpg/index.html.

Federal Trade Commission. "Fair Debt Collection Practices Act," August 12, 2013. https://www.ftc.gov/legal-library/browse/rules/fair-debt-collection-practices-act-text.

Filson, Jackie. "Trump Tips Hand, Sacking Top Official Focused on Lowering Costs for Working Families." Student Borrower Protection Center, February 1, 2025. https://protectborrowers.org/trump-sacks-top-official-chopra-focused-on-lowering-costs-for-working-families/.

"FSEOG (Grants) | Federal Student Aid." Accessed September 10, 2024. https://studentaid.gov/understand-aid/types/grants/fseog.

Gilmore, Ruth Wilson. *Abolition Geography: Essays Toward Liberation.* Verso, 2022.

Goldrick-Rab, Sara. *Paying the Price: College Costs, Financial Aid, and the Betrayal of the American Dream.* The University of Chicago Press, 2016.

Goldrick-Rab, Sara, and Katharine M. Broton. "Opinion | Hungry, Homeless and in College." *The New York Times*, December 4, 2015, sec. Opinion. https://www.nytimes.com/2015/12/04/opinion/hungry-homeless-and-in-college.html.

Gomez, Filiberto Nolasco. "Prison Labor in Minnesota, Part 2." *Workday Magazine*, May 11, 2018. https://workdaymagazine.org/prison-labor-in-minnesota-part-2/.

Gordon, Avery F. *Ghostly Matters: Haunting and the Sociological Imagination.* University of Minnesota Press, 1997.

Graeber, David. *Debt: The First 5,000 Years.* Melville House, 2014.

Grant, Jon E., Brian L. Odlaug, and Marc E. Mooney. "Telescoping Phenomenon in Pathological Gambling: Association with Gender and Comorbidities." *The Journal of Nervous and Mental Disease* 200, no. 11 (November 2012): 996–98. https://doi.org/10.1097/NMD.0b013e3182718a4d.

Granville, Peter. "Parent PLUS Borrowers: The Hidden Casualties of the Student Debt Crisis." The Century Foundation, May 31, 2022. https://tcf.org/content/report/parent-plus-borrowers-the-hidden-casualties-of-the-student-debt-crisis/.

Hager, Eli. "Debtors' Prisons, Then and Now: FAQ." The Marshall Project, February 24, 2015. https://www.themarshallproject.org/2015/02/24/debtors-prisons-then-and-now-faq.

Hall, Stephanie. "What Will Happen to Your Student Loans If Trump Closes the Department of Education?" *Teen Vogue*, February 13, 2025. https://www.teenvogue.com/story/what-will-happen-to-student-loans-trump.

Hammer & Hope. "The Supreme Court Shouldn't Get the Last Word." Accessed September 12, 2024. https://hammerandhope.org/article/supreme-court-abortion-student-debt.

Harris, Alexes. *A Pound of Flesh: Monetary Sanctions as Punishment for the Poor.* Russell Sage Foundation, 2016.

Heller, Nathan. "The End of the English Major." *The New Yorker*, February 27, 2023. https://www.newyorker.com/magazine/2023/03/06/the-end-of-the-english-major.

"Home | US Department of Education," February 21, 2025. http://www.ed.gov/.

References

Hoover Institution Library and Archives, "The Role of Government in Education," Collected Works of Milton Friedman Project records, 1955, https://miltonfriedman.hoover.org/objects/58044/the-role-of-government-in-education.

"How—and Why—America Criminalizes Poverty." Literary Hub. Accessed August 3, 2024. https://lithub.com/how-and-why-america-criminalizes-poverty/.

Hunter, Virginia. "Policing Public Debtors in Classical Athens." *Phoenix* 54, no. 1/2 (n.d.).

Inquest. "Debt Trapped" | Tim Curry & Tanisha Pierrette. October 5, 2022. https://inquest.org/debt-trapped/.

"Issue Paper: Student Loan Debt Relief," n.d. Department of Education. https://www.ed.gov/sites/ed/files/policy/highered/reg/hearulemaking/2023/session-1—issue-paper-student-loan-reliefom-committee.pdf.

Iuliano, Jason. "The Student Loan Bankruptcy Gap." *Duke Law Journal* 70, no. 3 (2020).

Kahn, Suzanne, Mark Huelsman, and Jen Mishory. "Bridging Progressive Policy Debates: How Student Debt and the Racial Wealth Gap Reinforce Each Other." Roosevelt Institute, The Century Foundation, Demos, 2019.

Kasakove, Sophie. "Why the Road Is Getting Even Rockier for First-Time Home Buyers." *The New York Times*, April 23, 2022, sec. US. https://www.nytimes.com/2022/04/23/us/corporate-real-estate-investors-housing-market.html.

Kim, Jodi. "Debt, the Precarious Grammar of Life, and Manjula Padmanabhan's 'Harvest.'" *Women's Studies Quarterly* 42, no. 1/2 (Spring/Summer 2014).

King, Lilly. *Writers & Lovers*. Grove Press, 2020.

Klein, Naomi. *Doppelganger: A Trip Into The Mirror World*. Farrar, Straus and Giroux, 2023.

Kliff, Sarah. "Mary Lou Retton Crowdfunded Her Medical Debt, Like Many Thousands of Others." *The New York Times*, October 12, 2023, sec. Health. https://www.nytimes.com/2023/10/12/health/mary-lou-retton-medical-bills-crowdfunding.html.

Lauer, Joshua. *Creditworthy: A History of Consumer Surveillance and Financial Identity in America*. Columbia University Press, 2017.

Lazzarato, Maurizio. *The Making of the Indebted Man: An Essay on the Neoliberal Condition*. Intervention 13. semiotext(e), 2012.

Lee, Leona. "House of Debt." *In the Red*, July 2023.

Leilani, Raven. *Luster*. Picador, 2020.

Lepore, Jill. "I.O.U." *The New Yorker*, April 6, 2009. https://www.newyorker.com/magazine/2009/04/13/i-o-u.

Levinthal, Louis Edward. "The Early History of Bankruptcy Law." *University of Pennsylvania Law Review* 66, no. 5/6 (April 1918): 223–50.

Liebenthal, Ryan. *Burdened: Student Debt and the Making of an American Crisis*. Dey Street Books, 2024.

Liebenthal, Ryann. "The Incredible, Rage-Inducing Inside Story of America's Student Debt Machine." Mother Jones (blog). Accessed September 8, 2024. https://www.motherjones.com/politics/2018/08/debt-student-loan-forgiveness-betsy-devos-education-department-fedloan/.

References

Lieber, Ron. "FAFSA's Expected Family Contribution Is Going Away. Good Riddance." *The New York Times*, December 30, 2020, sec. Your Money. https://www.nytimes .com/2020/12/30/your-money/fafsa-expected-family-contribution.html.

Lurie, Stephen. "The Long and Unequal Burden of Criminal Justice Debt." *Governing*, January 17, 2024. https://www.governing.com/policy/the-long-and-unequal -burden-of-criminal-justice-debt.

Mabie, Ben, and Melinda Cooper. "Family Matters." *Viewpoint Magazine*, March 19, 2018. https://viewpointmag.com/2018/03/19/family-matters/.

"Mapping Exploitation: Examining For-Profit Colleges as Financial Predators in Communities of Color." Student Borrower Protection Center, n.d. https: //protectborrowers.org/wp-content/uploads/2021/07/SBPC-Mapping -Exploitation-Report.pdf.

"Maximum Pell Grant Amount | BestColleges." Accessed September 12, 2024. https: //www.bestcolleges.com/research/pell-grant-amount/.

McClanahan, Annie. *Dead Pledges: Debt, Crisis, and Twenty-First-Century Culture*. Stanford University Press, 2017.

McGhee, Molly. *Jonathan Abernathy You Are Kind*. Astra House, 2023.

McGurran, Brianna. "College Tuition Inflation: Compare the Cost of College Over Time." Forbes Advisor, March 28, 2022. https://www.forbes.com/advisor /student-loans/college-tuition-inflation/.

McNair, Kamaron. "Federal Courts Have Halted the SAVE Plan for Now: 'Things Are Getting Much, Much Worse,' Advocates Say." CNBC, August 15, 2024. https: //www.cnbc.com/2024/08/15/federal-courts-halted-save-plan-for-now .html.

McNair, Kamaron. "If You Enrolled in the SAVE Plan, You May Not Have a Payment Due for Now—What Borrowers Need to Know." CNBC, July 19, 2024. https: //www.cnbc.com/2024/07/19/bidens-save-plan-blocked-what-borrowers -need-to-know.html.

Mezza, Alvaro, Daniel Ringo, Shane Sherlund, and Kamila Sommer. "Student Loans and Homeownership." *Journal of Labor Economics* 38, no. 1 (2020).

Minsky, Adam S. "Payments for Some Student Loan Borrowers Could Triple in 2025." *Forbes*. Accessed February 24, 2025. https://www.forbes.com/sites /adamminsky/2025/01/22/payments-for-some-student-loan-borrowers-could -triple-in-2025/.

Minsky, Adam S. "Republicans Take Key Step to Abolish the Department of Education, Imperiling Student Loan Programs." *Forbes*. Accessed February 24, 2025. https: //www.forbes.com/sites/adamminsky/2025/02/03/republicans-take-key-step -to-abolish-the-department-of-education-imperiling-student-loan-programs/.

Minsky, Adam S. "What Happens to Student Loan Forgiveness if Trump Abolishes the Department of Education?" *Forbes*. Accessed February 24, 2025. https://www .forbes.com/sites/adamminsky/2024/12/16/what-happens-to-student-loan -forgiveness-if-trump-abolishes-the-department-of-education/.

References

"Monetary Sanctions as a Pound of Flesh | Brennan Center for Justice," August 9, 2021. https://www.brennancenter.org/our-work/analysis-opinion/monetary-sanctions -pound-flesh.

Montague, Zach. "After Botched Rollout, FAFSA Is Delayed for a Second Year." *The New York Times*, August 7, 2024, sec. US. https://www.nytimes.com/2024/08/07/us /politics/fafsa-delayed-for-second-year.html.

Moore, Michael. "My Job Is Important—So Is Forgiving My Crushing College Debt | Op-Ed," *The Seattle Times*, October 20, 2023. https://www.seattletimes.com /opinion/my-job-is-important-so-is-forgiving-my-crushing-college-debt/.

"Morally Bankrupt: How the Student Loan Industry Stole a Generation's Right to Debt Relief." Student Borrower Protection Center, January 2022. https: //protectborrowers.org/wp-content/uploads/2022/01/SBPC_Morally -Bankrupt.pdf.

Moten, Fred, and Stefano Harney. *The Undercommons: Fugitive Planning & Black Study*. Minor Compositions, 2013.

"Moving Beyond Free: A College Affordability Compact for the Next Generation—Third Way." Accessed September 12, 2024. https://www.thirdway.org/report/moving -beyond-free-a-college-affordability-compact-for-the-next-generation.

MPR News. "These Students Are in College for Free under New Program for Lower-Income Minnesotans," October 16, 2024. https://www.mprnews.org/story /2024/10/16/north-star-promise-recipients-free-college-new-program.

Murch, Donna. "Paying for Punishment." *Boston Review*, August 1, 2016. https://www .bostonreview.net/articles/paying-for-punishment/.

NerdWallet. "How Borrower Defense to Repayment Works," May 1, 2024. https://www .nerdwallet.com/article/loans/student-loans/borrower-defense-repayment.

New America. "Student Loan History." Accessed August 30, 2024. http://newamerica.org /education-policy/topics/higher-education-funding-and-financial-aid/federal -student-aid/federal-student-loans/federal-student-loan-history/.

New America. "Student Loan History." Accessed February 24, 2025. http://newamerica .org/education-policy/topics/higher-education-funding-and-financial-aid /federal-student-aid/federal-student-loans/federal-student-loan-history/.

New America. "The Wealth Gap PLUS Debt." Accessed September 5, 2024. http: //newamerica.org/education-policy/reports/wealth-gap-plus-debt/.

Newfield, Christopher. *Unmaking the Public University*. Harvard University Press, 2011.

"North Star Promise." Accessed September 12, 2024. https://www.ohe.state.mn.us/sPages /northstarpromise.cfm.

Nova, Annie. "Biden Cancels $10,000 in Federal Student Loan Debt for Most Borrowers." CNBC, August 24, 2022. https://www.cnbc.com/2022/08/24/biden-expected -to-cancel-10000-in-federal-student-loan-debt-for-most-borrowers.html.

Nova, Annie. "Why Activist Astra Taylor Is Not Giving up on Student Loan Forgiveness." CNBC, August 11, 2023. https://www.cnbc.com/2023/08/11/why-activist -astra-taylor-is-not-giving-up-on-student-loan-forgiveness.html.

References

Nova, Annie. "Trump Wants Small Business Administration to Handle Student Loans. Here's What Borrowers Need to Know." CNBC, March 26, 2025. https://www.cnbc.com/2025/03/26/student-loans-could-be-managed-by-the-small-business-administration-.html.

"Perkins Loans | Federal Student Aid." Accessed September 10, 2024. https://studentaid.gov/understand-aid/types/loans/perkins.

"Private Student Lending." Student Borrower Protection Center, 2020. https://protectborrowers.org/wp-content/uploads/2020/04/PSL-Report_042020.pdf.

"Private Student Loans." Consumer Financial Protection Bureau, 2012. https://files.consumerfinance.gov/f/201207_cfpb_Reports_Private-Student-Loans.pdf.

"Qualifying Public Services for the Public Service Loan Forgiveness (PSLF) Program | Federal Student Aid." Accessed September 8, 2024. https://studentaid.gov/manage-loans/forgiveness-cancellation/public-service/qualifying-public-services.

Rardin, E. "Federal Correctional Institution Milan, Michigan Commissary Sales List," n.d. https://www.bop.gov/locations/institutions/mil/mil_commlist2025.pdf?v=1.0.1.

Ross, Andrew. "Probation Profiteering Is the New Debtors' Prison." *Boston Review*, November 10, 2021. https://www.bostonreview.net/articles/probation-profiteering-is-the-new-debtors-prison/.

"Sally Rooney: Renters Are Being Exploited and Evictions Must Be Stopped." *The Irish Times.* Accessed September 12, 2024. https://www.irishtimes.com/life-style/2023/03/18/sally-rooney-renters-are-being-exploited-and-evictions-must-be-stopped/.

Sather, Stephen W. "Dischargeability of Student Loans in Bankruptcy." The American Bankruptcy Institute, 2014. https://www.abi.org/feed-item/dischargeability-of-student-loans-in-bankruptcy.

Schirmer, Eleni. "A Speculative Endeavor." *Lapham's Quarterly*, 2022. https://www.laphamsquarterly.org/education/speculative-endeavor.

Schirmer, Eleni. "The Aging Student Debtors of America." *The New Yorker*, July 27, 2022. https://www.newyorker.com/news/us-journal/the-aging-student-debtors-of-america.

Schüll, Natasha Dow. *Addiction By Design: Machine Gambling in Las Vegas*. Princeton University Press, 2014.

Schwarz, Jon. "The Origin of Student Debt: Reagan Adviser Warned Free College Would Create a Dangerous 'Educated Proletariat.'" The Intercept, August 25, 2022. https://theintercept.com/2022/08/25/student-loans-debt-reagan/.

Seamster, Louise. "Black Debt, White Debt." *Contexts*, 2019.

Sheffey, Ayelet. "Adjunct Professors Should Be Eligible for Relief from the 'Crushing Burden' of Student Debt, Democrats Say in New Bill." *Business Insider*. Accessed September 1, 2024. https://www.businessinsider.com/student-debt-public-service-loan-forgiveness-adjunct-professors-durbin-booker-2021-7.

References

Shermer, Elizabeth Tandy. *Indentured Students: How Government-Guaranteed Loans Left Generations Drowning in College Debt.* Harvard University Press, 2021.

"Statement on President Trump's Executive Order to Return Power Over Education to States and Local Communities | U.S. Department of Education," March 20, 2025. http://www.ed.gov/about/news/press-release/statement-president-trumps-executive-order-return-power-over-education-states-and-local-communities.

"Stress Effects on the Body." Accessed September 1, 2024. https://www.apa.org/topics/stress/body.

Sweet, Elizabeth, Arijit Nandi, Emma Adam, and Thomas McDade. "The High Price of Debt: Household Financial Debt and Its Impact on Mental and Physical Health." *Social Science & Medicine* (1982) 91 (August 2013): 94–100. https://doi.org/10.1016/j.socscimed.2013.05.009.

Tax Policy Center. "How Do Taxes on Lotteries, Casinos, Sports Betting, and Other Types of State-Sanctioned Gambling Work?" Accessed September 12, 2024. https://www.taxpolicycenter.org/briefing-book/how-do-taxes-lotteries-casinos-sports-betting-and-other-types-state-sanctioned.

"Top 4 Questions: Direct Subsidized Loans vs. Direct Unsubsidized Loans—Federal Student Aid." Accessed August 30, 2024. https://studentaid.gov/articles/subsidized-vs-unsubsidized-loans/.

Totenberg, Nina. "Supreme Court Kills Biden's Student Debt Plan in a Setback for Millions of Borrowers." NPR, June 30, 2023, sec. Law. https://www.npr.org/2023/06/30/1182216970/supreme-court-student-loan-forgiveness-decision-biden.

Townsend, Jacinda. *Mother Country.* Graywolf Press, 2022.

"Tuition and Fees." Accessed September 1, 2024. https://simons-rock.edu/admission/tuition-and-financial-aid/tuition-and-fees.php.

"Types of Financial Aid | Federal Student Aid." Accessed September 10, 2024. https://studentaid.gov/understand-aid/types.

"University of Michigan Tuition and Fees." Accessed September 3, 2024. https://bentley.umich.edu/legacy-support/tuition.php.

"US Casinos Won $66.5B in 2023, Their Best Year Ever as Gamblers Showed No Economic Fear | AP News." Accessed September 12, 2024. https://apnews.com/article/casinos-best-year-revenue-gambling-betting-slots-6cefeecd6631fb6d102bac191179e3a0.

US Government Accountability Office. "Department of Education: Student Loan Relief in Cases of College Misconduct | US GAO." Accessed February 24, 2025. https://www.gao.gov/products/gao-24-106530.

US Government Accountability Office. "Direct Student Loans Could Save Money and Simplify Program Administration | US GAO." Accessed September 14, 2024. https://www.gao.gov/products/t-hrd-92-8.

US Government Accountability Office. "Public Service Loan Forgiveness: Education Needs to Provide Better Information for the Loan Servicer and Borrowers | US GAO," September 20, 2022. https://www.gao.gov/products/gao-18-547.

References

US Government Accountability Office. "Student Loans: Direct Loans Could Save Money and Simplify Program Administration | US GAO." Accessed August 31, 2024. https://www.gao.gov/products/hrd-91-144br.

US News & World Report. "What You Should Know About the FAFSA." Accessed September 10, 2024. https://www.usnews.com/education/best-colleges/paying-for-college/articles/completing-the-fafsa.

"Where Independent Minds Get Their Start." Accessed September 1, 2024. http://simons-rock.edu.

White, Jerry. *Mansions of Misery: A Biography of the Marshalsea Debtors' Prison.* Bodley Head, 2016.

White House, the. "Improving Education Outcomes by Empowering Parents, States, and Communities," March 20, 2025. https://www.whitehouse.gov/presidential-actions/2025/03/improving-education-outcomes-by-empowering-parents-states-and-communities/.

Williams, Jeffrey J. "The Teachings of Student Debt." In *Student Financing of Higher Education: A Comparison Perspective* (International Studies in Higher Education), n.d.

Wolfe, Anna, and Michelle Liu. "Want out of Jail? First You Have To Take a Fast-Food Job." The Marshall Project, January 9, 2020. https://www.themarshallproject.org/2020/01/09/think-debtors-prisons-are-a-thing-of-the-past-not-in-mississippi.

Zaloom, Caitlin. *Indebted: How Families Make College Work at Any Cost.* Princeton University Press, 2019.

About the Author

KRISTIN COLLIER is a graduate of the University of Minnesota MFA program. She has been a recipient of Minnesota State Arts Board funding and a Yaddo artist residency. Her writing has been published with *Fourth Genre* and *Longreads* and was recently anthologized in Coffee House Press's *American Precariat*. She is an organizer and high school English teacher, living in Minneapolis.